W9-AKU-854

SHARING

EXPERIENCE

STRENGTH &

HOPE

Nar-Anon Family Groups' Daily Reader

All rights reserved. No part of this publication may be reproduced, stored in, or introduced into a retrieval system, or transmitted in any form, or by any means (electronic, mechanical, photocopying, recording, or otherwise), without the prior written permission of the publisher.

Conference Approved Literature

B202 09-06-09 2nd Edition, 3rd Printing

© copyright 2007, 2009, 2011 by

ISBN 978-1-60585-002-3

Nar-Anon Family Group Headquarters, Inc. 1971
23110 Crenshaw Blvd. Suite A
Torrance, CA 90505
(310) 534-8188 — (800) 477-6291
www.nar-anon.org

Printed in U.S.A.

i

FOREWORD

The suggested daily readings on these pages represent the efforts of many Nar-Anon members who have shared their experience, strength and hope in writing. The purpose of this writing is to carry the message of Nar-Anon recovery to those who suffer the effects of another's addiction. Sometimes the writing happened individually and other times in groups or at an area or regional writing workshop. The contributors are sharing straight from their hearts and in keeping with tradition, remain anonymous.

Once written, there came the enormous task of editing, verifying, compiling, arranging, formatting, and indexing. Committed members of our fellowship came together to do all of these while working within the Twelve Traditions of Nar-Anon and group conscience.

We want to take this opportunity to thank each and every one of you who contributed your experience, strength and hope as well as your time. Together, we did it!

In this, our second edition, we now get to practice our slogan of "progress not perfection". A few writings were changed due to repetition, some grammatical corrections were done, the index was made more comprehensive and we have page numbers!

PREAMBLE

The Nar-Anon Family Groups are a worldwide fellowship for those affected by someone else's addiction.

As a twelve step program — we offer our help by sharing our experience, strength, and hope.

We carry the message of hope by letting others know that they are not alone; by practicing the Twelve Steps of Nar-Anon; and by changing our own attitudes.

We will respect your anonymity.

Our program is not a religious one, but a spiritual way of life.

MISSION STATEMENT

The Nar-Anon Family Groups are a worldwide fellowship for those affected by someone else's addiction. As a twelve step program, we offer our help by sharing our experience, strength, and hope.

VISION STATEMENT

We will carry the message of hope throughout the world to those affected by the addiction of someone near to them.

We will do this by:
• Letting them know they are no longer alone;
• Practicing the Twelve Steps of Nar-Anon;
• Encouraging growth through service;
• Making information available through Public Information, Hospitals and Institutions, and websites; and
• Changing our own attitudes.

SERENITY PRAYER

God, grant me the serenity to accept
the things I cannot change,
courage to change the things I can,
and the wisdom to know the difference.

PRAYER FOR THE GROWTH OF OUR FELLOWSHIP

God, we thank you for the peace and serenity we are finding as we learn to put our addicts in Your hands, one day at a time, and cease trying to change them. We are grateful that You helped us to find our way here, and we ask that You help those still alone and in pain because of the addiction of a friend or loved one. Please help them to find their way to these rooms, so that we may give back the gifts we have been so freely given, as well as give us a chance to share our experience, strength and hope with those suffering the isolation created by living with an addict. As we try to reach out to others with our fellowship, help us to be ever mindful of our traditions. We are trusting in Your love and concern for our addicts and us, and we ask that You help us to search always for Your will for us and for those we care about.

The beginning of each year is a good time to reflect on the past year. Our chairpersons will usually at this time of year present the topic, "What does recovery mean to me?" With that question in mind, each person in the meeting is invited to share his or her own experience, strength and hope, with special thought of the previous year.

For me, recovery means many things. It means knowing and accepting my past, and discovering who I am today, with an understanding of the forces that have brought me to the here and now. I have come to realize that my behavior was not always the best because I reacted to the addiction. Not being aware of this, I know that I did what I thought was best in the circumstances. I have discovered that I have both good qualities and imperfections. This has become a process for me to continue to discover the hidden facets of what has made me into the person I am. It means accepting what I have found out about myself and making the necessary changes in my life so that I can be comfortable and at peace with who I am. It means discovering the tools that will help me to shape myself, one day at a time, to become a better person.

To me, recovery is working the Nar-Anon Twelve Steps, Twelve Traditions and Twelve Concepts, and applying them to my daily life, my family and friends, and at work. It means working and applying this simple program with the awareness that I am doing this for myself, not for others or for the addict.

Recovery means keeping what I have by giving away my own experience, strength and hope. My gift to myself is my recovery, while my gift to the people in my life is what recovery means to me.

Thought for Today: I understand that my recovery depends on my perseverance, my regular attendance at meetings, my service to the fellowship, and the lessons I have learned from the Nar-Anon program that have become a part of who I am today.

"I'm sure that without this program I wouldn't be able to appreciate how much my life can be really wonderful, despite the hard times." ~ In All Our Affairs

The beginning of my recovery came when I worked Steps One through Three. I accepted that I am powerless, not only over the addict in my life, but also over events. I came to Nar-Anon with an open mind, ready to receive the messages, help and support that the program could so magically give. I changed my mind to a more sane way of thinking.

My reaction to addiction has made my life unmanageable. In these rooms, I learn that only chaos and confusion comes from trying to control the addict and his or her actions. I see the self-destructive patterns that have developed over the years and recognize that I need to change them. I also know there are consequences for my actions. I am so used to being there to pick up all the pieces and trying to fix all the addict's problems, so the addict will not have to suffer any consequences, and so that I will not be afraid.

The first three steps are realizing steps. Working these steps, I became aware of what I have become. Slowly, I realized that there was a better way if I chose to take the journey. The First Step gave me permission to change. What a relief - what a weight lifted off my shoulders to know that I am not a god! I cannot fix everyone. I cannot make them like me, even though I still want to try. My natural instincts do not always make me stop trying my way. The steps remind me I can change.

Thought for Today: I will let the first three steps talk to me when I am tempted to get caught up in another person's problems. I believe my sanity is restored whenever I ask for help. Today I surrender and find my real power by letting go of old ways.

"People have a hard time letting go of their suffering. Out of a fear of the unknown, they prefer suffering that is familiar." ~ Thich Nhat Hanh

The room where my home group meets remains the same. The chairs, the carpet, the lights, and even the walls are all the same as they were the first time I entered it. The difference is me. The person who sat there a year ago is not the person who sits there today. I feel as though all I did was sit in a chair faithfully and my life took on a whole new meaning. Some of the faces in the room are the same, but now they are important friends and people that I consider my family.

Before I came to Nar-Anon, my life was in chaos and my thoughts were scattered. The addicts in my life had complete control of my emotions because I had let them. I was afraid and angry; I was lonely and sad. I had told everyone in my life about my problems because I thought they would have a magic answer. I am sure they were all tired of hearing my stories. I even gave up church because I felt abandoned.

Thanks to Nar-Anon, my fear has changed to acceptance; my chaos has turned to serenity. I found spirituality with a Higher Power of my understanding and that Power is also my friend. My weakness has turned to strength and my scattered thoughts have been channeled into a new direction. The peace and serenity that the program offers has given me a new life.

I keep looking at the chairs. Are they magic? How could all this happen from sitting in a chair? In the beginning, there was no energy in me to take an active part in this program. I was suspicious and afraid. However, despite me, the changes came. Next week, I will get in my car, drive to my meeting and go in that door. I will find my chair and sit down. I will relax and wait for the blessings and growth that seem to come to me when I am sitting in my chair.

Thought for Today: If you are a newcomer, empty and lost, please sit down. The addict's drug of choice or how you look does not matter. It is simple and free to sit down and find yourself.

"In the depth of winter, I finally learned that there was an invincible summer." ~ Albert Camus

After attending Nar-Anon for many years, I now can say I am powerless over my husband's addiction, and my life is manageable. When I walked into my first Nar-Anon meeting, I knew that my husband was addicted to drugs. However, what I learned was that I was addicted to my husband. More importantly, I learned that I needed to practice my program to deal with the affects of living with addiction.

When I came into the rooms of Nar-Anon, I believed that I could stop my husband's drug use. I know now, that everything I was doing was causing me more pain. I was hurt so I cried, became angry and held resentments. I would beg him to stop and then threaten to leave him when he did not. I would plead with him that I would do anything for him if he would just not use. I made the situation worse because I did not carry out my threats or promises, so soon my words meant nothing. If only he would listen to me, I knew what was best.

I tried to protect my husband from the consequences of his using. I soon learned about enabling and saw that saving him from his consequences was only prolonging his disease and keeping him sick. I finally accepted that I had no control over his using and my attempts to control him were resulting in my own insanity.

I was at Step One for a long time before I finally got it. In the last eleven years, my husband has had periods of sobriety when he works his program with the help of his Higher Power. Little by little, I am improving. I worry less and less when I am able to step back and allow the addict to deal with his own addiction. I experience sanity, peace and serenity, which is a better way to live.

Thought for Today: My hard-learned lesson is that I cannot change the addict but I can change the way I react. As I stop taking care of his problems, surrender and work on myself, I am able to stop my crazy behavior and get my life back.

"Some people grin and bear it; others smile and do it." ~ Unknown

I am trying to find a balance between taking care of myself and helping others. I want to help those I love without taking on all of their burdens. I want to share my experience, strength and hope, offer my love and acceptance, and then let them go. I can give myself credit for the compassion and care that I feel for others. I realize that in my desire to help the addict, my helping actually hindered her from experiencing the consequences of her drug use. My helping may have prevented her from feeling she needed to change her self-destructive behavior.

As I am a person with a tendency to give advice, direct, and control, I made up a list to help me assist the addict without enabling:

- I do not do for the addict what she can do for herself.
- What is my payoff for enabling?
- Does enabling build my confidence in the addict or improve her self-esteem?
- Am I the problem solver?
- Do I nurture the idea that "all I have to do is ask" and I get?
- Do I participate in enabling because of my guilt if I do not help her?
- Is it easier to give in than to watch the addict suffer?
- What am I doing to enable the addict?
- Do I participate in the "drama" she creates?
- Do I tell her "I love you"?

Thought for Today: Step One taught me to stop controlling and enabling, and to take care of myself. When I tried to control the addict, I made myself insane and alienated my loved one.

"Every decision you make indicates what you believe you are worth." ~ A Course in Miracles

FAITH REPLACES FEAR

I remember the fear when I heard the siren, the fear when the phone rang. I remember carefully looking at the faces of people talking to me. Were they bringing me bad news? Was the phone call bad news? Was the siren an emergency involving my son? The fear was constant, unrelenting, debilitating, and gripping.

Working my Nar-Anon Twelve Step program was the start of the process that turned constant fear of disaster into faith that my Higher Power was taking care of me. My son got into recovery, and I was, in time, relieved of the constant fear of disaster.

Then, my fear of disaster shifted to fear of relapse. The feelings were equally constant, unrelenting, debilitating, and gripping. Again I accessed my Nar-Anon program and I found something that worked for me.

I used the analogy of recovery being a fixed deposit banking account. I looked back at the days, weeks and months of recovery and the newfound love, respect and admiration that had developed between my son and I, and I banked those days in a fixed deposit account. I told myself that nothing and no one could take those days away from me. Nothing could turn the clock back and erase those days. Our mutual recoveries were mine to keep forever.

Today I have faith that our respective twelve step programs will continue to bring days that I can bank one day at a time. As my faith grows, so my fear loses its power to dominate and have a hold over me.

Thought for Today: One day at a time, and with the help of my Higher Power, I will replace fear with faith.

"Only when we are no longer afraid do we begin to live." ~ Dorothy Thompson

Living in the here and now is a wonderful tool I acquired in Nar-Anon. I am focusing on today, each day, each hour, and each moment. I find tremendous comfort and relief when I stop worrying about the future that has not happened yet, and replaying the past that I can never change.

I am learning that staying in the present is all I need to do right now. This day, this moment, I do not need to solve all of my problems or take care of everyone around me. I do not need to make decisions that might affect me for a lifetime. I find serenity and peace moment by moment, taking care of myself first, while living my life in the here and now. I take life one step at a time, not projecting into the future but listening to my small voice inside that asks me, "Is this good for me right now?"

Thought for Today: Today, I will live my life in the here and now. I will focus on each hour and each moment. I will put myself first. I will take care of me and be cautious in my thinking and decision-making. Each moment will be precious to me, for it is all I am certain of.

"May your hands always be busy, may your feet always be swift, may you have a strong foundation, when the winds of changes shift. May you build a ladder to the stars, and climb on every rung - and may you stay - forever young. " ~ Bob Dylan

One of the reasons I had to be in control was because no one else seemed to want the job. I did not feel out of place or used because I liked things to run smoothly and to be orderly, and I was the only one who knew how to make that happen. Everyone else's life was more important than mine was.

I recognize now that my life was unmanageable and would be again if I focused on the addiction or the addict. I do not seem to have trouble recognizing that fact, just doing something about it. The old behaviors are waiting for me around the corner.

I wondered how the addict could not make better choices because they surely could see the consequences. Then I thought of my own life and I realized that I tended to do the same thing. I tried to ignore the fact that if I stepped in and started getting involved, then I would likely get hurt. No, I only saw that my actions would make someone else's life better. Who am I to say what is going to be the answer for someone else? How can I say their life would be better because I saw it that way? Did I learn my lessons by someone telling me, or do I learn my lessons by going through them myself? If I tried to get involved in someone else's program or inventory, my life became insane and unmanageable.

I thought my life was at the bottom when I came to Nar-Anon, but I continued going down before I started going up. I worried that I was going to be the only one in my family who was ever going to be in recovery. Then I realized that it did not matter. I was not there for them, but for me. I began to work my program, to let go and let God, to work the steps and to thank my Higher Power that I am not in control. I am here to carry the message and to practice these principles in all my affairs.

Thought for Today: We cannot force the flower to grow – we cannot change the tide. We can stand at the edge of the ocean and scream at the waves to stop, but they will not.

"Ten thousand flowers in spring, the moon in autumn, a cool breeze in summer, snow in winter. If your mind isn't clouded by unnecessary things, this is the best season of your life." ~ Wu-men

If I am willing to stand aside and let God's will be done, I free myself from personal anxiety and a mistaken sense of responsibility. One of the most commonly asked questions, when we find out about our loved one's addiction, is "Why?" Many times we really mean, "Why me?" We feel that the addict is punishing us for something. Over time, it becomes apparent that the "Why" is irrelevant. After all, no addict I have ever heard of makes a conscious decision to become an addict. So really, how important is it to know why? This whole exercise is merely a desperate attempt to find some logic in an illogical situation.

So what is important? For me, it is important to understand and accept the three Cs. I didn't cause it, I can't control it, and I can't cure it. For me, it is important to love and let it be. Letting go means I cannot do it for you; you are emotionally toxic for me. I will not allow your lifestyle into my home. It also means we can work this out together in our own programs. Sometimes it can be more compassionate for them and for us to ask them to leave.

I have to remember that sometimes it takes all the addict's focus to stay clean, and that staying clean does not necessarily mean they recover from their unhealthy behavior. This is a reality that though difficult, I must learn to accept. This is a simple program, but it is not easy.

Thought for Today: Accepting responsibility for what I can change is a growth experience for the addict and me.

"Exaggeration is truth that has lost its temper." ~ Kahlil Gibran

When I arrived to take my daughter to the hospital, she told me she had STD's. The old me would have lectured her. The old me would have broken down. The new me, strengthened by Nar-Anon meetings, remembered the slogan "Live and Let Live," and I was able to assist her without judging, controlling or criticizing. During the course of the next few days, I saw a side of my daughter that six months ago I would have missed because I would have been trapped by my emotions. I saw her angry and demanding things as if she were owed them. She was a foul-mouthed, manipulative and difficult person to live with.

Just like the addict, I needed help. That is why I came to these meetings. Before the program, I was trying to control my daughter. Now I realize that she was controlling me. Nar-Anon has shown me that this is not healthy; it is destructive and self-defeating. I realized that if I continued to let the addict control me, I would be destroyed as surely as she was destroying herself. Now I know that I cannot control the addict nor try to change her. I do not have to be upset. I must practice minding my own business and getting on with my own life.

Thought for Today: Just because one understands Step One, does not mean life will be easy. Nevertheless, it is getting easier for me to deal with. While the tension comes and goes, it is not making me sick anymore. While the stress is still there, it is not debilitating. I am beginning to see the bright, shining light that I thought had been lost.

"When I know I am not in charge, I can let one who is more qualified take over." ~ Meditations For People Who (May) Worry Too Much

I established a healthy boundary last night. My wife and I went to an awards dinner for my work, and we sat next to a co-worker and his wife. My co-worker is new, so I spoke with him at length about his life before becoming an agent with our company. I told him what it took for me to be successful and tried to give him some insight on what was in store for him. During the conversation, he asked me about my children. I thought, "Uh-oh, here goes."

I can talk at length about my oldest daughter, but what do I say about my addicted daughter? I told him about my oldest daughter and her 12-year-old son. All the while, I was thinking about what I should say about my addicted daughter. When I finished talking about my oldest daughter, I simply said that my youngest daughter is "not doing much of anything!"

My co-worker and his wife simply nodded their heads and we moved on to another topic. "Phew," I thought to myself. I do not have to explain to them about the horror we have gone through this past year. I do not have to listen to their show of concern. I do not have to explain. I do not have to compare in my mind their children to my addicted daughter. I do not have to have her in the forefront of my thoughts for the remainder of the night. I do not have to fight off the tension that surely would have followed. No, I do not have to do any of that. I felt relieved.

One of the women at my Nar-Anon meeting said that she enjoyed or looked forward to our meetings, as each of us knows what the others are going through. She can share her feelings at the meetings, and know that it is a safe place. She cannot do that with others in her life.

Thought for Today: I realize that I do not have to tell everyone I meet about my problems, even though they are real. I have the choice of not telling them to others or dwelling on them and ruining my day. I can share my concerns in my meeting with those that understand.

"We need to know how far we'll go, and how far we'll allow others to go with us. Once we understand this, we can go anywhere." ~ *Melody Beattie – Beyond Codependency*

Before my Nar-Anon program started to sink in, I would focus on every negative aspect of my life. Poor me, I am married to an addict. Poor me, the addict has finally left after I asked him to leave. Oh, poor me, the addict has found another person who is happy to live with him whether he is using or not. Poor me, I have been left alone to take care of myself. Who is going to help me and take care of me? Wait a minute, who was taking care of me before?

After years of attending Nar-Anon meetings, I am able to look at my situation differently. I married an addict and we had many good years, but unfortunately, for him, his disease progressed. He became sicker. His using was bothering me and so I asked him to leave and he did. I know he is safe and I hope he will get well. I am now free. Thank you, Nar-Anon and my Higher Power, for giving me another chance.

With an attitude of gratitude, I am freeing myself from my old way of thinking. I am changing. I am not always inclined to focus on things that are going wrong – negative things. I try to ask myself, where in my life is there good. I am grateful for these things. Sometimes when I cannot find anything good in my life I take a walk to the local reservoir. It is beautiful and serene. The lower trail is more than two miles. It seems like a bowl that opens up into the sky. "The firmaments of heaven" often occur to me. I feel closer to my Higher Power and my walk becomes a meditation for me. I return from my walk relaxed.

Thought for Today: When I look hard enough, I can be grateful for something.

"Though no one can go back and make a brand-new start, anyone can start from now and make a brand-new end." ~ Carl Bard

When I first came to the Nar-Anon program and heard about powerlessness, I did not understand what it meant. I thought I had control over everything and everyone including the addict. How enlightening to realize that the addiction of my loved one was out of my control, that I had no power over it or any responsibility for it.

I am also learning that powerlessness does not mean I do not have any power or that I am a victim or I am helpless. I do have the power to own my feelings and take care of myself. Powerlessness in recovery does not mean that I have to accept unacceptable behavior or make excuses for others' unacceptable behavior. I also should not make excuses for my own unacceptable behavior. I can use the Serenity Prayer and, with the help of my Higher Power, accept those things I cannot change and change the things I can. I have the power to forgive others and myself and accept that we are all flawed human beings. I can hold others and myself accountable and still love and accept them and myself, despite our shortcomings. I do have the power over my choices, how I see and react to the things that happen in my life.

I can turn the feelings of desperation that I had about powerlessness to feelings of joy, freedom and serenity, knowing that I have power over me. When I do, I start to feel grateful for the things my Higher Power and the Nar-Anon program have given me. The powerlessness of Step One has been the foundation for my recovery through the Twelve Steps.

Thought for Today: I know that I am powerless over the addict. It gives me a sense of freedom and serenity to know that I am ultimately responsible only for my own life and choices.

"We are powerless over our addictions, whether liquor, pills, people, food. We are not powerless, however, over our own attitudes, our own behaviors, our own self-image, our own determination, our own commitment to life and this simple program." ~ Karen Casey

For some time I thought about starting a Nar-Anon group near my home. What I heard today at a Nar-Anon convention helped to make that thought a reality. I spend a lot of time going to Narcotics Anonymous meetings with the addict in my life. I realized that I was doing a good job of helping, assisting, aiding, and supporting the addict with the addict's recovery. But I am not an addict, and I cannot relate to many of their struggles. I usually hear something that is useful, but I am not connecting to their stories.

Living with active addiction has taught me to use defense mechanisms. For example, many times I did not say what I believed because I was afraid the addict would not like what I said and then would get mad at me. Then, I expected that we would get into a fight, and the addict would go out and use. I thought I could control others by acting in a way that made them happy. My disease was one of fear and control.

The only times I had attended Nar-Anon meetings were when I went to a Narcotics Anonymous convention. The first thing I did when I arrived at the conventions was to see if Nar-Anon would be there. Every time I attended a Nar-Anon meeting, I felt at home and connected with the other members. I see now that by not working the Nar-Anon program I was depriving myself of my own recovery, and the growth and cleansing which I desperately needed in my life. As I continued to sit, listen and write, I realized that it had been a fear of failing that had stopped me from starting a meeting for myself. How could I control the success of the meeting? The result of my fear of failure was that I did not have the benefit of a Nar-Anon meeting close to me. It finally dawned on me that there was nothing to lose and everything to gain by starting a Nar-Anon meeting, which would benefit so many in my hometown.

Thought for Today: I will have the courage to do something new even though I cannot control or predict the outcome.

"The immature think that knowledge and action are different, but the wise see them as the same. The person who is established in one path will attain the rewards of both. The goal of knowledge and the goal of service are the same; those who fail to see this are blind." ~ Bhagavad Gita

I was almost done with my housework when I realized that the dishwasher had never turned on. Glancing at the microwave, I noticed that there were no readings. Thinking I had blown a circuit breaker, I went to the basement to check. I flipped the switches but nothing changed; still, no power. The electricity was completely out. I asked a neighbor what had happened. He said that the electricity would be out for several more hours because city workers broke an underground line. Although the house was completely powerless, I found myself flipping the light switch every twenty minutes to see if there really was no power.

Without power, I could not use the telephone, computer, television, lights, dishwasher, microwave, stove, vacuum, hairdryer, stereo, or washing machine. This situation helped me to understand the meaning of Step One in a much deeper and more practical way. Nothing I could do changed my situation. I had to admit, I was powerless.

Admitting I am powerless over other people, places and the disease of addiction, sometimes takes many failed attempts before I finally realize the truth and stop trying to control or change it.

Thought for Today: I have made many attempts to stop the addict from using. All these efforts have failed. Today I admit I am powerless over addiction and I can release the addict with love.

"Step One may be easy to read and easy to agree with, at least on the surface. We can freely admit to the fact that our lives are in real trouble. After all that is why we finally came to Nar-Anon." ~ The Nar-Anon Twelve Step Program

Addiction is a family disease. It not only affects the user but the non-users as well. I worried so much about the addict. I allowed the addict to consume my thoughts. The addict always had a crisis or was MIA on a binge. I was so distracted that I did not give the other family members much thought. It was not until I finally realized that there were other souls living in the house, including me, that deserved attention and tender, loving care, that I found the courage to make a tough decision. I applied the First Tradition to my family. For the common welfare of the family, I decided to offer the addict a choice – stop the drugs or leave.

Before I found my courage through the help of my Nar-Anon family, my husband and I allowed our addicted son to dictate the family dynamics. I did not understand the addict had choices, so I coddled him. The addict's behavior was destroying my other child's life. I allowed the addict free room and board while he spent his money on drugs, which was not setting a good example for either child.

In Nar-Anon, I learned that my son did not cause his disease. He was, however, responsible for taking care of himself. Like all of us, he had the ability to seek help and recovery. I had to take drastic measures and banish the addict from our home because of his behavior. Regardless of the support and love he was offered, he continued to be poisonous to the rest of us in the household.

I am thankful I had so much support from my Nar-Anon Family Group. Other members sharing about their own struggles gave me courage to act. I still do not know how our family's journey will turn out, but we are traveling in a healthier direction.

Thought for Today: None of us may have the ultimate answers, but we can all help each other feel less alone and afraid. It is because you have walked the same road as me and have shared your life and experiences with me, that I have become a better parent. The sharing of your experience, strength and hope is truly invaluable to me.

"Our common welfare should come first; personal progress for the greatest number depends on unity." ~ Nar-Anon Tradition One

Do I believe I will be here on earth forever? My favorite saying is "I'll do it tomorrow." Somehow, I never find enough time to do it, especially if it is for me. I schedule too much into my life. One of my character defects is procrastinating, and it has been a part of my life for a long time. I will work on it tomorrow, next month or next year. When I am honest with myself, I realize someday my time will be up, and my chance to do all those things will be lost. My bumper sticker says, "Be Patient, I Procrastinate."

Maybe I am giving myself permission to continue this behavior. I guess I have to learn the lesson that procrastination teaches. When I am gone they will write, "She never did today what could be put off until tomorrow and her tomorrow never came."

In Nar-Anon, I am starting to learn to put the focus on me and my character defects. When I do this, I realize it may be fear, the need to isolate, or the need to distract myself from my growth that makes me procrastinate. Perhaps it is because I feel I am not important enough to work on! I get an adrenaline rush every time there is a deadline. Am I setting myself up for failure or do I enjoy that feeling? What is my reward or payoff? What do I get from procrastination?

I am used to being the caretaker of others who are struggling to balance life against the weight of addiction. I feel guilty taking a moment to focus on myself or enjoy life. However, for my own sanity and growth, that is exactly what I need to do.

Thought for Today: The addict's roller coaster struggles in active addiction will continue, no matter what I choose to do. So today, it is perfectly fine for me to work on myself and enjoy a moment of satisfaction and happiness, without feeling guilty that I fell asleep on my watch.

"If we are to flourish as creative beings, if we are to grow into wholeness, we must bloom wherever we are planted." ~ Sarah Ban Breathnach

Before Nar-Anon I believed that I had to always give more so people would like me, or say the things people wanted to hear, not what I really thought or felt. I was a people pleaser and I did not want to hurt my friends' feelings. I did not respect myself enough to believe my own feelings had value. I had to forgive my addicted friends because they were not responsible for their behavior, because they were high. When I first learned that addiction is a disease, I mistakenly thought I had to accept unacceptable behavior from an addict because the addict was sick.

What I have learned in Nar-Anon about friendship is to be more open and honest in my relationships. I do not need to be mean or pushy, but I have a right to express my opinions. I can say what is on my mind in an appropriate manner whether the other person agrees with me or not. To be a friend does not mean that I have to agree with all of a person's values or opinions. I have learned to accept people for who they are, and not to expect them to be what I am or what I want them to be. I have also learned that everyone is responsible, including me, for his or her own behavior. I do not have to accept unacceptable behavior such as violence, verbal abuse or stealing. I can choose not to associate with someone who is behaving in a harmful manner, and I do not have to feel guilty or make excuses for their behavior.

Thought for Today: Nar-Anon has enlightened my mind and soul. I can now look at my part in a friendship. When there are things I do that are wrong and I need to make an amends or to take responsibility, I do. I also respect myself and protect myself from harmful behavior. Nar-Anon has given me a new set of friends that I can trust, and I feel close to them.

"How rare and wonderful is that flash of a moment when we realize we have discovered a friend." ~ William Rostler

Before I came to Nar-Anon, I did not have any balance in my life, but I did not realize it. My entire focus was on the addict, and I became lost in the shuffle. When someone asked me how I was doing, I would reply that I was not well. I then would tell them about the addict's problems. When the addict was out using, I could not sleep, eat or think straight. All I could do was focus on the addict. I would sit still and worry. I was paralyzed by fear and trapped in obsessive thinking.

When I came to Nar-Anon and I heard the steps for the first time, I embraced Step One because it so perfectly described my life. My life was unmanageable because I was trying to control the addict's life. Once I accepted that I was powerless over the addict and his choices, I was set free and was on my way to finding my balance and myself once again.

As I continued going to meetings and using the tools of the program, my life continued to change. When the addict was out using, I called a Nar-Anon friend and talked, went to a meeting or read my literature. Accepting the First Step helped me to move on. I was no longer stuck. I learned that worry never stopped anything from happening. I learned that my fear did not help the addict. I learned how to live my life again.

Thought for Today: As a person who loves an addict, I need to admit and accept that I am powerless over other people. I accept that my life is unmanageable when I am trying to control others. Then I can change my focus and find balance, peace, serenity and myself again.

"By letting go of the illusion of control over other people, their actions and their addiction…, we find an enormous burden is lifted and we begin to discover the freedom and the power we do possess – the power to define and live our own lives." ~ Paths to Recovery

How long will I continue to try to control other people, places and things when I know from working the Nar-Anon program that the only person I have any control over is me? My urge to control returns instantly when I take another person's inventory. I must learn to mind my own business and remember what my business is. If my name is not on it, I need to let it go.

Step One reminds me that I have no power over other people's lives. It goes on to suggest that my attempt to control other people, places and things is making my life unmanageable. If I come into Nar-Anon and honestly share my anxiety and frustration at my inability to accept the unacceptable, I open the way for help from the group and from the power that I feel present in these rooms.

Step One begins with admitting we are powerless over the addict, and then we admit our lives are unmanageable. If I practice this step each time I want to control a person or situation, not only will I be able to mind my own business, I will have more time and energy to do so. I will have the energy to set boundaries and make choices that benefit me.

Thought for Today: I will focus on the things I can change and I will release those things that I cannot change to my Higher Power. Knowing my limitations will prepare me for Step Two. I have begun my journey to serenity and peace of mind. My Nar-Anon program offers this priceless gift.

"There are two big forces at work, external and internal. We have very little control over external forces such as tornadoes, earthquakes, floods, disasters, illness, and pain. What really matters is the internal force. How do I respond to those disasters? Over that I have complete control." ~ Leo Buscaglia

My sponsor told me all progress is in direct relation to how much pain I am no longer willing to endure. When my son was almost killed, had crack psychosis and faced ten years in prison, I was so afraid for him. I did not think I could survive.

I was desperate for tools. When a woman in a meeting shared that she had three adult sons who were in prison, I knew she was the sponsor for me. She was someone who knew what I was facing. She had what I wanted – a way to survive with children in prison.

With my sponsor's help, I learned to let go and let this child be an adult and suffer his own consequences for using drugs. I did what she told me to do: read literature, write, work the steps and do service. I learned to have confidence that whatever the addict had to go through, no matter how dire, even death, it was his journey, not mine. His fate hung in the balance many times. Today, many years later, my sponsor and I are grateful that, unlike their fathers, our sons are no longer in prison and have found recovery.

Thought for Today: I do what my sponsor did for me, especially when a newcomer comes to a meeting, I share my story. With this, the newcomer may realize they are no longer alone but among people who can understand their situation.

"Sponsors – get one, use one, be one." ~ Unknown

I have been a caretaker for as long as I can remember. It started when I was a teenager when my mother needed my help to care for my ill father. I always felt that I had to be responsible for and take care of others. I chose a caretaking profession. In my first marriage, I felt that I had to take care of my husband and I allowed him to manipulate me constantly. He refused to work and expected me to manage everything. I kept my anger and resentment to myself, never realizing that it was destroying me. Then my children came along and I needed to take care of them. When my husband died, my anger and resentment died with him. I went back to what I thought was a normal life, but it wasn't. Everyone else's needs always came before mine. I could seldom say no to anyone and when I did, I felt extreme guilt. In my second marriage, things were quiet and peaceful for many years until my husband became addicted to crack. Once again, I became the caretaker, only the situation was much worse. I lost my sense of self.

One night when I felt as if I was going insane, I called the Nar-Anon hotline number. I went to a meeting the next day. I felt better after that first meeting, even though things were still crazy in my life. Through Nar-Anon meetings, I realized that I did not have to be responsible for taking care of others. They could take care of themselves. I needed to learn to take care of my needs. It was a long hard struggle to change the way I had felt for so many years, but the support that I received at my meetings helped me immensely.

Thought for Today: I can say no to the addict and to others and not have to feel guilty anymore. I am important. I have to take care of myself and allow others to take care of themselves. No is a complete sentence. The focus in my life has to be about me.

"Example is not the main thing in influencing others. It is the only thing."
~ Albert Schweitzer

Tradition One saved my family. Too often in the chaotic household of an addict, the needs of the addict are met at the expense of everyone else in the household. This was certainly true in my house. As the addict continued to spin out of control, vacations were skipped because I could not risk leaving the addict for any period of time. Holidays were ruined with one crisis after another. Financial savings were sacrificed to bail the addict out of yet another jam.

While taking a group conscience in a Nar-Anon meeting, someone reminded me of the first tradition, that "our common welfare should come first; personal progress for the greatest number depends on unity." It clicked in my head that this was also true for my family.

I realized that while I thought I was saving the family by saving the addict, I had harmed the addict and the entire family. By putting the needs of the addict ahead of the welfare of the family, I denied the family what was rightfully theirs. I also denied the addict the opportunity to be responsible for himself. This behavior led to an atmosphere of resentment. All members of the family felt cheated.

In order for the family to survive, the family had to come first. I now understand that an individual's needs are best met when the needs of the whole family are considered. Now when family decisions need to be made, each family member is given a voice. Not for what they want, but what they feel is in the best interest of the family as a whole. Each voice is considered and decisions are made that are right for the family.

Thought for Today: I will not act until I believe my actions will benefit all my family.

"Passing on our peaceful feelings increases the level of our own peace."
~ Karen Casey

In Step One, "I admitted that I was powerless over the addict and my life had become unmanageable." I now know that I am powerless over people, places and things. Powerlessness is not easy to accept.

Feeling powerless took my breath away! Most of my life I have been on my own and in control of my life – at least I thought I had control. I thought there was not much I could not do, so being powerless was something I could not accept easily. When addiction came into my life and turned me upside down, luckily I found Nar-Anon!

In the Nar-Anon program, I learned that I could admit I am powerless. Step One reminded me that I have no power over other people's lives. It also suggested that my attempt to control others was making my life unmanageable. When I come to Nar-Anon and honestly share my anxiety and my frustration at my inability to accept the "unacceptable," I open the way for help from the group and the power is present. I find it is okay to be powerless because I have a Higher Power in charge!

Thought for Today: When there is nothing I can do to help the addict or others, I can share my feelings at meetings. I do not have to be afraid. I see my powerlessness and release my problems to my Higher Power.

"'We will allow the good God to make plans for the future - for yesterday has gone, tomorrow has not yet come and we have only today." ~ Mother Teresa

I believe that there are two things I must do when taking the First Step. First, I must admit that I am powerless. Addiction is a difficult disease to understand. As the parent of a youngster, I believed that if I did my best, my little loved one would grow into a fine adult. How heartbreaking it was to discover that my child was an addict. I blamed myself. I remembered things I should have done and things I did not do. I tried hard to find out how I could help the addict now and cure this dreadful disease of addiction.

I had to accept that I was powerless. I did not do anything to make the addict use and I could not do anything to make the addict stop. This caused my life to become unmanageable.

Second, in Nar-Anon I must accept that my life is unmanageable and in need of improvement. The only person I can help is me. I can attend a meeting, share and listen. I can pray each day that my Higher Power will help me to know what I need to change.

Thought for Today: Accepting my powerlessness over others and taking the action I need to make my life manageable are things I can do.

"People who consider themselves victims of their circumstances will always remain victims unless they develop a greater vision for their lives." ~ Stedman Graham

Genuine kindness is difficult to give to another, and virtually impossible if I have not yet learned to receive it. Prior to Nar-Anon, I had trained myself to suspect and question everything, especially an act of kindness. Everything had a price. As a newcomer to the program, I brought with me that "kindness has a price" attitude. I found members who offered me their kindness through sharing, nods, smiles, and even hugs. I wondered what they wanted from me. What was their price? I felt uncomfortable with all of the unconditional kindness. Fortunately, I was encouraged to keep coming back in such a friendly way that I felt that they really wanted me to join. Little by little, I kept coming back, and shared my story, my nods, my smiles, my laughter, and, yes, even my hugs. It made me feel good. I was getting a gift as well as giving one.

It took some time, but I finally realized that genuine kindness has no price. To receive a smile, a hug, a shared laugh "just because" is a gift, truly a gift from the heart with no price tag attached.

Thought for Today: Acceptance is the highest form of kindness that I can give. Allowing others to be who they are without my judgment of whether that is good or bad, frees them and me of the burden of trying to change them to meet my expectations.

"We ask only for the grace to release our addicts with love, and cease trying to change them." ~ Nar-Anon Blue Booklet

I was aware that my life had become unmanageable, and I was certain that if the addict changed his behavior and stopped using drugs, everything would be perfect. Then I became aware of the fact that my life was unmanageable because I was not managing my life. I was trying to manage the addict's life.

By attending Nar-Anon meetings, I learned and accepted that addiction is an illness and that the addict was not the only one suffering from the disease of addiction. I too was suffering from the effects of addiction. With the loving support of my Nar-Anon family group and my acceptance that my Higher Power could do for me what I could not do for myself, I became ready to take the action needed to make my life manageable.

I began to practice the Twelve Steps. I sought guidance and the willingness to follow that guidance unconditionally. I healed one day at a time, as I began to attend to my responsibilities and take care of my own illness. I recognized my sick behaviors, attitudes and thinking. I also learned that I needed to stop doing for others what they could do for themselves. I needed to stop judging others, especially the addict. It is not my job to supervise anyone else's recovery. I will no longer enable the addict nor prevent him from avoiding negative consequences. I will stop trying to control the uncontrollable and get out of the way of his recovery.

Thought for Today: When I become *aware* of the truth and *accept* it, I then have choices and the opportunity to take appropriate *action*.

"Climb up on some hill at sunrise. Everybody needs perspective once in a while, and you'll find it there." ~ Robb Sagendorph

Living with an active addict is stressful and I constantly feel as though I am walking on eggs. When I harbor a mistaken sense of responsibility for someone else's well-being and safety, when my sanity and well-being is adversely affected by the actions of the addict, when I find myself worrying and losing sleep because the addict is out partying, when I worry that I may say the wrong thing and "cause" him to go back out, then I am not practicing detachment.

By detaching with love, I can stop feeling responsible for the addict's well-being and behavior. I have learned in Nar-Anon that addiction is a disease. It is not my fault! I didn't cause it, I can't control it, and I can't cure it. I have discovered by practicing detachment that I can relieve myself of the mistaken guilt and responsibility I felt.

Walking on eggs always results in broken eggs. Living with an addict causes stress. I think of detachment as a tight rope and the addict as eggs. I use the tight rope to walk above the eggs. I practice walking on the rope so I will not fall and break the eggs, but walking a tight rope is not easy; it takes a lot of practice. At first, I am sure to make mistakes, to slip and break a few eggs. However, if I practice and learn to walk the rope, I will eventually be able to achieve my goal. The same is true for detachment.

Thought for Today: Detachment is one tool I can use to separate myself from the chaos, fear and mistaken responsibility that result from living with active addiction.

"Feel the feeling. Choose the behavior." ~ Charles Rumberg

I expected my children to be perfect, to always do the right thing. I tried to control them by giving them direction and making them do things in a way that I felt was correct! When they didn't, I could not handle it.

I could not accept their drug use and felt that their behavior was a reflection on me. I was embarrassed for myself and scared to death for them. I would make big problems out of little ones. I became so distrusting of my children and others that I showed them no respect. I would meddle and invade their privacy by reading their diaries and their mail. I was looking for any excuse to challenge and confront them, thinking this would make them do what I wanted and make them stop using drugs. I was obsessed with their lives. All I could think of was how to change these addicts.

When I came to Nar-Anon, I learned that my interference and my attempts at controlling them were actually standing in the way of their recovery. I was not allowing them to change. I was afraid even to let them try. In Nar-Anon, I learned to let go of the control I never had in the first place.

Thought for Today: I will remember to yield a little here and there and "accept the things I cannot change" as it says in the Serenity Prayer.

"Help me find an appropriate balance of responsibility to my children. Help me parent through nurturing and discipline instead of control." ~ Melody Beattie

The slogan, "Let Go and Let God" has become a tremendous comfort to me. At first, I resisted the idea of letting go of my will and giving it over to a Higher Power. It made no sense to me. As a mother, I felt I was not being loving toward my son if I did not help him when he was in trouble. I felt guilty if I did not rescue him from jail.

I kept hearing at meetings to keep an open mind. When I did this, I heard members share how they found the serenity I wanted. Their wisdom, strength, and hope were an inspiration, so I kept listening. Many shared how they found serenity by letting go of self-will and control. This was difficult for me at first, but with practice eventually it became easier. I realized I was not helping by rescuing my son.

It was easier for me to "Let Go" than it was to "Let God." Trusting an unseen power was even harder since I was not even sure I believed in a Higher Power. When I let go of my doubts and grabbed on to faith, I found a wonderful calmness. I practice this often and it always brings me serenity.

Thought for Today: My faith keeps growing as I find that by "Letting Go and Letting God," seemingly unsolvable problems are resolved in ways I would not have thought possible.

"If we were logical, the future would be bleak, indeed. But we are more than logical. We are human beings, and we have faith, and we have hope, and we can work." ~ Jacques Yves Cousteau

The three Cs are similar to talismans. Their magic and power are available for me at the right moment. When I accept that I didn't cause it, I can't control it, and I most certainly can't cure someone else, I feel serenity.

I have over fifteen years in a twelve step program. My partner has a child who is in active addiction. I find myself wanting to save my partner from suffering, by trying to fix the addict. Indirectly I would be saving myself, as I am greatly affected by my partner's moods. When my partner is sad, I am depressed. My instinct tells me that I need to practice a new way of life. It was suggested that I could learn a better way to live in Nar-Anon.

Before Nar-Anon, I would try to fix the addict. I realize now that what I wanted was to make my partner feel better. I would make myself physically sick because I thought I had to be in control of my partner's feelings. I felt that the way to do that was to help her addicted loved one. I felt compelled to fix both situations.

I realized that my involvement was putting my recovery in danger. My life was in complete chaos. Today, I am learning to apply the three Cs in a new way, and learning to keep the focus on me. I am now feeling more peace and serenity, and less anxiety.

Thought for Today: I will place myself in the loving arms of my Higher Power. I know that with my Higher Power's help, I will make it. I can hold tight to the three Cs and let them take me on a safe journey. I only have the power to control myself.

"We do not need to search in order to find our true being. We already are it, and the mind which searches for it is the very reason why we cannot find it." ~ Roy Whenary

As the Twelve Steps are our guide to recovery, personal growth, and the solution to practically any problem, our Twelve Traditions provide us with the guidelines that make it possible for the Nar-Anon Family Groups to function and survive. The Traditions offer us spiritual principles that help us avoid distractions, errors, and pitfalls that can destroy the group.

As a person who came from an environment where active addiction resulted in chaos, confusion, abuse, and instability, I did not want to be a part of any program where I was going to have to follow anyone else's rules. Therefore, I was relieved when I was told the Nar-Anon program is merely suggested and that they would always respect my confidence and anonymity. The only thing asked was that I do the same in return.

As my recovery progressed, I was also just as relieved to find that there are Twelve Traditions based on spiritual principles that are designed to ensure the survival of our groups, and to fulfill Nar-Anon's one purpose, "to help the families and friends of addicts." Therefore, I believe it is important that I learn to respect and practice the Traditions.

Thought for Today: I am welcomed, supported and loved in our Nar-Anon group. The program is here for me today because of those who came before me, and their willingness to follow the Traditions. Today I will do my part to put principles above personalities, and adhere to the Traditions that help keep this program working for those who will follow.

"Our group experience suggests that the unity of the Nar-Anon Family Groups depends upon our adherence to these traditions." ~ *Nar-Anon Blue Booklet*

I have my own opinions and I need to be careful because sometimes my opinions, spoken out loud, will become gossip. I told a friend about another friend. Then that friend talked to the other friend about it. I was then confronted directly about my gossiping. If only I had not said anything in the first place. That is how my Higher Power shows me that I have stepped out of line. I did not mean for my other friend to find out what I had said about her. Now she was asking me about what I had said. Two old sayings came into my mind: "What goes around comes around," and "If you can't say anything nice, don't say anything at all."

To not participate in gossip, I need to begin with me. I need to remember that I should not talk about other people in a way that is harmful. I need to realize when I am being judgmental. When I recognize that a conversation is moving towards gossip, I need to be able to stop myself from participating.

I need to remember that my close friends trust me with their confidential stories, and if I repeat those stories, it will turn into gossip. I will pray to my Higher Power to show me what changes I need to make in my behavior and that I will be willing to make those changes.

Thought for Today: Nar-Anon teaches us that we are in a program to help one another by sharing our experience, strength and hope. Gossip contradicts this purpose, harms the unity referred to in Tradition One, and might eventually cause destruction of the group.

"Who gossips to you will gossip of you." ~ Turkish Proverb

Before attending Nar-Anon, I thought that being vulnerable was a weakness. It left me open to attack. I felt I was placing myself in emotional or physical danger where I could be harmed. I am learning that Nar-Anon meetings are a safe place where I can share my weaknesses with others without the fear of attack or harm. At a recent meeting, I heard another member share that she gets the most out of a meeting when she allows herself to be vulnerable. She found this especially true when she shared something about herself with a newcomer.

I tried her suggestion when I was asked to lead a First Step table, and found that she was right. By sharing openly about what was truly going on with me and how I had behaved, I was better able to look more clearly at my actions, feelings and doubts.

If I take the chance to be vulnerable with someone I do not know, I offer him or her the same gift of trust while I give myself an opportunity to grow. The newcomer always reminds me of where I have been and of where I never again wish to return. We are no longer strangers. This is the magic of the meeting.

Thought for Today: When I am terrified about how vulnerable I am to the effects of another's addiction and suffering, I am reminded that I have faced this before and lived to share about it.

"The foundation for the development of good relations with one another is altruism, compassion and forgiveness." ~ Dalai Lama

I am a member of the Nar-Anon Family Groups. My daughter is an addict who lives in our home and is working on her own path to recovery. I am learning to work the program for myself.

One Sunday, as we prepared to go to church, our daughter was late. Since my husband likes to be on time, I became anxious, wondering how they each would behave. I made a comment to my daughter that she should get up earlier because this same situation had happened last week and that maybe she needed to work on her time issues.

Immediately her cheeks became red and I saw that she was upset. I retreated to the bathroom and closed the door. When I came out, she said she was not going to church and she was angry. I told her that this was a trivial matter, and she should not blow it out of proportion. As we left the house, I began to worry. Could she be so angry that she would do something stupid? Would she try to get back at me?

My old behavior has a way of rising to the surface. As I shared this with a Nar-Anon friend, she asked me a question: "What are you afraid of?" I said I was afraid I would cause her to use drugs out of anger and I did not think I could go through that again. I saw her behavior as an indicator of an upcoming relapse. My friend replied, "So what could you do to stop her?" She continued to ask me about my fears and then she explained to me that I should not doubt my Higher Power, who knows what is best for my daughter and for me. She suggested I talk to my Higher Power about my fears and move on with my life.

Thought for Today: Trust! Today I will do my best to stay off the fear train, because I know it goes around in circles. Today I will have faith.

"Now that all your worry has proved to be such an unlucrative business, why not find a better job." ~ Hafiz

I came to Nar-Anon seeking answers, hope and guidance. I have learned to face my fears, doubts, anger, resentments, and pain. I continue to work on removing my negative thoughts and assumptions that can lead me into arguments with the addict, arguments that often lead me right back down the same road that first brought me to Nar-Anon.

Before coming to meetings, I felt helpless. I was torn between feeling protective of the addict and burdened by the responsibility. I have come to realize that I cannot make the addict change nor can I know what he is doing every minute. Nar-Anon has helped me to believe in myself, trust my feelings and feel safe again. This has become more important to me than controlling the addict, which is what I tried to do in the past.

I have found that if I live in the moment, I can face anything. I do not need to dwell on the negative or worry about what will happen next. I will read Nar-Anon literature, talk with my sponsor and attend meetings. I will also do service work which teaches me how to get along with other people, because our service structure is based on the Twelve Traditions and Twelve Concepts of Nar-Anon. This will keep me focused on my program and me.

Thought for Today: Just for today I will not criticize one bit, not find fault with anything (including myself), and not try to improve or regulate anyone but myself.

"To climb steep hills requires a slow pace at first." ~ William Shakespeare

Before Nar-Anon, I would have told you that I was the sane one and the addict was crazy. My addicted loved one was out-of-control. He disappeared for days, borrowed money he never paid back and stole from his friends and family. He did whatever it took to get high. He had been to numerous rehabs and spent years in jails but still continued this insane behavior.

I, on the other hand, pleaded, begged, cried, worried, and tried every trick, con and bribe to make him stop using. When that did not work, I made myself sick with worry and tried to clean up his messes by paying his debts. I spent thousand of dollars for collect calls from jails and halfway houses. I spent over half of my free time going to prisons to sit for hours in a visiting room. I did this all in the name of love, thinking that this was the last time; thinking that he will change; and thinking that he has had enough.

I started attending Nar-Anon meetings to keep an eye on the addict and to learn how to control his addiction. I went to meetings, I listened, I found a sponsor, and I read the Nar-Anon literature. I found that I was starting to learn about addiction and how I was affected by it. I saw that I was just as insane as the addict was. My behavior was compulsive and bizarre. It took time but I began to understand my limits and after listening to and saying the Serenity Prayer over a thousand times, I finally received the message. I was ready to take Step Two.

Thought for Today: I will turn to my Higher Power for help and have hope that my Higher Power can restore me to sanity. It is not my place, my duty or within my power to control others. When I feel the need to change or control someone else, I will remind myself that this is crazy thinking.

"I have faith that anything can come to one who trusts the unlimited help of universal wisdom." ~ Walter Russell

DECISIONS   **February 7**

When I first came to Nar-Anon, I was a decision-making mess. For over five years, I had lived with my husband's drug use and the mental, emotional, and sometimes physical abuse that came with it. It was easier to let him make all the decisions in our lives because if he was happy then we were all happy. The abuse seemed normal to me, but our four young children were so innocent and vulnerable. Many times, I thought I could take no more but it wasn't until I joined Nar-Anon that I realized that not only could I make decisions on my own, but that I would make one decision and stick to it. My children and I would not live with active addiction.

By working my Nar-Anon program and with the help of my Nar-Anon friends, I was able to make that one basic but oh so hard decision that has changed my life. My Nar-Anon friends helped me each step of the way to be a stronger and better mother for my children. Each day I am learning to make decisions. Though sometimes it is still not easy to make those life-changing decisions, I know that with Nar-Anon and my Higher Power, all things are possible.

Thought for Today: With the support and love I receive from my Nar-Anon group, I can begin to take control of my life and do what is right for my loved ones and me. Today, I know that I can make a decision.

"The wishbone will never replace the backbone." ~ Will Henry

I spent seven years trying desperately to hang on to my life and sanity. By the time I finally reached out for help and discovered Nar-Anon, I was very close to both murder and suicide. Like a drug addict, I had to reach a bottom that was so painful and humiliating that I could not go on without help from my Higher Power. A good friend in recovery took me to my first meeting and the people I met there told me to keep coming back.

What I heard that first night and many nights after that, was that I needed to detach with love and quit trying to change my husband. This was not what I came there to hear. They were supposed to tell me how to save him, not how to let him suffer and possibly die. It took a long, long time for me to comprehend what they were telling me; that my "helping" was what was keeping him from seeking recovery. He had no reason to stop using if he could use me to make his continued using possible.

Four and a half years ago, he finally reached a bottom that he did not have the stamina to overcome. He asked for help and went into recovery. Thanks to Nar-Anon and his recovery program, today we live a fairly normal existence, as long as we go regularly to our meetings to be around people who have suffered as we have and found a way out.

Thought for Today: I will not interfere and prevent the consequences of active addiction because in doing so I am standing in the way of recovery.

"The only person you are destined to become is the person you decide to be." ~ Ralph Waldo Emerson

I went to my yoga class today. My yoga class has a therapeutic approach, where the instructor formulates the exercises, stretches and poses based on the discomfort that each student is experiencing. The instructor asks each person how they are feeling, spiritually, emotionally and physically. He checks in with each student, and when it was my turn, I told him that I felt completely at peace.

Today, the past feelings of anxiety, fearfulness and pain are gone. As I meditated, I could remember those trying times, but they passed effortlessly, as quickly as they entered my mind, without upsetting me or sending me into a tailspin of trying to fix the impossible. No more "if only," no more "shoulda, coulda, woulda."

Because of the Nar-Anon program and years of practicing "letting go" and turning my loved ones over to the care of their Higher Power, I am able to enjoy this peaceful state of mind. Being active in Nar-Anon meetings and service has given me hope, peace and serenity. Through the sharing at meetings and the literature, I am learning how other members have changed their lives. With the loving support of my Nar-Anon family and the help of my Higher Power, I have been able to change my life. First, I had to see recovery in action, in others, to know it was possible. Then, as I worked the steps and practiced the principles, I felt the change in me. What a gift!

I welcome the newcomer because I know the program works. All I need to do is work the steps and trust in my Higher Power. I believe my Higher Power will guide me in the direction I need to go. I am also learning that in order to keep what I have, I need to share it with others.

Thought for Today: I will suggest to a newcomer that they come to at least six meetings before they decide if Nar-Anon is right for them. I will share with them how I have experienced the gifts of the program.

"Those who try to hang on when God is trying to move on will always be miserable" ~ Joyce Meyer

CRISIS

There is a saying, in German, *"denn wir haben eine Krise der Verzweiflung erreicht"* - for we have reached a crisis of desperation. When I read this the other day, I thought of my life before I started attending Nar-Anon. The desperation that had consumed my being was a crisis. I wanted to change the addict's destructive behavior and tried every trick in the book - anger, belittlement, and manipulation. None of them worked.

When I would look for the addict on the streets and did find her, I would be sick. When I thought about her, I would be sick. For the longest time, I was always feeling a crisis of desperation. Today, while I still long for the addict's healing, I have come to understand that the crisis that I was feeling was of my own doing. I was letting my thoughts of fear and doubt consume me.

When I see the addict today, I still ache for her healing and I do urge her, as Nar-Anon teaches me, to get some help. On the other hand, I realize that my urging her will not make her change. For me, this is one of the differences between then and now.

Now, I believe that I never cease requiring help to prevent my self-destruction. Nar-Anon is the source of that help. It has brought me back to the realization that I need to turn all of this over to my Higher Power.

I find myself asking for my Higher Power's help more often now, in all aspects of my life. I need guidance in this trial that I am facing. In the past, I envied the families of addicts who were seeking help and getting better. Today I do not envy them. Today I realize that although the addict is getting better, there are different problems they may face - a different crisis of desperation.

Thought for Today: I believe that, at the end of the day, I will be a better person because of my experiences. True wisdom comes from the overcoming of suffering and pain. All true wisdom is therefore touched with sadness.

"Practicing silence means making a commitment to take a certain amount of time to simply be." ~ Deepak Chopra

How ironic it is that it seems to be okay for women to cry, but it is not okay for men to cry. I say ironic because in my family, I am the one who wears my heart on my sleeve. My wife will not attend meetings because she says, "all I will do is sit there and cry"! I cry or tear up when I hear Taps played at a veteran's funeral. I cry when there is a happy ending to a film. I cry when I hear the "Star Spangled Banner" sung. I cry when I think too much about the addict.

I accept my wife's reason for not wanting to attend Nar-Anon meetings, but for me letting go of my emotions and pain is good! I accept my wife's reluctance to speak about the addict in our life, yet I find that speaking and crying helps me accept the disease of addiction better. I am able to accept the fact that I have no control, and thus have no expectations. For me, releasing emotions is part of the natural healing process. My Higher Power knows the hurt, pain, and other emotions that go along with my loving an addict.

I have been attending Nar-Anon meetings on a regular basis. When I share at a meeting, my pent up steam and emotions are not as ferocious as they once were. I attribute this to my practicing the principles of Nar-Anon. I benefit from listening to the stories of others and feeling the strength I receive from them.

Thought for Today: Attending meetings regularly is my strength and hope. The emotional release that I get allows me to move forward with my recovery.

"Surrender is the simple but profound wisdom of yielding to rather than opposing the flow of life." ~ Eckhart Tolle

The trials of being raised in a dysfunctional family sometimes made it hard for me to believe that there is a Higher Power. I could not understand why all these terrible things were happening to me. I did not choose to be born into this situation. Feeling abandoned by my Higher Power and not knowing where to turn for help, I was making poor choices. I chose to marry an addict and I assumed I could repair his problems.

When I came to Nar-Anon I found the hope that a Power greater than myself could restore sanity to my life; I gained the courage to move forward in this program. I am imperfect, but I choose to work the Nar-Anon program to the best of my ability. I tell myself that progress will be made on my own time schedule. Nobody has a time clock to judge my progress. I started to get better, sometimes gradually and sometimes, all at once. Yes, I hold myself accountable to a Higher Power, but that Power can and will restore me to sanity.

As I surrender to a Higher Power, I choose to lose my insanity. To work this step, I work on my stores of hope. Sometimes, hope is hard to come by because of past betrayals. Then I tell myself that no one can work this program for me. I need to do this for myself. Then, and only then, will I begin to heal.

Thought for Today: That I recognize the existence of a problem is the first step to my recovery. I have tried doing it my way and it did not work. I want the serenity and peace that other Nar-Anon members appear to have. I can work the Nar-Anon Program and trust my Higher Power to help me gain my own serenity.

"The way to end our stress is to investigate the thinking that lies behind it." ~ Byron Katie

There is one crisis after another in my life. How can I possibly be happy? Every waking hour of my life revolves around the antics of the addict. No matter how much I tried, I could not anticipate the emergencies. The telephone company turned off our service because the addict used the payment for drugs; the police impounded our car, and my checkbook disappeared. Friends with good intentions told me I should kick the addict out. They were sure that if I did this, I would be happy. One friend offered to take me to a Nar-Anon meeting saying, "Happiness is a gift we can give ourselves." What did I have to lose?

As I walked into the meeting, people were smiling and laughing. What did I have to laugh about? During the meeting, I heard one person say that happiness is being satisfied with what we have. Another said that she was happy because she set boundaries for herself and began taking care of herself.

That night I learned so much about myself. I felt that I was meant to go to that meeting to learn there was a Power greater than myself that I could rely on. All I had to do was let go. Today I know that happiness is being grateful for what goes right. I can let go and stop dwelling on the negative. My Higher Power will take care of me as the addict's Higher Power will take care of her.

Thought for Today: Just for today, I will be happy for what I have and for everything my Higher Power gives me.

"Thousands of candles can be lighted from a single candle, and the life of the candle will not be shortened. Happiness never decreases by being shared." ~ Buddha

If someone had told me twelve years ago that I would fall in love with and marry a man who had been a heroin addict for the previous fifteen years, I would have laughed, but that is exactly what happened.

I certainly did not feel I had a worry in the world. After all, I was 40 years old. I had grown up in the 60's. I had traveled to sixteen different countries. I had a good job that I loved. I was not naïve by any stretch of the imagination. I was well adjusted, happy, and confident that I could handle almost anything that came my way. I was not aware that I was a classic textbook example of a co-dependent and an enabler.

Five years ago, I stopped enabling. I had finally come to grips with the fact that both the addict and I were insane and one or both of us were going to die if I did not get away. I wish I had not waited so long. I wish that I had accepted my powerlessness over his addiction sooner and saved both of us years of self-destructive behavior. It took that long for me to believe what the people in Nar-Anon had been telling me all along: let go and allow him to suffer the consequences of his decisions and perhaps seek recovery. It was the hardest thing I have ever done in my life, but it saved me.

Thought for Today: Loving an addict requires detachment with love. I can love the addict without participating in destructive attitudes and behaviors.

"Every act of virtue is an ingredient unto reward." ~ Jeremy Taylor

My addicted son was out of food, so I ran out to buy some food for him, checking first to make sure I knew his favorites. His car motor was broken, so I gave him money to buy another motor. His clothes were dirty, so I washed and dried them. His cell phone had been turned off because he could not pay the monthly fee, so I paid it. After all, how could he find a job if he was weak from hunger, could not drive to interviews or work, had dirty clothes, and he could not be reached on the phone by employers I felt that if I did everything for him, he would be freed up to find a job. Wrong! He was freed up to do drugs!

I finally turned to Nar-Anon and found that the only person I could change was me. Instead of helping, I was enabling and trying to control the addict. I wanted the addict to have a job. He was willing to just get by which I was enabling him to do. I kept thinking about the Serenity Prayer. I had seen it a few times before and always thought it was a negative statement. Anything can be changed, I would think. Now I finally understand what the prayer meant: I can change anything about myself, but nothing about others.

Thought for Today: Today, I will enjoy the serenity of knowing that the only person I am in charge of is me. What a relief!

"In every crisis there is a message. Crises are nature's way of forcing change--breaking down old structures, shaking loose negative habits so that something new and better can take their place." ~ Susan L. Taylor

Asking is not always the easiest thing for me to do, but often it is the right thing. When I get lost, I ask for directions, and it usually helps me get to where I want to go. Why is it so hard for me to ask for help when I am floundering spiritually or emotionally when I am just as lost?

Since becoming a Nar-Anon member, I found that it has become easier for me to ask for help. I have learned that my Nar-Anon meeting is a safe place to share and ask questions. I am not judged and, I am with others who share the same problems. In the **Newcomer's Welcome**, I am reminded, "We have traveled that unhappy road too, and found the answer with serenity and peace of mind." I have also learned that when I ask for help in Nar-Anon, I will be given suggestions, not orders. I know that I still have the final choice.

In Nar-Anon, I have come to believe that I can ask my Higher Power for guidance. The God of my understanding became my Higher Power when I came to Nar-Anon. In Nar-Anon, I learned a new way to pray and ask for help. My prayers are no longer bargaining sessions. I now talk intimately with my Higher Power and accept the guidance I receive. I also believe that my Higher Power takes many forms, and often guidance is offered through other people, especially in these rooms.

Thought for Today: Sometimes I need to ask my Nar-Anon friends for help. Sometimes I need to ask my Higher Power for guidance as suggested in the Twelve Steps of Nar-Anon. However, in order to grow as a human being, I need to continually ask more from myself.

"The Nar-Anon Family Group is primarily for you who know or have known a feeling of desperation concerning the addiction problem of someone near to you." ~ Nar-Anon Blue Booklet

After beginning to work my Nar-Anon program, I became aware of changes in my life, both big and small. I am willing to admit that my life is not a bowl of cherries, and may never be. However, I can still find serenity and peace of mind. By attending Nar-Anon meetings and working the program, I have been able to accept my life. I have found a way to enjoy my life regardless of what the addict decides to do with his.

I had to make a decision that the addict, who enjoys verbal boxing, was not going to accept change from anyone, including his Higher Power. Since sparring back and forth had been going on for many years, it finally brought me to the realization that if I wanted this situation to change, it was going to be me who would have to make the changes. So I turned our relationship over to my Higher Power, and in doing so, I allowed my Higher Power to help me make decisions regarding my relationship with the addict.

It has been amazing how following the Twelve Steps has helped me to be a more understanding person with not only the addict but also everyone around me. I only need to let go of the control and the belief that everyone needed my help. The result is a healthier, happier twelve-stepper, who realized letting go is the only way to a healthy body and a happier me.

Thought for Today: I will turn my will over to a Power greater than myself. I will not try to change others. I will sit quietly and listen for direction.

"Letting go of our need to control can set us and others free. It can set our Higher Power free to send the best to us." ~ Melody Beattie

Accepting Tradition Two into my family life teaches me how to detach from my grown children. Tradition Two states, "For our group purposes there is but one authority – a loving God as He may express Himself in our group conscience. Our leaders are but trusted servants – they do not govern."

My role in the lives of my adult children is but as a trusted servant. I can guide and teach, but I cannot make decisions for them that they need to make for themselves. I can lead by example and share my own experience. I can offer guidance when asked, but I have to let go of the results and allow other people, even my own children, to make their own choices and accept the responsibilities of those choices.

Thought for Today: The best example I give my children is to ask for their help in respecting their decisions. It is not easy to remove the words, "You should," "Why don't you just," or "If I were you I would" from my vocabulary, but by asking them for a gentle reminder whenever I start on that path, I let them know that I want to try to let them be. Removing these words opened the door for healthier conversations. Now my children know that they can come to me for guidance without fear of my attempt to take over their thoughts and their lives.

"A power greater than any human being helped make this decision." ~ Herbert J Stiefel

About four years ago, in desperation I tried to kill my husband because of his addiction. Realizing that something was wrong, I went to see a psychiatrist. After the one-hour session talking about my husband, she suggested I attend a Twelve Step program and that program led me to Nar-Anon. The Nar-Anon program taught me that I needed to fix myself, not my husband. When I started to work on me, positive things started to happen in my life. One of the most important for me is friendship.

During the 20-plus years of marriage, I lived in isolation because I did not want people to know I was married to an addict. I did not allow people to come close to me. Now, I call members of my Nar-Anon family when I need help. During the past two years, I have given myself two birthday parties where I opened my home to my friends, who are mostly Nar-Anon members. This program has done so much for me that I would have to write in every newsletter that is written from now on in order to share it all with you!

With all that time alone, I can hardly believe that now I am telling a group of strangers, no, members of my Nar-Anon family that I have not yet met, that I almost committed murder! This was a secret for a long time. I was in the program for two years before I could tell anyone what I had done. Now I can say it without feeling bad about myself because the program has taught me not to beat myself up when I make a mistake. With the help of my Higher Power, which I choose to call God, my Nar-Anon friends and tools of the program, I have found a better, new way of life, and I am hopeful that I will never feel like killing anyone again.

Thought for Today: It is insanity to consider killing another because they fail to live up to my expectations, as much as it is insanity to live in isolation and unhappiness for long periods.

"Friendship improves happiness, and abates misery, by doubling our joys, and dividing our grief." ~ Joseph Addison

After overwhelming evidence, I can admit my powerlessness. I am unable to manage my own life. I am going to need a lot of help. I am feeling confused and weak when it comes to taking care of my needs. So where, how and when do I get help? With tremendous effort, I can go to a meeting. I am opening the door to committing myself to making my life saner.

At a meeting, I am reminded of Step Two's suggestion to believe in a Power greater than myself. Whether I have a strong religious background or none at all is irrelevant. Some of what I need is to believe in and practice determination, honesty with myself and open-mindedness. Other tools will follow in due time. The suggested guidelines are only that this power be loving, caring and greater than I am. Best of all, I can use this power long before I understand it. As long as this concept is helping me, the understanding part will catch up.

Thought for Today: This process of coming to believe will help restore me to sanity. The strength to move into action comes from this belief. I am beginning to understand this Higher Power concept.

"You do build in darkness if you have faith. When the light returns you have made yourself a fortress which is impregnable to certain kinds of trouble; you may even find yourself needed and sought by others as a beacon in their dark." ~ Olga Rosmanith

Step Two reaffirms to me that I may be powerless but I am not alone, and I am not helpless. After several months of three to four meetings a week, I realized that it was absolutely necessary for me to accept and believe in a Power greater than myself. I am being set free and encouraged to explore any method that will work for me.

I like the concept of doing it my way even though my belief and acceptance may not be orthodox. I use "act as if" as a tool. Pretending and play-acting were great tools that I used as a child. Therefore, I decided to give it a try. There is no reason for it not to work in my adult life. Tools only work when they are put to use. There is certainly nothing to lose, but so much to gain. There is always the possibility of relief if I act as if I am sane even when faced with the insanity of another's drug addiction.

Millions of people worldwide came to believe, each with unique viewpoints and understanding of a Power greater than themselves. I have managed to make the tool "act as if" work for me.

Thought for Today: There is much comfort and security in knowing that I have a Power greater than myself who is always available to help me through difficult times. I need only be willing to do my part and believe. Sometimes that means I need to "fake it 'til I make it."

"Whatever you do or dream you can do - begin it. Boldness has genius and power and magic in it." ~ Johann Wolfgang von Goethe

Admitting I am powerless is not a simple dismissal of uncontrollable actions by others. For me, it opens the door to gratitude. When I walk through that door into gratitude, each day is brighter. I feel myself healing.

Changing lifelong habits is an ongoing job. But today, it is the job I hold most dear. I find gratitude in the most simple of things and in the greatest of challenges life puts before me. As I walk my path in gratitude, my eyes are open to miracles I once trampled upon. Gratitude reminds me of my place in the universe. It allows me to see beauty within and without. Gratitude keeps my focus clear. It keeps me in today. I can see that love has nothing to do with a disease that can insidiously destroy me and those I love most. Gratitude humbles me. That which I am grateful for likely emerges as an awareness of my Higher Power's presence. When I am thankful and grateful, I am a better person and this radiates to all with whom I interact.

Thought for Today: Gratitude is the silver lining as I seek recovery. When I choose to live in and with gratitude, I am one step closer to finding serenity.

"As we express our gratitude, we must never forget that the highest appreciation is not to utter words, but to live by them." ~ John Fitzgerald Kennedy

One of my favorite lines in the <u>Nar-Anon Blue Booklet</u> is "keep an open mind… you will soon feel very much a part of the group." When I first came to Nar-Anon, I had strong opinions on what the addict in my life should and should not be doing. I also firmly believed that I could make him stop using. I was convinced that if I could say that one word or convey that one thought, the addict would see how much his using was hurting our family, himself and me.

Fortunately, I kept an open mind and continued attending meetings. By listening and sharing in meetings, I soon discovered that my obsession with the addict was keeping me from my recovery and growth. I was so focused on the addict that I was neglecting me.

An open mind enabled me to change my focus. I learned about the disease of addiction and the tools of the program. This knowledge helped me to determine what my responsibility is. Most importantly, I learned what I can change, with the help of a Higher Power, and what I cannot.

Thought for Today: Today, I stay focused on my recovery by going to meetings. I try to live every day in a manner that will make a difference. I pray with an open mind for guidance, wisdom, and the ability to release the addict with love. Today, I know that it is the best thing I can do.

"Your mind is like a parachute. It only works if it is open."
~Anthony J. D'Angelo

I have gone through the insanity that is referred to in Step Two. I have an addict in my life and I tried everything to get through to him. I thought logic would work. I thought love would work. I thought maybe I did something wrong but when I did what I thought was the right thing, the addict still used. I tried tough love and sending the addict to rehab. All I wanted to do was to fix and control the addict's habit. I cried, I yelled, I screamed. I cried some more. I became frustrated, felt lonely, felt lost, thought I was in an impossible situation, and felt inadequate.

Then I was introduced to Nar-Anon and the First Step. I admitted that I am powerless. I gave up my struggle to control the addict and realized I have choices. I could choose to stay. I could choose to leave. I could set boundaries. I could detach with love. I found it was okay to be helpless. I could mange my life but not the life of another. I learned to take my focus off the addict and put it on me, my actions and reactions. I saw the part I played. I learned to react differently. I went from feeling lost to having direction. Laughter came back into my life as I looked at things differently. When I gave up trying to change the addict and let go and let God, I found that all things were possible. I saw changes, not in the addict perhaps, but in me. I started to believe in a Power greater than myself and saw that my life was being restored to sanity. This is Step Two.

Thought for Today: My Higher Power can restore my sanity, bring me serenity, and turn my sadness into joy. As I use the tools of Nar-Anon, I find new friends, do things for myself and get my life back.

"Insanity was the result of our past behavior. Letting go of the control that created such a hold on us can be frightening, but, as we listen and learn from others, we can begin to feel and see miracles." ~ *The Nar-Anon Twelve Step Program*

Why was "Live and Let Live" such a hard concept to wrap my mind around? With the help of the Nar-Anon program, I can now see that when I am dealing with the disease of addiction, I feel an urgency to fix everything that goes wrong in my addicted loved one's life, and to help him with his daily struggles. I realize that when I try to control and manage the addict's life, it is based on my own fears and a lack of respect for him. I appear to be saying that I think the addict is clearly not capable of doing things for himself and he will be harmed.

What I am really doing is enabling as I am trying to make myself feel better. I want to fix things to relieve my fear and anxiety, while lifting some of the guilt, shame and responsibility I feel for the addict. This is my illness and it can be overwhelming. I ache so badly for him. I want him to get better and to live a healthy, prosperous life. All the while, I may be slowly killing him with kindness! I am not helping. In fact, I may be standing in the way of his recovery.

The addict can find his own way and learn to function and take responsibility for himself. He must be allowed to deal with his own mistakes and be accountable for his actions as we all are. In Nar-Anon, I learn that enabling is teaching the addict dependency instead of responsibility. I was enabling him to stay sick in order to feel better myself.

Thought for Today: I can help my addicted loved one best by allowing him the freedom to live his own life and make his own choices. In turn, I must remind myself daily to live and let live!

"We might be tempted to help release the butterfly from her cocoon. It is human nature to want to assist, but if we do, she will fall to the ground and die; the struggle to free herself strengthens her wings enough to survive and fly." ~ Eunice Brown, The Compassionate Friends Magazine, February-March 2006

Prior to recovery, I found myself in dangerous and insane situations. More than once, I put myself, or other family members, in immediate danger by going into a known drug area to retrieve the addict's car. At the time, I thought this was the sensible thing to do, because the addict needed the car for work. Was this the act of a sane person?

Step Two talks about sanity. I felt I was the sane one in my house and that the addict was the insane one. I was the person that was holding everything together, by ensuring the addict had a car so he would not lose his job. How else would the bills be paid? I now realize I had an active part in the insanity. I participated and even helped my loved one continue to use and to be a happy addict.

When I started practicing Step Two, I felt a great burden had been removed from my shoulders. I discovered that I could rely on my Higher Power and accept the outcome of any situation without question. What a great relief!

Thought for Today: I no longer have to rescue the addict. I can let the addict assume responsibility for each consequence of his using.

"Today, more than ever, we need to pray....for the light to know the will of God.....for the love to accept the will of God....for the way to do the will of God." ~ Mother Teresa

It took me a long while to embrace the hope that is offered in Step Two. What little belief in a Higher Power I had had been severely shaken by the disease of addiction. I had prayed and prayed that God would make the addict in my life stop using, as I was sure that would solve all our problems. I had never prayed for anything before so I assumed that God would accommodate. When it did not happen, then I gave God an ultimatum. If the addict does not stop using, then I know that God does not exist.

When, in desperation, I started coming to Nar-Anon meetings, I was reluctant to accept this step, as I was still angry about not getting my prayers answered. I had serious doubts about the existence of a Higher Power; after all, the addict had not even slowed down. Then I heard what other members had to say. I heard them speak of the group being their Higher Power at first. I heard that this step was about the belief that I could be restored to sanity, that it was not about the addict using. With just that much, I was able to find the hope that I could be happy again and that these steps could work for me, if I worked them.

Thought for Today: By working on Step Two, I found hope in my life again. Accepting that there was a Higher Power, whether it is a spiritual presence or simply the power of the Nar-Anon group, was comforting. I knew I was no longer alone and my life could return to sanity regardless of addiction.

"Once you choose hope, anything's possible." ~ Christopher Reeve

I do not seem to be able to think about anything but my loved one. I keep projecting all the "what ifs" and how my life "could have been." All the old hurts and anger keep pouring in. I keep thinking how stupid I was. Why didn't I do this or that? There are days when my old enemy, fear, consumes me, sometimes for no apparent reason. Something has brought back old memories and fear has taken over. I am ready for a change.

It takes courage to transcend the fear-based isolation I make. For so long, I have stayed away from friends and avoided others. This program gives me the courage to make a call to a Nar-Anon friend. I can re-establish old acquaintances and make new friendships. I had been alone for so long that it was difficult to change. Now, I can draw on the Nar-Anon program for the courage to dial that first number.

I need not fear, fear itself, but I can use the tools of the Nar-Anon program to get through this period by going to more meetings, calling program people, writing and meditating. Then, I am not left alone with the fear. There is hope. There is a power that can help me to concentrate on the reality of today. The Nar-Anon program teaches me how to stop belittling myself, guides me to love myself, and heals the old wounds. I am experiencing freedom from my past feelings, thoughts, and fears.

Thought for Today: Hope keeps me company in times of fear.

"You are no longer alone." ~ Nar-Anon Twelve Step Slogan

I have found the slogans to be of great help. During the early days of my recovery in Nar-Anon, the slogans gave me hope and comfort, especially "One Day at a Time." Taking one day at a time was a new concept for me because I had been a worrier all of my life. I even thought that if I failed to worry, bad things would happen. I felt such fear and despair that I could not live in the present. My habits of dwelling on the past and worrying about the future made my life unmanageable.

In the backyard one day, I decided to try this new "One Day at a Time" concept. I began walking and with each step, I meditated on one step at a time, one day at a time. I concentrated on my feet, on the ground, and then on my surroundings. I was able to enjoy the moment. The past was gone. The future was of no concern. Only this moment was present and with it, came calmness.

Thought for Today: There are times when I slip back into my old worrying behavior. I bring myself back to the present by concentrating on one day at a time and one moment at a time. I can choose not to worry. It gives me such a feeling of peace to know that I am capable of living in the moment.

"I got the blues thinking of the future, so I left off and made some marmalade. It's amazing how it cheers one up to shred oranges and scrub the floor." ~ D. H. Lawrence

Tradition Three defines Nar-Anon members, what we do as members, and one important limitation.

> *"The relatives of addicts, when gathered for mutual aid, may call themselves a Nar-Anon Family Group, provided that as a group, they have no other affiliation. The only requirement for membership is that there be a problem of addiction in a relative or friend."*

Nar-Anon Family groups are the relatives of addicts. Relatives can have many definitions, but my understanding of relatives as it relates to Tradition Three is anyone who has been affected by the addiction of another person. As the family and friends of addicts, we come together to provide mutual aid. At Nar-Anon meetings, I learn I can help another person when I share my experience, strength and hope. Through this exchange, I also receive the courage I need to recover.

Tradition Three also assures me that Nar-Anon groups will not promote or be influenced by any political, social or religious theories. Tradition Three does not imply that, as an individual member, I cannot be associated with other political, religious or philosophy groups or theories regarding addiction and recovery. It simply states that the Nar-Anon groups should not be associated with these other beliefs. This is necessary to maintain the purity of the group's purpose to provide mutual aid and allows members to find their own path to recovery.

Finally, it defines the only requirement for membership, "that there be a problem of addiction in a relative or friend." This allows me and every other member the right to decide if we qualify for Nar-Anon.

Thought for Today: I am grateful that Nar-Anon is a program of choices. I can choose if I want to be a member. I am not required to be associated with any specific group to be a member. The program allows me to choose my own path to recovery, yet gives me a structure within which to work.

"Alone we can do so little; together we can do so much." ~ Helen Keller

Our twenty-nine year old son is an addict, hopefully in recovery after a stint in jail. My wife and I have found it difficult to cope with his disease of addiction. After being Nar-Anon members for only a few months, one of the most helpful things we had learned was the three Cs. We had come to realize that we did not **cause** our son's disease, we could not **control** him, nor could we **cure** him. This has been a profound and comforting revelation for us.

In the past, we had debated with police, recovered his impounded cars, paid traffic tickets, bailed him out of jail, paid his rent, and even provided a stipend while he looked for work over a period of years. We unquestionably believed that this was our responsibility as parents, and for several years, we had no idea that he was using drugs.

Because of our experiences in Nar-Anon, we are reassessing our interactions with our son and our mutual responsibilities. On the one hand, we realize that it is unfair of us to set or mandate expectations for our son to meet. However, on the other hand, we realize that he must take responsibility for his own actions, and the resulting consequences. How to achieve this is the question.

Our plan is simple, but it is not easy: we will love him, but not try to control him; we will provide support, but not bail him out of any self-generated misfortunes; we absolutely will not tolerate any hurtful or harmful behavior by him towards us.

Thought for Today: Every individual is responsible for his/her own existence. Any attempt to avoid that responsibility or to usurp it from another will result in heartbreak.

"So often times it happens that we live our lives in chains, and we never even know we have the key." ~ *The Eagles*

Before Nar-Anon, my anger towards the addict was beyond anything I had ever experienced in my life. I used to allow it to consume me. Attending Nar-Anon meetings has shown me the futility of this emotion. My anger not only made me miserable, but everyone else around me as well. It was the addict I was hoping to change, but being angry with the addict made no difference in his behavior. My anger only seemed to push the addict further away from me.

Through Nar-Anon, I came to realize that anger is not the answer. In fact, it only made the situation much worse than it should have been. I truly believe that if not for the Nar-Anon message and all the members who share their experience, strength and hope at our meetings, I would still be on the road to self-destruction.

By recognizing the anger in me, I can see the cycle beginning to break. I can stop the process of anger that is consuming and destroying me in my daily life. I have become a gentler and more loving person.

Thought for Today: Feeling our feelings is one important part of the recovery process. Learning how to balance my feelings with an appropriate action is another. Anger is a secondary emotion resulting from troublesome thoughts. I can ask my Higher Power for help in changing the way I think, and pray that the anger will go away.

"When angry, count to ten before you speak. If very angry, count to one hundred." ~ *Thomas Jefferson*

ROBOT VERSUS HUMAN

March 4

A modern robot is an amazing piece of work; it is extremely smart and sometimes is almost human. I wonder if a robot can think and feel, and if there is any difference between a robot and me. Of course there is. The robot does not have a heart and its computer is engineered to perform a specific set of analytical tasks. The whole point of its sophisticated circuitry is to make certain that the robot cannot transcend its programming, ever. Its existence is defined by its predictability.

I am different; I am unpredictable. Unlike even the most fabulous contraption, I can choose to act differently than I did in the past. My quirky unpredictability sets me apart from machines – it makes me human, at least until I am confronted with the reality of having an addict in my life. Almost from the moment when I recognize that someone I love is undeniably an addict, I try to cope with the situation by saying and doing the same things over and over. I nag, I give instructions, I yell, I worry, I rescue again and again, turning into a robot. In fact, I use an especially revealing expression to indicate this transformation: I say the addict "pushes my buttons."

Participating in Nar-Anon is an alternative to living in a robotic haze. I gain practical tips from the experience, strength and hope shared by my fellow members. I have learned it is fine to fully feel my feelings, as long as I remember that I have a choice about how I am going to translate my feelings into action. I can pause, I can consider my motivations, and I can estimate the effects of my behavior on me. I can choose to be mindful, and unpredictable. Slowly but surely, I am getting to be more and more unpredictable.

Thought for Today: Thanks to Nar-Anon, I am becoming human again. The buttons still get pushed, but they are not hooked up to the switches that spark the same automatic behaviors. Moreover, the situations I encounter in the rest of my life no longer evoke the same robotic reaction.

"Make the most of yourself, for that is all there is of you." ~ *Ralph Waldo Emerson*

:

ONE DAY, ONE MINUTE, ONE HOUR March 5

Today, I can see the wisdom in the slogan "One Day at a Time." I have come to believe that my program is one day at a time, one hour at a time, or even one minute at a time.

Why does this work for me? Well before I was introduced to this slogan, I was thinking about what I could have said in the past to stop my daughter from her destructive behavior. I would think about how I might be able to help her in the future. I would worry and get sick thinking about how she was living her life. Where was she sleeping? Who was she seeing? What drugs was she taking? Was she being promiscuous? Was she going to wind up in jail or dead somewhere? All this and more was going through my mind.

The slogan "One Day at a Time" means just that, to take the day as it comes and not worry about what has been or what will be. If there is a crisis during the day, deal with it. If there is no crisis, do not make one up in my mind and worry about what will probably never happen. I am learning this wisdom in Nar-Anon. The worst of my worries never came to pass. The scenarios that my fertile mind imagined never happened. Therefore, if it is not so, do not think it is.

By not worrying about the past or the future, I am able to think about what is. I now realize that I have no control over my daughter or anyone else. I have learned, with the help of my Higher Power, that the only person I can control and affect a change in is me. What a powerful thought!

Thought for Today: All the worrying I did over the addict and the pain I put myself through was for naught. The pain is still there, but my reaction to the pain does not have to destroy my life. Working my Nar-Anon program helps me to accept these painful circumstances and to learn how to live with them.

"When I spend my time preparing for what might happen, I am missing what is happening." ~ Anne Wilson Shaef

Have you ever wondered what it means to hear a "still small voice"? There are many times I have trouble sleeping. It seems my mind wants to go into overdrive when I lay down. Many a night I lie awake, tossing and turning, full of worry. I keep thinking about my addicted son. Is he okay, or is he on the verge of another relapse?

To find some peace and serenity, first I must remind myself that when I lie down at night, I have all of the day's business still floating around in my mind. Next, I remind myself that the day is over, and that I am reliving a past that I cannot change. I ask my Higher Power to help me let it go. These are only my thoughts and interpretations of the day's events that are causing me to worry. They are not real and cannot be trusted. In addition, by worrying about a relapse my son has not even had, I fear the future. I need to stay in the present moment.

I then recite a first person version of Step One: "I admit I am powerless over the addict and my life has become unmanageable."

I make a decision to use this restless night as a "reason" to pray for my son. In doing so, I let go and turn him over to his Higher Power. I listen carefully for the "still small voice" of my Higher Power. It is not long before I am free of worry and fear, which has now been replaced with faith.

Thought for Today: I believe that faith is strength that I can feel if I am listening to my Higher Power. I believe a Power greater than myself will speak to me with a "still small voice" when I am quiet enough.

"Faith is taking the first step even when you don't see the whole staircase." ~ Martin Luther King Jr.

FAITH RESTORED

For the last twenty-three years, I felt it was up to me to help the addict to overcome his problem and to make his life a little easier in any way I could. He left home at the tender age of fifteen by his own choice after experimenting with marijuana and alcohol. I am sure he stopped maturing then, as the following twenty-three years were pretty much a series of successes and failures with work and two failed relationships due to his inability to cope with everyday life. His drug abuse seemed to escalate and that is when my life became unmanageable and insane. I devoted every waking moment to analyzing, and mentally repairing the addict. I soon found that I could no longer go on this way.

Nar-Anon helped me to accept a new concept of my Higher Power. I already had an abiding faith, but it had been sorely tested over the last few months. My faith was restored when I heard the message of Nar-Anon that I need to step aside and let God do the work. The program has helped me to realize that detachment is the only way for me. In my own mind, I believed that if I showed someone enough love, it was possible for him or her to overcome anything. That was before I realized that addiction is a mental, as well as, a physical disease. It renders the addict incapable of receiving and processing the love and help we have to give them.

Thought for Today: I am learning to love the addict in a new way, by letting go and letting God do his work.

"Every evening I turn my worries over to God. He's going to be up all night anyway." ~ Mary C. Crowley

I need constantly to remind myself that the addict did not need my help when he decided to use drugs, and he does not need my help to stop. Therefore, I need to detach if we are both to survive the insanity of addiction. Nar-Anon tells me that the efficacy of faith can be demonstrated only when I let my overwhelming problems go, and let a Power greater than myself (who I choose to call God) take over.

I am ready to lay my burden at God's feet. I am too tired to continue down the same old path. I know that I must stay strong for the addict's sake, and let him suffer the consequences of his actions and seek his own recovery. I know if I do not break his pattern of coming to me for help all the time, he will never recover. Every day, I realize increasingly that it is okay to stand back and do nothing. Inaction is okay!

I know that when I consciously surrender my will to my Higher Power's will, I can see faith at work in my life. I can take comfort in unwavering faith, for without it I am helpless and alone.

Thought for Today: A thought for all other newcomers like me to consider: I believe there is hope. I believe that I am a work in progress and God is not finished with the addict in my life or with me. I have not arrived yet, but one day I will if I keep working the Twelve Steps and keep coming back, because the program works.

"Our history is not our destiny." ~ Alan Cohen

I have always believed in a Higher Power, but never has my belief been as strong as it is now that I have become a part of the Nar-Anon fellowship. It took my participation in the program to reaffirm that I can turn over my challenges in life to a Power greater than myself, if I will allow it to happen. That meant having Step Three printed indelibly upon my forehead. I needed to put my will aside and allow God's will to unfold. With two addicted loved ones in my life, I had taken on all of their burdens and had not allowed them to experience the consequences of their drug abuse. I was always trying to manage or fix their lives instead of allowing their Higher Power to handle them. In the process, I lost sight of God's plan for me.

Now that I have embraced the Nar-Anon program for life, I can focus on that plan and do what is best for me. I can now recognize when situations will not work in my best interest and I can release them to my Higher Power. One of my favorite sayings is, *that is not good for me*, and it applies to my relationships with children, mates, family members, friends, co-workers or anyone else in my life.

Thought for Today: The Nar-Anon program has taught me that I can only manage one life, that of my own. Trusting in a Higher Power and detaching from the problems of my children has made me stronger, and my sons have learned to be independent.

"Depending on our Higher Power can increase our independence from the opinions, needs and demands of others. We need no longer look outside ourselves to other people for validation." ~ Paths to Recovery

Many people come into recovery frightened and insecure; I did. I felt weak and alone. I was uncertain of my direction and did not know where to go for help or answers. In Nar-Anon, it was suggested that if I could find some faith in a Power greater than myself, I would find security and guidance. I wanted that feeling of safety and strength. However, for me, faith did not come overnight; it took time and effort to grow.

When I ask my Higher Power for help and then acknowledge the source of that help, I see the benefits brought about by planting my tiny seed of faith. I nurture that tiny seed of faith with the sunlight of my daily prayers and my faith grows. It is a reward for living life on life's terms. One day, I find that my faith has become similar to a huge, spreading tree. It does not stop the storms of life, but I know that I am safe in its shelter.

Thought for Today: Just for today, I know that faith in my Higher Power will not calm the storms of life, but it will calm my heart. I will let my faith shelter me in times of trouble.

"Faith is the bird that feels the light and sings when the dawn is still dark." ~ Rabindranath Tagore

When I come to Step Three, turning my will over to the care of a Higher Power, I begin to accept the fact that I can let go of my need to be in control. I am making a decision to let the God of my understanding lead me on my path of recovery.

Faith in a Higher Power did not have to strike me with a lightening bolt. The focus and emphasis of my daily life changed as I let my Higher Power take control. I am seeing different results from my actions. I feel more confident in the challenges and choices that my life presents. I can begin to feel, enjoy, and trust again. My faith in a Power greater than myself frees me from the anxiety I carried.

Insanity is doing the same things over and over again, expecting different results. Letting go of the control that had such a hold on me is somewhat frightening. As I listen and learn from others, I begin to feel and see miracles in myself. Trust and acceptance in my Higher Power is bound to follow.

Thought for Today: I will release my will to my Higher Power. In doing so, I am only giving up an illusion of control and seeing the reality of my situation.

"For if you have faith the size of a mustard seed, nothing will be impossible to you. " ~ *The Bible*

I obtained a better understanding of the disease of addiction when I was diagnosed with breast cancer. I came to see clearly that although I did not have power over this disease, I did have power over how I would react to my illness and what I could do for myself to aid in my recovery.

I did not choose to have cancer. The doctors and my surgeon explained my options to me. These options were: lumpectomy, mastectomy, radiation, chemotherapy, and trust in a Higher Power, or I could do nothing and have no chance of recovering from the cancer.

I believe it is the same with the disease of addiction. A person does not choose to be an addict. The family, a physician, or even law enforcement can explain the addict's options. If the addict wants to recover, the options are: Twelve-Step meetings, treatment centers, and seeking the help of a Higher Power. Alternately, the addict can choose to do nothing and not recover from the disease of addiction.

As a family member, I have choices, too. My options are: attend Twelve-Step meetings, take care of myself, release the addicted loved one, and work on my spirituality, or choose to do nothing and not recover. By doing what is needed in recovery, I can find happiness, growth and freedom whether the addict is using or not.

Thought for Today: Addiction is a disease and I have no power over a disease. To recover and heal from the effects of addiction, I must take the necessary steps with the help of my Higher Power.

"Today, I will trust that God will do for me what I cannot do for myself. I will do my part – working the Twelve Steps and letting God do the rest."
~ Melody Beattie

I used to try to manipulate the affairs of my loved ones to reduce their pain. That way, I had hoped to be spared the chaos that their pain would bring to me. I could not stand to watch other people make mistakes and make what I thought were wrong choices. I knew that I could show them a better way to live. In reality, I do not remember any time that what I did worked. In fact, I usually made things worse and I prevented other people from learning the lessons that life had for them. I found that enabling was a weakness in my character, and at some level, I would always be fighting my compulsion to interfere. When I fall back into my old behavior, my Higher Power will gently tap me on the shoulder with reminders such as, "Does this have your name on it? Are you in control?"

Practicing Step Three helps me to stop before I meddle in another person's life and choices. I know that this is one of my life lessons and I am okay with that. It is progress, but not perfection. I know that sometimes my old feelings will still arise, but now I have the tools to daily turn my will and my life over to the care of my Higher Power. Nar-Anon helps me to grow and to realize where I was and where I am now. This gives me the strength to keep working my program.

Thought for Today: I need to continue to detach with love, to let go, to surrender my life and the lives of others to my Higher Power. I need to look for God's will, not my own.

"We can only learn to know ourselves and do what we can -- namely, surrender our will and fulfill God's will in us." ~ St. Teresa of Avila

I came to Nar-Anon to help my addicted loved one. I quickly learned that to be of any help to others, I must first take care of myself. When I took my inventory, I saw that I was a distrustful person. Trusting has always been difficult for me. I have lived my whole life feeling as though I was a victim; therefore, I acted like a victim. Today, I want to change and be able to trust rather than see myself as the eternal victim, living in fear and still suffering from the wounds of my past. I want to learn to trust in a safe and healthy way.

TRUST: *"Assured reliance on the character, credibility, strength, or truth of someone or something. One in which confidence is placed; Dependence on something future or contingent. Hope, etc..."*

When I look at the definition of trust, I see it has more to do with where or with whom I choose to place my trust. From this, I gather that trust conveys the assurance of consistency and confidence in the thing or person I am trusting. I do not have to fear when I am fairly certain of how this person or thing will act or be.

My part is to use my experience, conscience, and common sense before I make a decision to trust someone or something. When I am in doubt, I can turn to my Higher Power through prayer and meditation, ask for guidance, and wait for direction. I believe that my Higher Power is trustworthy.

Thought for Today: Today, I turn my will and my life over to the care of my Higher Power. When I place my trust in my Higher Power, I have no reason to fear.

"Trust is that rare and priceless treasure that wins us the affection of our heavenly Father." ~ Brennan Manning, *Ruthless Trust*

Before I came to the Nar-Anon Family Groups program, I had lost the ability to make a personal decision. I could not tell you what kind of food I wanted to eat or which movie I wanted to see. When asked what I wanted, I could only respond with an "I don't know, what do you want?"

Making decisions that affected my life was not safe for me – neither in childhood nor during two decades of living with the progressive disease of addiction. What if others did not like my choice? What if I made the wrong decision? What if my decision was not the decision the other person wanted from me? What would happen next? Would I be yelled at, put down, threatened, or hit?

As I recover in the Nar-Anon program, I am remembering who I am. As I get reacquainted with myself, I have decided to keep some parts of myself that I had before twenty years of living with active addiction. I have decided to add some new traits to myself that I saw and liked in others in the program. In Nar-Anon meetings, I am learning how others have changed their lives and I am attempting similar changes. Now, I listen to suggestions from other members, but am able to make my own decisions. This eliminates my perceived threat of being scorned or ridiculed for my choices.

As I work the Nar-Anon Twelve Steps with the help of my sponsor, meetings, program literature and service, I get to know myself better and get stronger in making decisions for myself. Now that I am learning how to make decisions, I have been able to decide to turn my will and my life over to my Higher Power who I know I can trust.

Thought for Today: I am grateful for the Nar-Anon program; it has helped me know myself and has given me the confidence I need to make decisions.

"Don't be too timid and squeamish about your actions. All life is an experiment. The more experiments you make the better." ~ Ralph Waldo Emerson

As a parent of two teenage addicts, my life was full of frustration and turmoil. Although I was responsible for their actions as minors, my example and teachings were cast to the wind. My children were raised not to smoke, drink or use. I expected them to refrain from smoking since that is what killed my mother before she knew her grandchildren. I held to my expectations firmly even though the results were always the same – the pain of disagreements and resentments. I would lecture, scold, whine, or otherwise try to manipulate them.

One day while I was driving home, I thought of the ashtray on the front porch. I bet there would be butts in it – my children who I expected not to smoke were smoking. This was simply unacceptable to me. My blood pressure rose as I was filled with anger and frustration.

In Nar-Anon, I am learning that addiction is a progressive disease and that a relapsing addict will begin where the active addiction left off. So it is with me. I was fully in the grips of my own disease. In my anger, I reached for the program. The phrase: "An expectation is only a premeditated resentment" came to mind. In a moment of refreshing clarity, I thought, "They were smoking yesterday. They were smoking all last week, last year! It would be reasonable to expect that they smoked today and probably will tomorrow." In that moment, I accepted reality. I still did not approve, but I accepted it.

When I crossed the front porch my serenity was back, my blood pressure was normal, and I did not even notice the ashtray; it did not matter any more. My children have problems and I hope that someday they will solve these problems themselves. After all, people quit smoking all the time. In one of those quirky twists of life, within months, both quit. The fruits of that twenty-minute drive did not stop there. I am learning I am in denial. I am not accepting the realities of the family disease of addiction. My expectations had been unreasonable and even irrational.

Thought for Today: I am responsible for my expectations. I set them and I can change them. In so doing, I have control over my recovery and some of the hurts in my life.

"Within every adversity lies a slumbering possibility." ~ Dr. Robert Schuler

I thought I had always believed in a Higher Power. I had been raised in a religious home and went to church every Sunday. I had attended twelve years of religious school. Since I prayed every day, when it came to the Second Step, I did not have any trouble believing that a Higher Power could restore me to sanity.

The Third Step should have been easy, but I found out that my old way of praying was not working. My prayers were long "want lists," always asking to please change the addict or other things in my life. When I concentrated on Step Three, I realized that there was no bargaining and no taking back of my problems. I had to turn over my will to my Higher Power. I had to accept that what was happening in my life was my Higher Power's will. I found that the Serenity Prayer helped me as well as another prayer that described Step Three for me: "Guide my every thought and may these thoughts guide all my actions."

Thought for Today: Each morning I pray to my Higher Power. This reminds me that I have made a decision to turn my will and my life over to the care of my Higher Power who I believe knows what I need.

"I have held many things in my hands, and I have lost them all; but whatever I have placed in God's hands, that I still possess." ~ Martin Luther

In the Nar-Anon program, I learn that the present moment is all I have and that it is enough. Only by living in today can I be fully capable of experiencing what is happening in my life. Otherwise, I may be missing vital information and lessons that I need for my recovery and growth. When I dwell on the things that have already happened or what may occur in the future, I close the door to the present.

I have found it to be true that excessive worry about things that had not happened was wasted energy and caused me illness, anxiety and exhaustion. After all, the events that I had obsessed over did not happen the way I thought they would or, in some cases, did not even happen at all!

When I live in the present, I have a sense of freedom and calmness because I am not overwhelmed with unnecessary feelings, thoughts and worry about the future or the past. I have a choice to obsess or take things as they come. Choosing to go with the flow allows me time to process what is needed and move forward when the time is right.

If I listen, I have found that my Higher Power tells me when the time is right. I will get a feeling of uncertainty when the time is wrong and a feeling of excitement or energy when it is right. When I go against those feelings, I make my biggest mistakes and wish I had done otherwise.

By living in the moment, I can look at each thought in detail and experience the feelings associated with that thought. I can move forward when I am certain, and I am not rushing to find an outcome.

Thought for Today: Learning to live for the moment can be very liberating and relaxing. I get a sense that the decisions, feelings and thoughts I am processing are not forced.

"Faith is different from proof; the latter is human, the former is a Gift from God." ~ Blaise Pascal

At the age of fourteen, my daughter started using alcohol and within six months, I started attending a Twelve-Step program. Six years later, she told me she was using several illegal drugs and I found the Nar-Anon fellowship. When I became addicted to prescribed anti-seizure medication, I sought help in the rooms of Narcotics Anonymous. I call myself a triple winner.

One holiday weekend at an open NA meeting, I was listening to several addicts complaining about their drug-using, non-recovering relatives. They said their relatives did not want anything to do with them during the holidays, not even a shared family dinner. When it was my time to share, I shared what I had learned in Nar-Anon, that I have no control over other people, places, or things. I only have control over myself. Another addict with many years of recovery said, "And that is only with the help of your Higher Power." I was shocked; no one ever cross-talked in this meeting, and someone was interrupting me! After the meeting, we talked about it; and he repeated what he had said. It took a few more years for me to understand the meaning of this addict's statement.

The first three steps tell me I am powerless and that I can be restored to sanity if I make a decision to turn my will and my life over to my Higher Power. In other words, I must trust in a Power greater than myself.

Now I understand that by myself, I am this small source of power. When I turn my tiny power over to my Higher Power, I tune into a magnificent power. This infinite magnificent power is what gives me the strength to control myself. I cannot do it alone.

Thought for Today: With time comes wisdom and understanding. With time comes spirituality. With time comes peace in our hearts and in our homes.

"I want to feel my life while I'm in it." ~ Meryl Streep

After I had attended Nar-Anon meetings for several months, something new happened. I was in the middle of a big fight with the addict, who was still in active addiction. Both of us were loud and raging; then the addict began saying derogatory things about me.

My usual reaction began. I would go into the hurt mode, huddle-over, feeling as though he had kicked me in the stomach. I felt the pain of a victim that I had gone through so many times in my life, but this time something new happened. Instead of going all the way into the usual negative spiral that I had experienced at such times, I questioned my actions. Then the three Cs popped into my mind: I didn't cause this rage, I can't cure it, and I can't control it. Instead of bowing over in pain, I stood up straight and looked at the addict with love and for the first time I could see the addict's feelings.

Another strange response happened when the addict calmed down and stopped raging. We were both stunned. I realized, for the first time, how my reactions were related to the addict's behaviors. My behaviors were also responsible for the mess we made. I knew then that changing my reactions and me was going to help our family. I may not be able to cure or control addiction but I can change my reactions and end my fight in the losing battle that I was engaging in.

Thought for Today: I will change my reaction to old situations and hope that others will notice my new behavior.

"For daily need there is daily grace; for sudden need, sudden grace, and for overwhelming need, overwhelming grace." ~ John Blanchard

I woke up one morning with a headache, feeling very needy. I wanted to be loved and to be reassured by my partner. I was looking at my partner to make me feel safe. I wanted him to tell me that we would try to stay together forever. I realized quickly that I would not get what I was looking for from the addict. As soon as I would ask for his reassurance, I would regret it or would not believe it, even when I was getting what I asked for from my partner. I would then hate myself for being so needy and dependent.

Because of the Nar-Anon program, I am now able to identify a way out of this thinking trap that I created and know so well. I will turn my focus to my Higher Power. I will start telling myself that my Higher Power loves me unconditionally. I am safe; my Higher Power will take care of me. I can let go of my crazy, needy thinking and turn it over. I am then okay, even if I am feeling weak. A warm feeling starts to grow in my stomach. I feel love and am encouraged to be myself. I am okay with all my strange feelings. There is newfound freedom when I no longer depend upon my addicted loved one. I know I am okay with who I am and where I am now. I thank my Higher Power for my life; it is exactly as it should be right now. I now depend on my Higher Power and receive the reassurance I need.

Thought for Today: I will accept that I am powerless over another person. I believe that there is a Power greater than I am. I will make a decision to hand my insecurities and doubts to my Higher Power. This saves my day!

"Hope is faith holding out its hand in the dark." ~ George Iles

Hello, Higher Power, I have been waiting for a miracle for nineteen years. What is the problem? I have attended Nar-Anon meetings, worked the steps, gotten a sponsor, been a sponsor to others, done service work, prayed and meditated but nothing has changed for my addicted loved one.

At times, the waiting has been exhausting. I am so tired of doing what the program tells me to do. I want results now! I want my loved one changed and healthy.

Waiting has never been easy for me but maybe it has taught me patience. In Nar-Anon, I learned how to wait. Program tools get me through the waiting process with peace and serenity. I say the Serenity Prayer and find acceptance. I use the slogans and I am able to be patient with myself, my addicted loved one and you, Higher Power.

You know, Higher Power, during the last nineteen years I have also found many good friends in the Nar-Anon fellowship. They understand this problem of addiction, as others cannot. So today, I am no longer waiting alone. They support me when I am weary of waiting. They love me when I cannot love myself. They continue to assure me that there is no situation too difficult, and no matter what happens to the addict, I will be okay. I know today that with the Nar-Anon fellowship, I can overcome any unhappiness.

Thought for Today: With the patience and loving support of the Nar-Anon program, I can endure and persevere, however long I have to wait. Maybe the miracle in my life is not whether or not the addict finds recovery. Maybe the miracle in my life is Nar-Anon and my own recovery.

"Today, I will wait, if waiting is the action I need, in order to take care of myself. I will know that I am taking positive, forceful action by waiting until the time is right. God, help me let go of my fear, urgency, and panic. Help me learn the art of waiting until the time is right." ~ Melody Beattie

I was a person whose life revolved around the addict. It was, I thought, my job to anticipate what he wanted and needed, and to give it to him – no matter the cost. I would have sacrificed anything for him. I would have even chosen him over my children. Certainly, I sacrificed myself for his every whim and problem. This was especially true when I stepped in to save him from the consequences of his drug use.

I waited up at night, unable to sleep. I feared for his life when the runs lasted for days. I called hospitals and even police stations looking for him so I could find relief in knowing he was okay. I was one of those "We have a court date" people. Part of me did not even understand that only his name was on the court's docket, not mine. My obsession was his happiness and well-being. He had become my world.

In Nar-Anon, I have slowly learned to put the focus back on me, one step at a time. First, I had to learn (it took practice) to take the focus off him. I had to learn to put the focus somewhere else as I could not yet put the focus on myself. Therefore, I started by focusing more attention on my children who needed it, on Nar-Anon service work, on my elderly grandfather, ailing mother, and on my work. That enabled me to slowly take my focus off the addict.

I used the slogans: "Easy Does It," "Keep it Simple," "Think," "How Important Is It?" and "One Day at a Time." These slogans guided me in this long difficult process of turning from the distraction of obsession to facing reality. It was only after I was free from my obsession that I could begin to focus on me and begin my own transformation to a happier and healthier person.

Thought for Today: Obsession leaves as we practice using all of the tools of the program, and change the focus to ourselves.

"If you work on your mind with your mind, how can you avoid an immense confusion?" ~ *Seng-Ts'an*

One of the benefits I receive by attending Nar-Anon meetings is that I see and do things differently than I had in the past. "Easy does it" was hard for me. I had always believed that there were only two ways to do something, the right way and the wrong way. I also believed that the easiest way generally was not the right way. In an effort to make things right as I saw them, I complicated a difficult situation, tried to force what I thought were the best solutions, and thus assured myself that I was helping. As it turns out, I was doing very little right, but instead was making my life a complicated mess.

In Nar-Anon, I have learned not to be critical of others' or my own actions. I do not have to see everything as right or wrong. So today, I do the best I can, as I have always done, but now without the personal recriminations that I am not trying hard enough and things are not happening fast enough. I am more accepting when things do not go the way I planned. Life throws enough challenges my way, so I do not need to seek them out or create new ones on my own.

Thought for Today: I would not plan a trip by selecting the route with the most road construction. By applying the slogan "Easy does it," I can work with what I have, and let the rest go. The road construction is there for a reason and will eventually make my life better, but all I can do in this moment is drive slowly through while I await the results.

"Be mindful of each moment in your day. Slow down! Your journey is not only about arriving at your destination. The journey is the journey. The end is not the journey. The destination will be what it will be, but did you enjoy the way?" ~ Ron Rathbun

Since I am not able to think like an addict, my first instinct is to react to their attitudes and choices with anger, fear and frustration. This keeps my focus on other people and other people's problems, not on my own. I, of course, have no problems, because I am not an addict. I am the one with all the answers. I am the one with all the strength. I can control any situation. I can get others out of any problem they may face.

I can relate this behavior to leaking pipes. I am able to put some tape on the first few leaks, but when I run out of tape, I cover them with anything I can get my hands on. I try to hold all the leaks in until they are bursting out of control. I cannot spread myself thin enough to cover them all up.

Now, when I find myself knee-deep in water, I have to give up and admit that there is a problem that I cannot fix. This is when I came to Nar-Anon. I came to the program not knowing what to expect, but I knew that I had no idea what to do next. I needed direction. I came with my self-righteous attitude that I could fix anything. I came with all my baggage and habits and techniques that I was sure would work for any situation. I learned that I was living in chaos, and thriving on a way of life that helped me survive the effects of a loved one's addiction.

Thought for Today: In Nar-Anon, I find ways not merely to survive but to live.

"Man cannot discover new oceans unless he has the courage to lose sight of the shore." ~ André Gide

When I was young, I thought I had a lot of faith, but after the years of living with an addict, my faith seemed to disappear. How could so many heartrending events happen to such a good person? I volunteered at my church and visited my mother regularly. Could not the God of my youth see all the good, charitable things I was doing? It took some time before I realized the part I had played in all of this, and that my lack of connection with my Higher Power was a big part of it.

Even after my spouse's first incarceration, I had faith that our life would get better. However, after years of living with active addiction, survival became the new order of the day. I learned to read his irrational behavior and then adjust my own behavior accordingly. I took to sleeping with my purse and car keys in my pillow, crying myself to sleep. I no longer believed that the protection I wanted was available to me. I became disillusioned by my youthful faith that I thought was a result of my good works. Today in Nar-Anon, I am learning that faith is a trust in a Power greater than I am that can restore me to sanity.

Thought for Today: Today I have a spiritual relationship with a Power greater than myself. I know that only daily contact with this Higher Power can see me through. I have faith that this Power is available and willing to guide me in all my decisions. I have a bookmark that reads, "I do not know what the future holds, but I know who holds the future." I now believe this.

"Nar-Anon is not a religious program, but a spiritual way of life." ~ Nar-Anon Blue Booklet

The key words in Step Three for me are "decision, will, and care." Each time I read this step, I think about my part in making my life better.

My part is to make a decision to let go of my willful controlling and put my life in guiding hands. It sounds so easy! I have found that prayer and meditation are essential to letting go of my will. I consciously resolve to do this step daily in order to stay aware of what I can change and what my responsibility is.

How do I know that the result of turning it over will be miraculous for me? From experience! When I surrendered my will and paid attention to the guidance of a Higher Power, I experienced miracles! I continue to experience miracles when I practice the tools of the program, attend meetings, read Nar-Anon literature, work with my sponsor, pray, and meditate.

Evidence of this care includes newfound positive relationships with relatives and friends, forgiveness, acceptance and unconditional love. I have a healthier body, less diseased by stress. I have a brighter spirit and a positive outlook on life rather than toxic doom and gloom.

Thought for Today: I believe in a caring Higher Power. I trust that Power to work for good in my life. The miracles, big and small, are what I have to look forward to when I let go of my own self-will.

"Decision: something that somebody chooses or makes up his or her mind about, after considering it and other possible choices." ~ Encarta World English Dictionary

CHOICES

Before Nar-Anon, I would have said that my life was in control. I knew what I wanted. I thought that if only the addict would stop using, everything would be okay. Now, I realize that the addict had control over me. I was always thinking about him and his life. I worried about him constantly and did not want to upset him. I did what he asked even when I knew it was not the right thing for me to do. His needs and wants came first. I had lost control.

Nar-Anon gave me back my life. I learned we both had choices. I learned to let him make his own choices and not try to tell him what to do. I also learned to make my own choices because they were right for me, even though some of them made the addict unhappy.

Once I understood that I was powerless over him, his reactions and everyone else, it did get easier. In Nar-Anon, I learned how to do that by practicing the Twelve Steps, and by applying the Serenity Prayer and the slogans to my life.

Thought for Today: When we look outside ourselves to other people, places or things for our happiness and well-being, we have lost control. True happiness comes from within.

"Control is an illusion, especially the kind of control we've been trying to exert. In fact, controlling gives other people, events and diseases control over us." ~ Melody Beattie

I have always felt that I could solve everyone's problems but no one would listen to me. I felt more and more helpless as I watched a loved one slowly destroy himself with drugs. With each passing day, I was more determined to do everything I could to make the addict change. If he would realize the importance of getting his life in order by attending Narcotics Anonymous meetings, keeping appointments with his probation officer, and working, then he would be fine. I became obsessed with finding ways to make this happen. Even though I had been attending Nar-Anon meetings for almost a year, I was still having a problem separating helping from enabling.

With the help of my Nar-Anon friends, I slowly recognized my own addiction for fixing. I had not yet learned how to let go and practice the acceptance, courage, and wisdom promised in the Serenity Prayer by taking Step Three: "Made a decision to turn our will and our lives over to the care of God *as we understand Him.*"

I was not getting the answers that I wanted, so I kept taking the job back. Needless to say, nothing changed. Then at a meeting someone shared these words, "when I asked why God hadn't helped, my Higher Power replied, you would not get out of the way and let Me in." Suddenly my mind was filled with this thought, "The water on the lake was like glass," and I felt suddenly calm. I had at last put my "right" foot up onto the Third Step. With the support of my sponsor, I am keeping it there.

Several days later, I learned that the addict's Higher Power had helped him find his answer. There was a bus, which on its route passed his home, his work, the probation office, and to top it off, three Narcotics Anonymous meetings.

Thought for Today: I realize that what may seem impossible can be possible if I am patient. As for me, I have finally learned to let go so that now my loved one can grow on his own.

"...giving him an opportunity to become himself, to develop the best within him, regardless of what that best may be..." ~ *Nar-Anon Blue Booklet*

As our two sons were growing up, my husband and I stressed that they should always be honest with us. We told them repeatedly that they would not be punished for telling us the truth. Just do not lie.

When I found out that our youngest son had been using drugs for two years, I realized that he had told us many lies. I was devastated by the amount of deceit that it took for him to hide his addiction. When he finally went into a rehab program, the truth about his addiction began to reveal itself. Little by little, his honesty began to return. It was as though an enormous weight was being lifted from his shoulders.

Now that my husband and I are in Nar-Anon, I see that honesty is a problem for both of us, not just for the addict. There are many times when I do not want to see the truth about myself. With every meeting I attend, I learn a new bit of my truth. I practice my program daily and use it in all my affairs. By living these principles with the help of my Higher Power, I come much closer to being honest with others and myself. I also feel an enormous burden being lifted from my shoulders.

Thought for Today: Total honesty requires perfection. I am not perfect. I am doing the best I can today with the help of my Higher Power and the Nar-Anon fellowship. I will allow others this same luxury.

"There's always room for improvement, you know-it's the biggest room in the house." ~ Louise Heath Leber

I have always wanted to belong to something or to someone, or to have someone belong to me. This longing and desire was the driving force that propelled me to seek to be accepted and to fit in. I was confused, isolated, and lost. I existed to please others. The funny thing is the very secrets that I protected belonged to the addict. They are the things that separated me from a healthy lifestyle. Secrets killed my recovery program and distanced me from others. I could no longer hide and pretend that I was okay.

Through the shared experience of the Nar-Anon meeting, a new awareness of me has emerged. I do not seek to feel accepted; now I am accepted. I know, because I accept myself. When I hear feelings honestly shared in a meeting, the passion of that honesty opens the door for healing, not only for the one sharing, but also for me as I, in turn, am inspired to truthfully share my thoughts. I connect, I experience empathy and I understand others, but, more importantly, I understand myself. This is my Higher Power at work. I come to meetings to recover trust in myself. I am excited and motivated to change.

Today I have more energy. My hidden layers are peeling away. I finally can see the light of my higher self. My top priority is for living a healthy life, physically, mentally, and spiritually. I like myself better now. I have a new, more interesting relationship with myself. I trust my spiritual intuitions to guide me down the recovery path of new choices.

Thought for Today: Honesty gives me the gift of a serene, connected life of freedom and choice. I am grateful for the unconditional love and support of my Nar-Anon home group. I feel their healing energy and I give back. I am honestly connected to the Nar-Anon way.

"Listening is a gift to ourselves." ~ Karen Casey

In Step Four, I learned that many of the beliefs that I impose on others might result in my own pain and disappointment.

I believe that trust is a part of any loving, close relationship. When addiction becomes active in my loved one, I no longer trust him. I have learned that my beliefs and expectations of others are in error. My own beliefs result in my feelings of betrayal, pain, anger, and resentment. I also believe that if the addict lies to me, then he does not love me. I believe a relationship built on trust is a safe haven, a soft place to fall. So why would the addict not want the same? Why would the addict want to taint the relationship with lies? Why risk such a cherished thing?

What is really happening is that my rules for a relationship are being broken. I create expectations for the addict. This causes frustration for both of us. I want him to earn back my trust but when he attempts this, I am scared that because of his past actions he will burn me once again. He feels guilty and ashamed. He would like me to forgive and forget after a few trustworthy attempts at amends, to get the relationship back on track.

In Nar-Anon, I am learning that addiction is a disease and that the addict has lost the power of choice when it comes to drugs. This knowledge gives me compassion to accept the addict.

Thought for Today: I can prevent myself from being hurt by not creating expectations of the addict. When I do, I am opening myself to pain and disappointment. Today I can separate the addict from the illness and love the person. I can allow myself to mistrust the disease. I can do what is necessary to take care of myself.

"Love truth, but pardon error." ~ Voltaire

MAKING JUDGMENTS   April 2

I heard someone say, "human beings make mistakes but they are not the mistakes." This made me wonder about all of the times I sat in judgment of the addict in my life. Did I let the addict think, or did I think that the addict was the mistake? I have not been able to get this thought out of my mind. Human beings make mistakes. I make mistakes. That is how I know I am human. This reminds me how quick I am to judge.

From the Nar-Anon program, I have learned to take my own inventory and to avoid taking the inventory of others. I have learned to set boundaries for myself. I ask myself if this is my issue or the addict's. If it is the addict's, I give it back. I am learning, one day at a time, to forgive myself when I don't and to start over again. I am learning that life is a journey not a destination. I am also learning to make amends quickly when I make a mistake. I know that I cannot control someone else's behavior, only my own. Daily, I ask my Higher Power to help me, to be with me. I am learning to put my Higher Power first, myself second and then others. By taking care of myself in this way, I can be of help to others if they choose to ask. I am learning the relief of not being responsible for the addict's behavior.

Thought for Today: I will not sit in judgment of others including the addict. I will take my inventory, make my amends and humbly ask for my Higher Power's help. In doing so, I will experience a change for the better.

"If you have made mistakes, even serious ones, there is always another chance for you. What we call failure is not the falling down, but the staying down." ~ Mary Pickford

When I started attending Nar-Anon, I had a great deal of anger and held much resentment toward my addicted loved one. I blamed him for everything that happened. I felt that I was the one suffering from his addiction. I was the victim, he was the cause of my pain and suffering and I had a right to be angry with him. I hated him and yet I loved him. I stayed with him because we have children. Blaming the addict helped me to justify any and all of my actions, good or bad.

I never thought that I needed to take a look at myself. It was so much easier to not focus on me. I never thought that I had faults and shortcomings. Maybe I was making some bad choices but I was not the addict. In Nar-Anon, I am learning that I am not powerless over myself, I am not the victim and that I have to take responsibility for my choices. I am doing this by working the steps. Step Four has been especially helpful in my recovery as it asks that I take a fearless look at myself. I am asked to identify my character defects. Then I begin to see and understand the part I play in this family disease of addiction.

I now realize that putting the blame on others started long before the addict came into my life. It had always been easier to blame others than to admit the part I played in my troubles, and how my attitude affected my feelings and behavior. Today, I am learning that I need to deal with my anger and resentments. I am doing this for myself because I want peace and serenity.

Thought for Today: Step Four is one of my recovery tools. It helps me see my weaknesses and strengths, so I can play an active role in my recovery.

"Change the behavior and the attitude will follow. I have to put action into my program. I have to take care of myself to believe that I am worth taking care of." ~ Anonymous

ARROGANCE

If you had disagreed with me in the past, I would have had to argue with you until you changed your mind and saw the light, my light that is. Because I was always right, you needed to recognize that fact; and if you did not, I would either disregard you completely or show you nothing but contempt. This attitude of pride and arrogance only resulted in me being mad at the world and disliking most of the people in it. I was a bitter and unhappy person. This state of mind left no room for peace and serenity. Then I meet the addict who, on the surface, was a very agreeable person that fed my ego and pride. I fell in love and we were married six months later. This relationship eventually brought me to Nar-Anon.

In Nar-Anon, it was suggested that I take my focus off others and put it on myself. During a Fourth Step inventory, I shared with my sponsor the need to always be right. She asked why it mattered to me. She also suggested that I might need the approval of others to validate myself. She also reminded me of the Serenity Prayer, and who I could change. Only because I was so unhappy did I even consider her point of view.

Therefore, I practiced letting go of my need to be right. At first, I stopped arguing. To my surprise, when I stopped arguing, other things changed. The lack of conflict also reduced my level of anger and bitterness toward others. To my surprise, I could even be okay with not having everyone think the same way as I did. Finally, I was even able to accept others most of the time.

Thought for Today: Change is not easy and I do not change quickly. I have to practice new ways of thinking and behaving. If I do not practice, I can see myself falling back into my old behavior. When I practice new ways of thinking and behaving, unexpected things happen.

"When they discover the center of the universe, a lot of people will be disappointed to discover they are not it." ~ Bernard Bailey

I am grateful for so many things today that before the program I did not even see. I did not believe that anyone or anything could help me with the weight of the world on my shoulders. Today, I am able to think about something, talk it over with other Nar-Anon members and give it to a Power greater than myself, that can do for me what I cannot do for myself. That does not mean that everything will turn out the way I would like it to. It means that it is not all my responsibility to do, decide, carry, or work things out for others. I can let others be themselves and do whatever they want to or need to do. I have learned that other people are not my responsibility. That is a great relief.

After doing Step Four and talking with other members, as well as having a sponsor who lets me see what works and does not work for me, I know I am not responsible for everything and everyone.

I understand that addiction is a disease. Nar-Anon has helped me to be grateful for what I have. Today, I am grateful for things I used to take for granted: food, a home to live in, a car to drive, and friends. I have learned I can take something I am responsible for and turn it over to my Higher Power – knowing that the result does not depend on me. For this, I am eternally grateful to this program.

Thought for Today: Today I know what it means to be good to myself. I understand that I can take care of myself and that I have the resources to become the person I want to be. I believe I can become a much better person by using the tools of Nar-Anon and by having the courage to change. I am grateful for who I am today.

"For today and its blessings, I owe the world an attitude of gratitude." ~ *Clarence E. Hodges*

People such as me, whose problems have brought them to the point of despair, come to Nar-Anon seeking advice and looking for solutions. As soon as I attended my first meeting, I felt as if I had come home. I was among people who understood me. I was a fortunate newcomer. I appreciated those who had gone before me and shared their experience, strength and hope. It encouraged me to keep coming back. As a newcomer, I discovered that it is by giving, receiving and sharing that I am able to heal. I was slowly able to once again regain control of my life.

My group also showed me that there is work to do on me, not the addict. Nar-Anon is not just a sounding board for continually reviewing my miseries, but is a way to learn how to detach myself from these problems. When I change the focus from my addicted loved one to me, I begin to change and grow. This is how I can recover and heal.

Thought for Today: I will learn by listening, reading Nar-Anon literature, and by working the Twelve Steps with the help of my sponsor to gain a better insight into myself. The more I read and study, the more knowledge I gain. Knowledge is power and it will increase my ability to work the steps. I can help others and myself by sharing my experience, strength, and hope at meetings. Submitting written shares also helps convey my thoughts to the larger audience of all Nar-Anon readers.

"Turn your melodrama into a mellow drama." ~ Ram Dass

I consider myself a fortunate husband: my wife and I both attend Nar-Anon meetings. We are both in recovery, and we can support each other in ways we were never aware of when we took our marriage vows. We can share at meetings and at home. In addition, when we meet a newcomer or someone starting on the painful road of dealing with the effects of living with an addict, we can share from both our viewpoints. In our Nar-Anon group, we are fortunate because we are able to share our thoughts with other couples who are going through the same pain we are. It is important that we do not make judgments of each other's reactions to a crisis.

My wife is a stronger person than I am. I used to have more dark times than she did. Maybe it is because I am a typical man who wants to be in charge, telling everyone how to live or what to do. Nar-Anon has not only provided a recovery program that lets me live a happy life, in spite of having an addicted family member, but I have also learned about myself. I try to work on controlling my "expert" attitude just as I work on controlling myself when confronted with the uncontrollable – addiction.

I use a journal to write down my thoughts, my feelings, my desires for the addict and me, my sadness in dealing with this situation, and my victories over the darkness. I think it is similar to exorcizing a demon from my being. I am more able to block the madness from overtaking me as it once did. This is good – good for me, good for my wife, and good for the addict as well.

When a crisis happens, my wife and I support each other, work the program together, help each other, and laugh again.

Thought for Today: We thank our Higher Power for Nar-Anon! Together we can.

"The world is seldom what it seems; to a man, who dimly sees, realities appear as dreams, and dreams realities." ~ *Samuel Johnson*

In our local Nar-Anon region, there is a yearly announcement of a special retreat, which is a gathering of Nar-Anon members who wish to work their Fourth Step. The first year I saw this announcement, I did not understand the significance of this step. However, I saw my friends return from the retreat as if they had returned from a trip to a faraway land. The following year, the retreat was held in the spring and it seemed like a perfect time for me to get away from home. That weekend changed my life. The Fourth Step, which seemed to be a potentially uncomfortable confrontation with my demons, actually turned into an opportunity to meet someone I had not seen for a long time. Myself! I spent time learning that the hurt and unhappy woman I had become, started out as an innocent young girl who had her life interrupted by the occurrence of alcoholism and drug addiction in her family. I was given an opportunity to heal the hurt of that child and choose a new direction for the grown woman.

Over the years, I have unfortunately missed out on some opportunities to revisit the Fourth Step Weekend. Therefore a new chance to spend some time with heroic members of Nar-Anon was too good to pass up. Their strength lifted me in the middle of this dreary winter. I found myself lying in bed at night, listening to the laughter and joy in voices that had come to Nar-Anon tearful and distraught. What a wonderful healing program this is!

Thought for Today: Taking a fearless and moral inventory is not a punishment. It is a freeing experience where I can discover myself. I am not perfect but I am okay.

"And the day came when the risk it took to remain tight in the bud was more painful than the risk it took to bloom." ~ Anaïs Nin

I have expectations of myself. Have you ever heard the expression: "Expectations are disappointments waiting to happen"? I used to have expectations of the addict in my life. Those expectations were somewhat out of focus, more like a dream sequence in a movie than reality-based. In my fantasy, I expected the addict would go to college somewhere, find a fulfilling career and have a happy life. Through attending Nar-Anon meetings and working the program, I have learned I can have expectations that are real, and they are only about me.

A few months ago, I held a little funeral for those groundless expectations. I celebrated what was, looking back on the time when he and I were close. Then I said good-bye to my expectations—and yes, I grieved for that significant ending in my life. Because I work my program, I am able to enjoy something new - my own reality and all that I am able to achieve. I am free from rancor, regret, disappointment, and resentment. I have learned that when I live one day at a time, I am able to see life clearly, rather than as a fantasy.

Thought for Today: Today, I will have expectations only of myself that are real and reflect my conscious commitment to living life one day at a time.

"The most painful state of being is remembering the future, particularly one you can never have." ~ Søren Kierkegaard

The other day I took my grandson to the pier to go fishing. I wanted to get away from it all and not think about anything. I needed a clear head. While on the pier, a man came up and started talking to my grandson. He looked like what we used to call a bum. I listened as he told me about his three daughters and how one of them was all messed up such as he was.

He told me how he liked his beer "now and again" and that he was not ashamed to be in the situation in which he found himself. I asked him how a fellow like him ended up where he is. He proceeded to tell me something that did not make much sense. I thought about him for a long time after that.

Before I started attending Nar-Anon meetings, I would not have given this man the time of day, but something inside of me now tells me that this person was not a low-life bum, but rather a human being that had a big problem. He had a problem so terrible that he did not know how to get out of it.

Thought for Today: I am learning compassion and acceptance through Nar-Anon. I am learning that not everyone is as fortunate as I am. I am learning how to look at people differently. A saying I had learned earlier now has a new meaning to me: "Love the sinner, not the sin."

"It's not what you look at that matters, it's what you see." ~ Henry David Thoreau

It is my belief that I have every right to ask to be recognized and understood. That is why I always wanted to explain my reasons, opinions, excuses and needs as clearly as I could, using far too many words although I was seldom satisfied with the results. I always felt that the other person did not understand me.

When I started attending Nar-Anon meetings, I did feel that I was understood, but I still felt that everybody was different from me and that my situation was somehow special. I now recognize that this is one of my shortcomings. I would focus on the differences between people, not on our similarities. I loved to feel unique although I felt isolated. Another shortcoming I recognized is that I placed expectations on the outcome of being understood. I thought if the addict understood how I felt, he would stop hurting me, or frustrating me.

I am now learning that I can enjoy my uniqueness without isolating. I can share my experiences with other Nar-Anon members to unite us in recovery. Communication is important because it allows me to share. However, I cannot use logic or detailed explanations to make people act the way I see fit. I do not have that power. I can express how I feel, but when I start repeating myself over and over, it is likely I am trying to control or manipulate rather than communicate.

Thought for Today: I will not use my words to control but I will share my experiences, strength and hope to grow in my recovery.

"Skillful speech not only means that we pay attention to the words we speak and to their tone, but also requires that our words reflect compassion and concern for others and that they help and heal, rather than wound and destroy." ~ Bhante Henepola Gunaratana, Eight Mindful Steps to Happiness

I affectionately dubbed my 17-year-old son "rehab boy." Today, he completed one month at a drug rehab facility with three more months to go. The court mandated this treatment as part of his sentence for crimes committed as a young offender. Most of his crimes were for petty theft, drug dealing, and prostitution for drugs, all pretty ugly stuff.

For about two years, I had tried all of the conventional measures to help my son. He was 100% out of control, despite all the usual avenues that parents take to find help for their child. Absolutely nothing prevented him from using and wreaking havoc at home and anywhere else he could. I honestly did not know if there would have been any other way to help my son, other than what I did. I told him he was no longer welcome in my home. It was a tough choice to make as a parent, to evict my child. He lived on the streets for one year, homeless, stoned and out of control.

During this time, I gained the strength, support and faith I needed from the Nar-Anon Family Groups. I now believe that if I had not done what I did, my son would be dead. I am thankful he did not die during that year he was living on the streets. I am also thankful he did not hurt anyone else in my family or outside of the family. I feel that he may not have received the help he is now receiving, had I not finally received the courage to get out of his way so he could reach his bottom.

Thought for Today: The addict has a Higher Power and I have learned that it is not me. No matter how much it hurts me, I need to get out of the way and let the addict experience the consequences of his using.

"There is no education like adversity." ~ Benjamin Disraeli

Some of my Nar-Anon friends who entered the program after I did were already seeing their addicts in recovery. I thought that this was not fair, and I realized that I envied them. When I started working on Step Four, I discovered that envy is one of my deep-rooted character defects. I needed to ask my Higher Power to help me deal with this matter and I learned to do this one day at a time. I needed to get on with my life and stop dwelling on the addict. By attending Nar-Anon meetings, I am doing just that.

Becoming entirely ready to have my character defect of envy removed required some research on my part. Why did I envy my Nar-Anon friends whose loved ones were in recovery? Is it because I believed that my peace of mind and serenity was dependent on the addict's recovery? Have I not stated that I had no control over the addict and made up my mind that I was going to think of my wife and myself first? Was the addict not the one who made her choice and, therefore, she was the only one who could make a difference in how she was living? Yes, there it is. My focus is still misdirected.

Thought of Today: The message of Nar-Anon is starting to take hold. I will change my focus and become entirely ready to have my envy removed.

"I hope we can be happy where we are, be grateful for our blessings-now-here, accept the challenge that is ours and make the most of it, and don't be envious of others. God help us to be grateful." ~ Ezra Taft Benson

How did I become such a martyr, sacrificing my own well-being as I tried to change and take care of others? As I listen to the committee in my head, I hear and understand the woman who raised me also had in her head the voice of a martyr. The church community I was raised in valued acts of self-sacrifice. Naturally, I believed this was how a good woman should behave, always giving to others and putting herself last. To behave otherwise would be selfish.

I married into addiction because it was familiar. I knew it so well from my childhood and it was prevalent in my community. My "committee" voice said, "I sacrificed so much for you! Yes, I took care of you as if you had no father, because I felt your father was too out of it to be a parent and a good influence." Naturally, I was always stressed out. "Everything would be perfect if ..." Yes, I spun my wheels trying to create the perfect marriage and perfect children.

In reality, my mother modeled to her children, and I later would model to mine. We taught our children to deny their needs, ideas, wants, feelings, and their souls for others. We were training martyrs.

Then I found Nar-Anon and learned that, although I loved the woman who raised me, I could take a different path. I could take care of myself and not feel guilty or selfish because I put my needs first. I also learned that catering to addiction only made matters worse.

Thought for Today: A martyr is somebody who makes sacrifices or suffers greatly in order to advance a cause or principle. When I make sacrifices to prevent the addict from the consequences of his actions, I am advancing the addict's disease.

"How much a family is affected by substance abuse depends on how long they have lived with it, how advanced it is, how much shame and secrecy surrounds it, and the roles and responsibilities of the person with the disorder. If the problem is left untreated, family members will also develop destructive behaviors, such as denial, enabling, and co-dependency." ~ *The Partnership for a Drug-Free America*

My daughter chooses to keep her distance from me because all I did was worry about her. I worried about where she was, what she was doing and what she was using. The truth was that I was obsessing about her because I felt so angry with her. My anger was what I used to hide from and I did not deal with my fears and sadness. All I could think about was how horrible and ungrateful she was. I could not keep her out of my mind. I was exhausted with worry as my negative thoughts consumed me.

Slowly, I began to see that my obsessive, stinking thinking was controlling me and making me sick. With the help of my Nar-Anon group, I came to realize that only I could change my thoughts. So one day, I decided to think differently. I made a list of my daughter's strengths. Then each time I had a negative thought about her, I would look at my list of her strengths, choose one, and think about it for a short time. Example: I think, "how thoughtless she is"; but my list also says she is "spiritual," so I change my focus and think about her positive quality of spirituality.

Gradually, over time, I realized I was hardly thinking about her at all. My obsession with her and my negative thoughts had dissipated. The Nar-Anon program gave me the knowledge that I am not powerless over my thinking and I have a choice. It also gave me the encouragement and tools to use so that I could change my thinking to what I wanted.

Thought for Today: If I am obsessing about the behavior of others, I only need to change my attitude and focus. I can focus on the addict's valuable and useful abilities. Perhaps one day I can change the focus to myself.

"Our ultimate freedom is the right and power to decide how anybody or anything outside ourselves will affect us." ~ Stephen Covey

I find it amazing that the working of Step Four can help dictate how one reacts to life's challenges. This step made me realize that my reaction to any given circumstance is controlled only by me with the help of my Higher Power. I realize that I had previously let anger and impatience control how I reacted to any given situation and that I need to work on those defects of character. The change that came over me was profound!

My feelings towards the addict have changed because of Step Four. Where once I would get angry when I saw her, I now realize that anger accomplishes absolutely nothing on the path to recovery. I have seen a difference in the addict and in myself since I stopped getting angry with her. One benefit of this is that I am not constantly in a foul mood because of my anger. I am now able to reach towards what I have always been seeking…serenity! I feel better physically, spiritually and emotionally. I have no more stomach aches, my blood pressure has not gone up, and I am able to appreciate the sunshine in my life. Indeed, the other day I could listen to the magic and beauty of a bird singing.

By working Step Four, I am accomplishing many things. I am seeking my Higher Power's guidance and solace. I am also realizing that the addict is a person who suffers and deserves compassion.

Thought for Today: I thank my Higher Power for helping me embrace the Nar-Anon program and giving me the strength and courage to take Step Four. I am not the stressed out, frantic, angry and impatient person that I once was.

"Today I am going to use my inventory to help me find a better way of life." ~ Today a Better Way - Families Anonymous, Inc.

My favorite "Just for Today" saying from the <u>Nar-Anon Blue Booklet</u> is "I will be unafraid. Especially I will not be afraid to enjoy what is beautiful, and to believe that as I give to the world, so the world will give to me." What an inspiration! During the years of living with active addiction, I was afraid of everything, but especially afraid of enjoying beauty. With addiction, happiness is always temporary. I knew that even if something did make me happy, there would soon be something horrible to take its place. So I taught myself to ignore happiness when it came along, priding myself on how much wiser it was to stay at a level of constant sadness, and avoid the inevitable fall into deeper disappointment.

Then I came into Nar-Anon and learned that happiness is not temporary; it is optional. Years of self-imposed misery could be years of growth and joy instead. It had been my decision all along, and no matter how I tried, I could no longer blame my unhappiness on the addict. As I went to more meetings, it became clear that at any point in our relationship I could have tried improving my attitude. Instead, I blamed him for everything that went wrong and took no responsibility for my life.

Slowly, the program started to sink in. "Just for today I will be happy." Today is all I have. If I waste it thinking about what might go wrong tomorrow, there is no one to blame but me. Instead, I will open my eyes and look around me. Once I do that, I can see all the beauty and wonder in the world. The choice is mine and I have to be the one to open my eyes. It seems frightening to be happy. I have to remind myself that this is a big change in my life and change is often scary.

Thought for Today: Thanks to unfailing support from my Nar-Anon friends and my sponsor, my life is filled with beauty and more joy than I thought possible. I have been given back a wonderful gift, the gift of laughter. As long as I can lighten up and laugh, I will be able to enjoy life without being afraid of what I cannot see.

"Have a wonderful day, unless you've made other plans." ~ Unknown

If I saw an insane person on the street, I would not try to talk sense to that person. Why do I think I can try to talk sense to an addict? Why do I think I can cure addiction by talking? I learned in Nar-Anon, I could not.

I used to think that if I were the perfect parent, spouse, friend, child, or sibling to the addict, the addict would get clean. If I were good to the addict, the addict would get clean. The truth is I never heard an addict say, "I got clean because my parent, spouse or child was so good to me."

I kept trying to do one more thing. I was certain that this "one more thing" would be the *one* that would work. The addict would hit bottom, see the light, go to a meeting, and find recovery. It took me so long to learn and accept that there was no "one more thing" for me to do. It was not my responsibility. There was no "one more thing" to stop the addict from using.

Nar-Anon showed me how to change my focus by thinking about the addict in another way. The reality was that he was using. By believing otherwise, I was kidding myself. I was obsessed with the addict's behavior and my thinking was distorted. I have learned from Nar-Anon that addiction is a family disease.

Thought for Today: In the safety of my Nar-Anon meetings, I can work the steps, talk to a sponsor and do service. In these ways, I practice changing my thinking. Slowly, a new way of thinking and a new way of life emerges.

"...there are two entirely opposite attitudes possible in facing the problems of one's life. One, to try and change the external world, the other, to try and change oneself." ~ Joanna Field

Nar-Anon has taught me to love the addict, but hate the disease. I learned that I could not change the addict. What I can do is take care of my children and myself.

After six months of attending Nar-Anon meetings and working my program, I became stronger and decided to ask the addict to move out. I also asked her not to call. Nevertheless, her behavior was out of my control and she called me every three weeks. Then I received an email message from her with one simple word: "testing."

For the next three days, I was spinning and obsessive thinking took over again. I was glad she was 600 miles away. Otherwise, I do not know if I could have stayed away from her. I broke it off because her active addiction was so harmful to me. I also needed to protect my children. I finally admitted how toxic living with active addiction was for me.

I was still so angry that drug addiction had taken her away from me. Then I remembered a dream I had while we were still together and the addict was clean. I dreamed that a bigot came up and shot my beloved dead. I beat him up, crushing his skull, and woke up screaming. Two weeks later, she relapsed.

I now realize that drug addiction had taken her from me just like the sick person in my dream. I came to the realization that addiction was the killer. This thought allowed me to feel compassion for the addict and relieved me of the guilt I was feeling.

Thought for Today: I will allow myself to do what is right for me without guilt. I will take care of myself and release others with love to do the same.

"Remember you, too, are always changing, and you can direct that change consciously if you so desire. Yourself, you CAN change. Others you can only love." ~ Nar-Anon Blue Booklet

The phone rings and it is a friend asking if he could pick my brain about some principles that I am learning from my Nar-Anon program. He asks, "What do they tell you to do when you care about an individual and you cannot help them or change them?"

Of course, I did not want to give a long detailed explanation for "minding your own business," but I kindly responded, "We learn to detach with love." "Explain," was his reply.

I shared with him what I was learning in Nar-Anon. It is possible to detach from other people's problems with love. Detaching means to allow someone to find their own way and not tell them what to do, or try to control them. We cannot tell another person how to live or what choices to make. It is impossible to manage another person's life.

We talked about how a doctor can treat several illnesses everyday but remain emotionally detached in order to help his patients. He could diagnose and prescribe medicine but the patient has to want to take the medicine and follow the doctor's orders. I was able to paint a verbal picture when I said, "A doctor cannot make a patient take his medicine anymore than he can take the medicine for his patients."

Thought for Today: We should not fail to plan, but we would be mistaken if we thought we could plan the results.

"Sometimes people we love do things we don't like or approve of. We react. They react. Before long, we're all reacting to each other, and the problem escalates." ~ Melody Beattie

My mother had intense mood swings, and my father was emotionally unavailable. To protect myself from my mother's emotional and physical abuse, I went into a world that felt safer: My trance. I had no close relationships, and I was sure I had no personality; there was something missing in me. This is how I lived my life; this was my trance, my way of not being.

My husband was the first person with whom I felt comfortable. He loved to talk, and I was a good listener. I believed that with him I would become a real person. In my denial, I did not realize that in those early years of marriage he had deep psychological problems. This led to his suicide. Ours was a dysfunctional family. Neither my husband nor I knew anything about nurturing and bringing out the best in our sons. Both boys eventually used drugs. Our youngest was fortunate not to have the disease. The other tragically was an addict and committed suicide at the age of thirty-five.

My real fear was that people would discover my invisibility. I could not relate to my husband's or my son's pain or needs because no one had seen to mine. It took most of my energy to keep up the appearance of being normal. My fear of living was like a wound, and I was sure I was unlovable.

The Nar-Anon program allowed me to start reconnecting and stop being at war with myself. It was as if I was aroused from a deep sleep. I began a spiritual journey that led me to recovery and my Higher Power. By practicing the program and working the steps, I received the help I needed to find myself. It is still painful, but I am discovering the peace and serenity of having an inner and outer persona that match.

Thought for Today: My Higher Power can do for me what I cannot do for myself.

"Prayer and meditation will direct my efforts today. My purpose can be fulfilled." ~ Karen Casey

As a newcomer, it was suggested that I attend several different meetings because each meeting has it own atmosphere and reflects the personality of its members. When I was recently asked to start a new Nar-Anon meeting, I was not sure what I wanted to do or, to be more specific, what I could not do. Therefore, I asked one of the long-time members for instructions. It was suggested that I study the Twelve Traditions.

I learned from Tradition Four that each group decides when, where, and how they will conduct their meetings. They also determine how they will open and close their meetings. Some groups open their meetings with the reading of the Serenity Prayer and close with Friendship – Nar-Anon Style. Others open with the preamble and several readings from the <u>Nar-Anon Blue Booklet</u> and close with the Serenity Prayer. Every group is free to choose its meeting structure and program topics, such as table meetings open to all to share or having a single speaker per meeting.

Tradition Four gives Nar-Anon groups freedom regarding nearly all aspects of their structure. We are asked that the group ensures its decisions are made with the overall purpose of the Nar-Anon fellowship in mind. We should refrain from discussing non-Nar-Anon philosophies in our meetings, and try to limit group discussions to Nar-Anon principles.

Thought for Today: Nar-Anon has taught me that I have choices and I am free to practice my program as I choose. However, our Nar-Anon Family Groups should remain clear about their primary purpose and why they were formed.

"Each group should be autonomous except in matters affecting other Nar-Anon Family Groups, or N.A. as a whole." ~ Nar-Anon Tradition Four

Before Nar-Anon, I used to make agreements with the addict, thinking that I was helping her. In reality, I was trying to manipulate her into recovery. I tried to keep her off the streets by offering to pay her rent if she would go to meetings every day, and offering to take her to the meetings. Of course, she agreed to go along with my demands in order to get the money. It did not work and now I know why. I should have let her do it for herself.

The situation I find myself in reminds me of the need to be constantly learning the messages of Nar-Anon. One fellow member, who had recently started attending the program, said he had hoped he would not be doing this for the rest of his life. He now realizes this might be the case. I have had this thought, too.

What is the alternative? To slide back into the complete and devastating darkness that once controlled my life. No, I do not want nor desire that! I have a sister who was a drug user when she was young. When I spoke with my father about my daughter's addiction and situation, he said, "I could still cry thinking about your sister." This was almost 35 years after she stopped using. Of course, I know he still suffers so much because he has never gone to a Twelve-Step program. Then I thought this is the reason why I keep coming back. I am sure that I need to keep coming back!

Thought for Today: The help and comfort that I receive from the members in Nar-Anon cannot be measured. This is truly a new and better way to live.

"You cannot travel on the path until you become the path itself." ~ *Buddha*

In the depth of despair, I found I was ready for bed before the sun had gone down. I figured my metabolism required more sleep than most people do. I felt continually exhausted from trying to solve all the problems that arose from addiction. It had become a 24-hour job. No wonder I was always exhausted! I had no time for myself because I was spending all my time on someone else.

Once I started working the Nar-Anon program, I made time for me. In the beginning, giving myself a half hour for a meeting was amazing. It was a small amount of time to spare, but to me, it was a monumental change. It felt good! Another change was learning to use acceptance to quiet my mind. I never realized how the constant scenarios going on in my head were contributing to my mental and physical exhaustion.

It is amazing to now discover how little sleep I actually do require. I was trying to figure a way to escape a future that was not even here yet. I had a negative attitude about the addict and was surprised to find after attending meetings how my negative belief was wearing me out. Releasing the addict was a freeing experience for me and gave me a newfound energy. My life was no longer in constant turmoil, always waiting for the next crisis to get involved in. I now have more energy to do the things that are important to me.

Thought for Today: Although my life is far from perfect, it is much more manageable today. I do not know what will happen; I only know there is a loving power that I can trust to care for me. When I begin to think crazy thoughts, I will remember to let go of my fear and be free.

"Whenever you fall, pick something up." ~ Oswald Avery

The Nar-Anon program gives me spiritual freedom. It encourages me to find a personal understanding of my Higher Power and allows others the same freedom. Until I could think of my Higher Power in terms that were meaningful to me, I was not able to truly turn my life over.

Our Nar-Anon area sponsors a Twelve Step weekend workshop. To prepare for it, worksheets of the first three steps are provided for us to review before we attend and we then work Step Four at the workshop. The experience of taking my own inventory, from childhood to the present, made it clear to me why I was so hesitant to turn my life over to the God of my understanding – someone who I felt allowed bad things to happen in my life. What I learned was that my Higher Power was not making these bad things happen to me. My Higher Power was there to help me get through those tough times. Each situation that had happened in my life made me stronger as it prepared me for the next. I realized that my Higher Power was always there.

Thought for Today: Each day with the strength and guidance of my Higher Power, I can detach from the addict with love and live my own life by turning the addict over to his Higher Power. I relapse too, and when I do, I pray to my Higher Power. I need the help of the god of my understanding to live my life fully.

"I know God won't give me anything I can't handle. I just wish he didn't trust me so much." ~ Mother Teresa

In Nar-Anon, we work the Twelve Steps for ourselves. Step Four, "Made a searching and fearless moral inventory of ourselves," can appear to be a difficult and intimidating step. Possibly, because we have been focused on others for so long, especially the addict, we fear we do not know ourselves. Perhaps, like many people who are affected by the disease of addiction, we are suffering from low self-esteem and are frightened that a searching and fearless inventory will show that we are not worthy.

I find that a searching and fearless moral inventory is a journey of self-discovery; one that I need to take for personal growth. In order for me to recognize growth, I first need to know where I am. I need to understand what kind of person I am and to picture the person I want to be.

When I take my Fourth Step inventory, I thoroughly and honestly examine my attitudes, responsibilities, and understanding of important concepts such as self-worth, love and maturity. I look at myself and record my character traits, both my strengths and my weaknesses. I get to know myself and record the findings. I am then prepared to assess what has worked for me and what has not, what I like and what I wish to change. With help, as I work the succeeding steps, I start to make positive changes to become the person I want to be.

Thought for Today: When I take my inventory, I give myself a gift of honesty, which leads to a willingness to grow.

"You have to leave the city of your comfort and go into the wilderness of your intuition. What you'll discover will be wonderful. What you'll discover is yourself." ~ Alan Alda

At times, detachment has been hard for me. My sickness leads me to believe that I can say or do that one thing to help change the addict's life. However, my way of helping, shaming, blaming, and complaining, never improved either my life or the addict's life. Through the program with the help of my Higher Power, I am learning to release with love.

Even though I am in Nar-Anon, there are still many days that I want to interrogate the addict to make sure my prescribed course of action is being followed. Instead, I remember my program and choose a more healthy approach. Reminding myself of my powerlessness over the disease of addiction helps me to detach from another's actions. The addict's recovery is the addict's business. I can only be responsible for my own recovery.

Serenity comes when I understand that there is a Higher Power who loves and cares for each of us, for me as well as for the addict. Detachment with love is not abandonment, but it is surrendering my will and the addict into the loving care of a Power greater than me.

Thought for Today: Nar-Anon literature reminds me that without practice, detachment is merely a theory mentioned in a brochure. Detachment may take time and practice. My Nar-Anon friends keep me on track. Each day, I will work toward the freeing feeling of detachment.

"The real voyage of discovery consists not in seeking new landscapes, but in having new eyes." ~ Marcel Proust

One of the hardest things for me to grasp in Nar-Anon was the idea of having no expectations for the addict in my life. Having always had high expectations of everyone involved in my life (especially myself), it seemed foreign to me to let go of those expectations.

By attending Nar-Anon meetings on a regular basis, I can honestly say that I am now able to lower my expectations. Our <u>Nar-Anon Blue Booklet</u> suggests that I "Take no thought for the future actions of others. Neither expect them to be better or worse as time goes on, for in such expectations you are really trying to create." Expecting the addict not to behave like an addict is denial of reality. I have found I am much happier when I lower or surrender my expectations of the addict, others and myself.

Before Nar-Anon, I could go into a fantasyland of creation, planning for events or happenings before they even came up. In my mind, everything would be so perfect. I would invariably be disappointed. I know it was because of my having such high expectations each time.

Thought for Today: When I lower my expectations, or let go of them altogether, I find myself enjoying and appreciating my life and the addict in my life so much more.

"An expectation is a premeditated resentment." ~ Anonymous

How do I make the transition from caretaker or enabler to helper? The best way to help addicts is to seek help for myself first. One of life's toughest lessons is that I cannot change anyone except myself.

Somehow, my behavior may be contributing to the addict's continued use of drugs. It does not mean I am responsible but I do need to look at my part. By finding ways to bring order and peace back into my own life, I give addicts the opportunity to find a way to recovery.

Allowing addicts to take responsibility for their actions may provide them with the motivation to find their own way in life. It may not be the way I would like them to do it, but there are many roads to the same destination.

It has been said that by doing the right thing to bring sanity into my own life, I end up doing the right things for the addicts in my life. I give them the chance to take charge of their lives. In the end, I get a chance to live in a positive and enriching way.

Thought for Today: I will look at myself and the role I play in the family disease of addiction. I will change the things I find are harmful and self-defeating and leave the rest to a Power greater than me.

"Few things help an individual more than to place responsibility upon him, and to let him know that you trust him." ~ Booker T. Washington

I had picked up and pasted the pieces of my son's life back together for so long that I did not know how to stop. I felt shackled to this addicted adult child. I knew the terrible difficulties and emotional agonies of drug addiction were destroying me and I realized I needed help.

I found Nar-Anon meetings and started attending on a regular basis. Each meeting I attended gave me more clarity. When I became willing to focus and work on what I needed, there were so many tools to use. I had a problem knowing which was best for me. It proved very difficult for me, accepting that drug addiction is a disease, practicing detachment, getting myself a Higher Power and taking an honest inventory of myself.

Changing what I could became easier as I went along because I started seeing results, not so much for my son, but for me. In the bigger picture, communication between the two of us improved. My life became almost normal again even though I could see no improvement in his life. He continued to make bad choices, but now I understood and accepted that those were his choices. I am completely convinced that I can control no one but myself.

Thought for Today: Sometimes I am tempted to fall back into familiar behaviors. When that happens, my newfound detachment and acceptance kick in and I get back on track. Most importantly, I am okay with myself. Because of Nar-Anon, I am aware of what I can change and what I cannot change.

"I will have great happiness with other people today if I accept them and try to change only me." ~ Karen Casey

I wrote this poem in the early days of my frustration and confusion that came from trying to deal with the craziness of our addicted son. I was so angry because of the stress, and I was filled with resentment. I felt a regular teen was difficult enough to raise.

No Harmony

There is no harmony in the way he plays us.
He is young and took no lessons;
it comes naturally.
There is no guile.
He does not know the strength of his song.

He does not know that every child
in search for his own way
sings the same clanging, weeping song
of torturous disharmony that tears
and pulls at one or the other.
His parents should stand strong, together,
with the same chorus of standards that should be known.
It's not his fault they know no song to sing
in rounds or rhyme.

At times of stress, she sings LOUD
and is a clanging, repetitive sour note
who thinks she is a righteous tone
until he cringes, pulls back and groans,
tone deaf,
out of time with her song of sorrow,
one lonely note with infinite possibilities.
ALONE
NO HARMONY

Thought for Today: Thanks to the Nar-Anon program, my harmony is restored. Surrendering my self-righteous attitude, thoughts of blame and the need to be right, frees me of the feelings of anger, sorrow, frustration, and despair.

"Live and Let Live." ~ Nar-Anon Twelve Step Slogan

Over the last week or so, the addict had been saying that she really meant it this time when she stated that she was ready to go into a rehab program. There were signs that she meant it. I told her to make some calls. To my surprise, she did.

In the past, I would be over the moon with joy and I would be up all night with questions in my mind. Is she going to make the calls? Will she go in when they say to come in? Will she complete the program or stay only a day or so? I remember the last two times the addict agreed to go into a rehab program, I was full of hope and joy and anticipation. When she left before finishing, I became upset. I was so disappointed that my anger took control of my being. I was sick for weeks and emotionally distraught because she was not doing what I knew was best for her.

However, this time is different because I have learned the beauty of living my life one day at a time. I have also come to realize that my desires for my daughter are just desires. The message of Nar-Anon teaches me that I do not have control over the addict. I should not expect her to seek help and I should not have any expectations. I can only hope she will seek recovery, but I no longer expect it. I will not be distraught. I will not get emotionally and physically sick. I have learned that I must think of myself first and not let her addiction destroy me.

Thought for Today: With the tools of Nar-Anon, I know that I can resist expectations and have hope. I realize the strength that I now have comes directly from my Higher Power. It is with gratitude that I acknowledge the source of my strength.

"When others, especially our children, deal with life differently than we would, or have stressful situations to face, we can respect them by assuming they have everything they need to handle that situation." ~ Anne Wilson Schaef

Before discovering Nar-Anon, I was fairly certain that I had all the answers when it came to knowing how to stop the addict from using drugs. Of course, I tried everything from anger to threats, from manipulation to acquiescence, all in the hope that the addict would change. Never before in my life did I think I needed assistance from others to reach a goal. Reaching goals either came naturally to me, or through hard work and persistence. Now here I was, helpless in saving the addict in my life.

It was only when all my actions failed that I began to realize that I needed help. That was the beginning of humility for me, to realize that I also needed outside help, either from other people in Nar-Anon or from my Higher Power, or both.

One day at a time, I gave up my self-sufficiency and came to discover humility in every step, in every slogan and even in every tradition in Nar-Anon. I also discovered that the biggest obstacles to my progress were my weaknesses of character, pride, impatience, intolerance, expectation, anger, and the necessity to control others. When I work the Nar-Anon program, I find that I no longer need to have all the answers to all the questions.

Thought for Today: Humility means to surrender to God's will, not to a destructive and shameful way of life.

"Humility gives me back the capacity of seeing with clarity without distorting myself spiritually or emotionally." ~ Today a Better Way

I do not know if I have yet learned how to let go, or if I ever will. Lately, I have been concentrating on myself and not focusing on the addict. This seems to be helping me. Before Nar-Anon, my mind was always going a-mile-a-minute. Today, I no longer feel the emotional turmoil I once felt. The suffering is still there but does not seem to dominate me as it did before.

In letting go, I am learning how to concentrate on myself. For some, this may seem cruel, but they do not understand. They do not know that emotions can destroy us if not kept in check. They do not understand there is nothing I can do for the addict as long as he does not want any help.

I feel that my resolve to let go is a sign that the Nar-Anon principles are finally beginning to work for me. I realize that I am able to let go, and move on with my life, loving my son and hating the drugs that he uses. I have thought for some time now, that I may never get over this situation, but I am learning how to deal with this terrible time in my life. I ask God to help me to let go entirely so that I may continue to heal.

Thought for Today: We can make progress by changing from rejection to releasing with love without doing it perfectly. Gradual effort, one day at a time, will eventually get me entirely ready to have my defects removed.

"Some people think that it's holding on that makes one strong. Sometimes it's letting go." ~ Sylvia Robinson

Sometimes it feels as if my problems will never end. Recently, I felt that my life would not ever get better. My computer wore out. My father was so weak that I had to hospitalize him and then he died. I ran my car into a pole ruining the front bumper. I had a huge financial set back dealing with all of these problems. Then the addict left the rehab program she was in after only a few days, and was immediately arrested.

While all of these life problems were upsetting me, as each one occurred, I kept remembering the simple, short objectives and easy to remember messages of Nar-Anon: "One Day at a Time." "I have no control." I kept repeating the Serenity Prayer to myself. If I cannot find the serenity to accept the things I cannot change, the courage to change the things I can, or the wisdom to know the difference, I will keep remembering to take it one day at a time. If I can make it through this day, I pray that I can face whatever situations may arise.

Thought for Today: I have made a determination that I will not worry about tomorrow. Why worry about the future when I have enough to deal with at this moment? After all, I have found that when I do worry, things rarely, if ever, turn out the way I had imagined.

"If you're climbing the ladder of life, you go rung by rung, one step at a time. Don't look too far up, set your goals high but take one step at a time. Sometimes you don't think you're progressing until you step back and see how high you've really gone." ~ Donny Osmond

One of the reasons I came to Nar-Anon was to find a way to get the addict clean. Whatever it took, I was willing to find the solution and solve the problem. I came to meetings and I listened to the members sharing. I learned that there were tools that I could use in this program. A slogan I took to heart was "Listen and Learn." I also slowly learned that this program was not for the addict but was for me. I was the one who needed recovery, maybe even more than the addict did. I had become so addicted to her that I needed to turn the focus back to myself.

The addict recently told me that she finally learned the meaning of "One Day at a Time" when she went to prison and found that she had no way to change her situation. She is now trying to stay clean without the help of a Twelve Step program. While I have my doubts that this can work, I cannot tell her what is best for her. I realize that one of the best ways I can help her is to continue working my own program. My one-year medallion that I received from my group states: "Rarely have we seen a person fail who has thoroughly followed our plan."

The addict's steps in the direction of recovery relieve some of my tension and the darkness I have experienced, but I still find myself needing the wisdom of the Nar-Anon message. I have learned that the envy I once had for those whose addicts were in recovery had no meaning. The worry, anxiety and fear are still there, just in a different way.

Thought for Today: I am learning not to worry about the future and to take life one day at a time. My program works!

"A master blesses calamity, for the master knows that from the seeds of disaster (and all experience) comes the growth of self." ~ Neale Donald Walsch

One morning I found myself crouched on our front porch steps. All the lights were out inside and outside of the house. I was watching the cottage next door for half the night while my husband was crouching in our car with a gun and a rifle. This was when I finally had to admit to myself that I could not protect my addicted son twenty-four hours a day. A drug dealer was after him. The stress of having to move to another residence, coupled with a breakup with his girlfriend, sent my son veering out of control and acting as if he was having a nervous breakdown. I finally decided to join Nar-Anon and found the help I needed.

At my first meeting, I heard other members share their pain and successes. It was with great relief that I heard for the first time the three Cs: "I didn't cause it, I can't control it, and I can't cure it." I repeated that phrase in my head over and over again in the following weeks. Another precious piece of information I received that evening was that I could only change myself. I embraced that one thought and felt an overwhelming weight lifted from my shoulders.

I now understand that for my son to recover and have a chance to gain wisdom, strength and confidence in his decisions, I need to get out of his way as he experiences the ups and downs of his everyday life. I continue to remind myself that "I didn't cause it; I can't control it; and I can't cure it."

Thought for Today: I will work my program because I now know I can only change myself. I must step aside and allow the addict to deal with the consequences of his using and get out of God's way.

"Do you prefer that you be right, or that you be happy?" ~ *A Course in Miracles*

Since joining Nar-Anon, I have learned many things. I have learned that many wonderful people are like me. Many of us were trained from an early age to take care of others. Therefore, it was not surprising when I started doing the same thing with my son. I had no consistent boundaries. He learned that if he yelled at me loud enough and long enough, I would usually change my mind. I worried about what he did and did not do and eventually took on the responsibility of doing everything for him. Through years of difficulties, and with the fear of what might happen if he was left to fend for himself, I became obsessed with my son and his problems.

While reading the Nar-Anon literature and listening to other members, I learned that I was not allowing my son to experience the consequences of his own actions. As hard as it has been, I am detaching with love and letting him choose his own path. I have found that as I have changed for the better, so has my son. Thank you, Nar-Anon!

Thought for Today: Today I will not take on jobs that others can do for themselves. I will spend my time working on tasks that are important to me.

"So many gifts await us when we accept the program and its principles. We dispense with the baggage of the past. We learn to live this day only. And we come to believe that there is a power greater than ourselves that has us and everything in our lives under control." ~ Karen Casey

PATIENCE

I came to Nar-Anon expecting a quick fix for my problems. I soon found that it does not happen that way. I did not get instant recovery, but I learned to be grateful for the lessons the program has given me.

One thing I am learning from this program is patience, which is defined as "the ability to endure waiting or delay without becoming annoyed or upset and to persevere calmly when faced with difficulties."

It takes time – time to learn, time to grow, time to accept the changes. Nar-Anon allows me the time I need to do things at my own pace. No one tells me I should move faster. No one scolds me for not learning my lessons a little sooner. I know that I will make mistakes, but I also know that I will continue to learn and grow with the help of my program, my group and my Higher Power.

Thought for Today: I know that I have peace and serenity that comes with working this program, which I never want to give up. I know that there will be rough times and I will falter, but it is okay. I want to accept my part, learn my lessons and move on.

"There are different types of patience: the patience of being indifferent to the harm inflicted by others, the patience of voluntarily accepting hardship, and the patience developed through reasoned conviction in the Dharma." ~ Dalai Lama

RELEASE THE ANXIETY

When I came to Nar-Anon, I had to be anxious about everything. I had to project what the next crisis would be, find out who would be involved, contemplate all the solutions available to me, and then pick which one would be right. This, in itself, was a lot of work. Then I had to figure out which solution I would use and start implementing it right away. I decided that if I did not practice worrying about it before it happened, then how would I be able to handle it when it came along? This was my twisted thinking which I thought was rational at the time.

The understanding that this was not a good way to live came through attending Nar-Anon meetings. I realized that being anxious made me avoid thinking about my feelings. It robbed me of the present moment. I was living in the future, in a world that might never happen. I was trying to deal with burdens that perhaps would never come my way.

The burdens lifted, as I was able to deal with my anxiety. I had to get honest and be willing and open to my Higher Power's guidance. I started to "Let go and let God." In doing so, I was able to help me. I could now sort out what I was feeling and why. I was able to start making choices that were good for me.

Thought for Today: By releasing the anxiety in my life, I am better able to make the right choices at the right time for myself. By not worrying about a future that I have no control over, I can take the weight off my shoulders today.

"It has been said that our anxiety does not empty tomorrow of its sorrow, but only empties today of its strength." ~ Charles H. Spurgeon

When I heard that my area was sponsoring a Fourth Step weekend, I knew that God had decided that it was time for me to attend. Never in my wildest dreams did I realize what I would uncover about myself when I got there. Working Step Four gave me an understanding of who I really was and what I needed to do to continue my path of recovery in Nar-Anon. I determined that in order for me to get the full benefit of working Step Four, I would need to move on to Step Five, "Admitted to God, to myself and to another human being the exact nature of my wrongs." What a wonderful healing experience it is to share with a sponsor or fellow member of Nar-Anon what I have learned about myself!

Admitted to God: Because of this step, I am more open to the presence of God in my life and the guidance I receive from him. Today, I can not only admit my wrongs to God, but I can thank him for giving me the lessons I needed to learn. I am where God wants me to be. I could not apply this program without my Higher Power's presence. As I admitted my wrongs to God, I felt the healing taking place.

Admitted to myself: The key to Step Five for me was admitting who I am to myself. I had to be totally honest. I could try to fool others, but I could not fool myself, and I certainly could not fool God. I have found a better understanding of myself when I am open-minded enough to accept my shortcomings and realize that I need help.

Admitted to another human being: When I share my thoughts with another Nar-Anon member, and experience no condemnation for my actions or feelings, I feel very grateful and humbled. I felt only love, concern, and acceptance after taking this step.

Thought for Today: In the years since, I have taken my inventory many times and have found hidden qualities, characteristics and weaknesses that God has helped me channel into strengths and new abilities that I did not know I had. I am glad I have the Twelve Steps to continue learning about myself and improving my life in the process.

"The vision must be followed by the venture. It is not enough to stare up the steps - we must step up the stairs." ~ Vance Havner

One of the practices of my home group is to study one of the Twelve Steps on the first meeting of each month. Each person discusses what the step means to him or her and how it has helped in his or her recovery. Visiting a different step every month helps me to obtain a deeper understanding of the Nar-Anon program. I am learning by re-visiting the program's principles and seeing how I can apply these principles in my life. This journey of discovery and growth often reminds me of peeling an onion. Layer by layer, and sometimes with tears, I peel away. I do this in order to remove the damaged layers so I can move forward in my recovery. I focus on each step month by month and write my reflections in a journal. I can then compare my progress with earlier years.

I came to believe the steps are my path to serenity and peace. I take these steps beside my program friends and we are led to a new understanding and insights, personally and collectively. I feel blessed and grateful to have a structure for measuring my progress. As I grow in my recovery, the understanding of the steps helps me to grow, change and mature.

Thought for Today: Studying the steps is important to me, as they are the foundation of my recovery. I can apply them to all of the problems I encounter. They also remind me that I do not have to face life alone; I have my Higher Power and my Nar-Anon family.

"The steps offer me a road map for living that leads to a spiritual awakening and beyond." ~ Courage to Change

When I came to Nar-Anon, I felt life was unfair. Why did my husband have to be an addict? Don't I deserve a normal, healthy family? This was my second marriage and I was determined to make it work. I thought if I were kind and giving, he would want to get better and act the same towards me. I gave with expectations. My giving and what I thought was love had strings attached. However, as my husband's addiction progressed, I could no longer maintain the illusion of a loving, normal family or relationship. I worked so hard at hiding his addiction, and trying to cure him, but both our behaviors became more and more bizarre and unhealthy. It was apparent that there was a problem, and it was not just him. When we finally broke up, I felt my world had fallen apart. I felt alone, a failure, discouraged, and wanted to isolate.

I had started attending Nar-Anon meetings before our divorce was final, and I continued afterwards. It became the only time I went out, except for work. After a year of program, I was asked to be a group service representative and I accepted, thinking it would be another night out, which I knew I needed. At my first area meeting when one of the officers announced she could no longer serve, I volunteered. This time the results were different. What I discovered is through Nar-Anon service work, I can carry the message of recovery as I experience it. I learn I can help others in a healthy and supportive way when I give freely.

Thought for Today: For me, giving back to the Nar-Anon fellowship is an expression of unconditional love and part of the healing process. When I give freely, without expectations, I help create a healing environment for others and myself.

"Kindness in words creates confidence.
Kindness in thinking creates profoundness.
Kindness in giving creates love." ~ Lao-Tzu

After my mother abandoned me, my grandmother told me that regardless of her actions, I should always love my mother. Without her, I would not be alive. In my opinion, my mother was a promiscuous rebel. She did not raise me; my grandmother did. I was a good child by my grandmother's standards because I usually did what I was told. As an adult, I still did not want to do anything wrong, because I learned pleasing people made me feel good and lovable. I wanted to be loved, but I did not want to be like my mother.

I married early and had three children. With the fourth child on the way, my husband took a walk and never came back. I felt abandoned again. I worked long hard hours, always with a smile on my face, while my gut ached. I stayed busy, supported my family, but had no help. I never looked for any. I was too busy trying to survive and prove that I was a strong person, doing the right thing, still proving that I was nothing like my mother.

After my children were raised, they began to use drugs. I felt abandoned one more time. I have also reared three grandchildren and tried to make a difference in their lives. I cared for them out of love and gave them everything. Once again, I took a back seat in my own life.

I finally sought help by joining Nar-Anon. Through the Nar-Anon program and my Higher Power, my life was saved. I realized that I had taken a back seat in my life and had abandoned myself. Today I am so grateful and I no longer look for closure from my experiences of abandonment. I am a new person now because of the loving support from my Nar-Anon family. I have received so many good things from the Nar-Anon program and have learned a better way to live. I can now contribute to others along the way and yet not abandon myself!

Thought for Today: I have found that I can forgive and not fear repeating what I consider the mistakes of my mother. I can do what is right for me without giving up my love for others.

"Love is a part of everyone who lives and breathes.
Love is a force that binds all people together like drops of water in a mighty ocean.
How can you not be of love?
If you do not see love within, you have not looked." ~ Ron Rathbun

I have come to the realization, after much thought, that I have been a "know it all," especially where my daughter was concerned. After all, she was an addict. I used to think that my daughter could not do anything right and did not know anything. I felt I had to do everything, because, after all, she was an addict. Whenever something broke, it was her fault, because, after all, she was an addict. When things were missing, it was her fault, because, after all, she was an addict. I did not listen to her when she spoke, because what could she know or say of importance, because, after all, she was an addict.

I have been attending Nar-Anon meetings for about four years, and I finally realized how unfair I had been to her. I am slowly learning through listening, listening and listening, that I do not know it all just because I am not an addict. I recognized that many things are my fault even though I am not an addict. Through Nar-Anon, I have learned that my daughter, though an addict, is not a non-person; that she has thoughts and feelings that are real, and that she deserves respect and recognition, whether she is using or not.

Thank you Nar-Anon for creating an environment where I can listen and grow, and realize and admit my shortcomings, without being judged. I can also see others as they are and give them the same respect.

Thought for Today: I will focus on myself and on those things that I can change. I will not judge others. I will ask my Higher Power for guidance and accept the choices that others make. I will practice acceptance and respect. I will not judge.

"When we judge them, we judge on what we believe we know of them, failing to realize that there is much we do not know, and that they are constantly changing as they try for better or worse to cope with life." ~ Nar-Anon Blue Booklet

For some reason, my Higher Power has decided to put a variety of addicts in my life. Not only my immediate family suffers from addiction, but also other relatives, friends and acquaintances. I felt my job was to make them all well. Each time a new addict came along, I took it as my personal responsibility to fix them. In my thinking, they needed to know about the Twelve Steps, they needed to know about our program and the Narcotics Anonymous program and meetings. I had them ready for recovery, commitment and service. All they had to do was follow my plan. The problem was that my plan did not work when I tried to apply it to others.

When I start taking control, my Higher Power seems to let me know, gently at first, that I should not be getting involved in someone else's program. I should not be getting too comfortable, thinking that I have conquered the "letting go" part. I need to remember that I do not have all the answers. That is the job of a Power greater than I am, and if I decide not to listen, I am nudged a little harder and reminded that there are many more lessons where those came from!

Thought for Today: My Higher Power is there to teach me and remind me that I have to "Let Go and Let God." I am powerless over everyone but myself.

"I am still learning about the major themes of my recovery – patience, judgment, isolation and detachment." ~ Paths to Recovery

I spent many years denying the fact that my son had a serious disease. He was the victim. I thought that an easy solution was that he just needed to stay away from the other people who were using. I fought this disease with my whole body, soul, emotional and spiritual being. I cried and I became angry. I was frustrated, disappointed and a total emotional wreck. My whole life revolved around my son. I followed him around and I gave him money time and time again for everything but drugs. I answered his calls for help, picked him up in the middle of the night, and gave him rides to get drugs. He would get out of jail and I would pick him up because I knew how to enable. Then the cycle would start all over again. No job, things disappearing from the house, me asking him which one of his friends he was letting in while we were at work and who was taking our belongings. He was a money pit. I was under the impression that things were going to get better, because jail made an addict stop using so he would not have to go back. This, however, was my philosophy, not the addict's.

My growth in Nar-Anon has been a slow process. I listened to the Steps and I heard that I am powerless, but I did not hear that my life was unmanageable. I could still be in control. Step Two suggested a belief in a Power greater than myself, but I still felt my help was needed. Step Three said that I could turn my will over to my Higher Power. I thought if He could make the addict get clean, then I would have serenity.

I am grateful today for the Nar-Anon members who listened to me, who shared with me and taught me who was really in control and who needed to change for me to have peace and serenity. Now, I know that there is life after addiction. I know that in order to learn a lesson, I have to go through my situations, not around them. Today I think before I react. My son is still an addict. He is spending most of his time in prison, but in spite of this, I now have my life back.

Thought for Today: I want to love the addict and support him, but let him discover his own path. Today, I trust my Higher Power to lead me on my own path of peace of mind and serenity.

"If you find a path with no obstacles, it probably doesn't lead anywhere."
~ Frank A. Clark

I came to Nar-Anon because someone I loved was out of control. My life had become out of control as well, but I had not been able to admit it. I was desperate for my life to be normal again. As I attended Nar-Anon meetings, I realized that I could not go back, I could only go forward. My initial goal was to get the addict clean so the rest of the family could be happy. I shared my story at meetings because if I said it enough times, I would find a way to fix them. I was hoping to find some magic key that would make the disease go away. I kept enabling and I was obsessed with the idea that I could straighten out the chaos. The insanity of this disease is that continually reasoning cancels out all the unreasonable and unbelievable things that happen. This could not be happening because it was not logical. I adapted to whatever my family threw at me. I was the crazy one because nothing seemed to bother any of them. I felt as though the disease of addiction tore my heart out and made me believe that I could live without it.

I realize that I can share things with my Nar-Anon group that I cannot share or admit to myself. I am finding that the only way to change my way of thinking is to say my thoughts out loud. I need to learn to separate the addict from the addiction. I need to get honest with myself and admit that I need help. I am finding that my Higher Power does not make me work on every part of my program all at once. I am given what I need to learn slowly, one day at a time. I am finding that addiction changes things. Yes, my life will never be the same, but now, because of the Nar-Anon program, it is going in a healthy direction. I am learning to enjoy life and be grateful just for today.

Thought for Today: By focusing on me, I am better able to focus on others. By being able to experience my feelings, by welcoming them instead of fearing them, I have been able to learn and grow. I can now be a friend or a listening ear to a newcomer who is in pain and hurting. I can share with them my experience, strength and hope and I can help them find the gift of serenity that was so freely given to me.

"Treat people as if they were what they ought to be and you help them to become what they are capable of being." ~ Johann Wolfgang von Goethe

My son is an addict and I loved him by rescuing him. Each time I rescued him, I believed that this was the rescue that would work, and he would see the error of his ways and stop using. Instead, I kept rescuing and my son kept using. After years of this cycle, I found Nar-Anon. Taking the focus off the addict and putting the focus on me made no sense to me when I first started to attend Nar-Anon meetings. How would not helping the addict help the addict?

Members of my Nar-Anon meeting shared their experiences, wisdom, strengths, and hope. I learned from them the difference between enabling and helping. I learned how protecting someone from the consequences of their actions was not only disrespectful, but by doing so, I was standing in the way of their recovery. This was not my job and my behavior was harmful. I needed to get out of the way and let things happen, despite my fears. I had to learn to trust something greater than myself. I had to learn to trust that by letting go of my son, serenity was available to me.

The slogan "Let Go and Let God" comforts me in my recovery, and reminds me that my son has a Higher Power, and it is not me.

Thought for Today: I will remember that I am not in control. I will trust in a Power greater than myself. I will release my addicted loved one and all the other problems that I cannot solve to my Higher Power. Today I know that is the best thing I can do.

"Stop trying so hard to control things. It is not our job to control people, outcomes, circumstances, life. Maybe in the past we couldn't trust and let things happen. But we can now. The way life is unfolding is good. Let it unfold." ~ Melody Beattie

Before I was in recovery, I had days when I was miserable because things did not go as I planned or wanted. In the Nar-Anon program, I learned that I have tools that help me cope with life's disappointments. I still have days where I am unhappy and disappointed in events and situations that do not unfold as I desired, but I have learned that life is neither all good nor all bad. Even when I think times are bad, I can choose to take care of myself with the help of my Higher Power by focusing on the positive and being grateful.

I was recently confronted with the loss of a loved one. I was angry, hurt and full of resentment. I felt because I was working what I believed to be a good program and asking my Higher Power for direction, that only good things would happen and I would be happy. When I shared my feelings at my Nar-Anon meeting, my group suggested that I might not be using the steps and practicing the program's principles, which could help me through this loss. One member suggested that I try using gratitude. By actively practicing gratitude, I could change my attitude towards the event. It is my choice. Do I want to be a victim of circumstances by focusing and obsessing about things that do not go my way, or do I want to focus on the good things happening in my life and be thankful for the things I have?

Thought for Today: When I look at the word gratitude, I see attitude. When things are difficult, I can acknowledge the good and be grateful. I can change my focus and thinking to promote a good attitude, which is a step in the right direction.

"Practicing gratitude will help us more fully appreciate what has been offered us. Being grateful influences our attitude; it softens our harsh exterior and takes the threat out of most situations." ~ Each Day a New Beginning - Daily Meditations for Women

Many newcomers are taken aback when they learn that we are working the same Twelve Steps as our addicted loved ones. Tradition Five explains why this is necessary and how it helps. The Fifth Tradition demonstrates the loving nature of our program. I learned by working the steps that the answer to recovery is not only to love and accept the addict but, more importantly, to love and accept myself.

One of most important lessons I learned is to stop the fighting and let go of the resentments. This is essential for my recovery. When I accept and practice the First Step, I accept that I am powerless over the disease of addiction. So what benefit would I get by going to meeting after meeting, reliving my war stories about the addict and complaining and blaming the addict for all of my problems? This behavior hurts me and does nothing for the addict. Further, it adds little or nothing to my fellow members' recovery.

The second part of this Tradition is our fellowship's role in sharing our message of hope and healing to others who are suffering. We can do this by supporting a newcomer or fellow member in crisis, providing information about our program to local drug abuse treatment centers, schools and prisons, and letting others know there is a better way to live.

Thought for Today: I am grateful for my Nar-Anon program, which teaches me that changed attitudes and encouragement to others will help me far more than focusing on my problems. In helping others and supporting my Nar-Anon group, I can reap the rewards of recovery.

"Each Nar-Anon Family Group has but one purpose; to help families of addicts. We do this by practicing the Twelve Steps of Nar-Anon, by encouraging and understanding our addicted relatives, and by welcoming and giving comfort to families of addicts." ~ Nar-Anon Tradition Five

When I came to Nar-Anon I was alone, frustrated and confused. The members of my group welcomed me. I was happy to find that they cared about me and they understood me. After I had attended several meetings, I heard about sponsorship. In my area, the Nar-Anon Family Groups have sponsorship meetings. I decided to go to one, as I thought it would help my recovery to share with a fellow member in between my regular meetings. It helped me in ways I had never imagined.

In a sponsorship meeting, members are encouraged to choose a sponsor from among long-time members with whom they can share their thoughts and feelings. When I chose my sponsor, I looked for someone with whom I felt I shared a common bond.

My sponsor not only gives me suggestions and support, but a new way to look at an old problem. It is so helpful and comforting to have someone I can call when I am in a crisis, to have someone that already knows me with all my character defects. My sponsor is a good listener and that gives me an opportunity to talk about my resentments and anxieties. He also shares how he dealt with similar problems. I feel comfortable sharing my personal story in detail with my sponsor. What I did not know was that sponsors receive the same benefits from our relationship and private sharing. Sponsorship is a process that works both ways.

Thought for Today: Thanks to Nar-Anon, I have a special person who listens to my old problems and suggests new ways to respond to them. My sponsor shares his experiences with me. Sponsorship is a gift for both the sponsee and the sponsor.

"It's good, the doing of the deed, that, once it's done, you don't regret, whose result you reap gratified, happy at heart." ~ Dhammapada, 5, translated by Thanissaro Bhikkhu.

During my Fourth Step, I cleared the way for self-understanding by examining my strengths and weaknesses and listing them. Then I looked at Step Five and once again was intimidated. However, as I gathered the courage to bare my soul, I realized that I had already completed two thirds of the Fifth Step. Step Five asks that we "admit to God, ourselves and another human being the exact nature of our wrongs."

When I took Step Two, I came to believe that "a Power greater than myself could restore me to sanity." If my Higher Power could do that, I realized I did not need to admit again, for the sake of my Higher Power, the exact nature of my wrongs. My Higher Power already knows of my wrongs.

Through the process of writing a searching and fearless moral inventory, I was admitting to myself the exact nature of my wrongs. Yes, I had virtues, but I also saw traits that I did not like. The only other thing left to do was to admit my shortcomings to another human being. Like many members of the Nar-Anon family, I chose to share my character defects with my sponsor. My sponsor has many years in the program and was there when I first came to Nar-Anon. At the beginning, many of my wrongs were the very behaviors I thought were the right things to do.

Thought for Today: When I admit my wrongs, I am making room for change. I am clearing the debris of the past and opening the door for a better future and a better me.

"Each time we face our fear, we gain strength, courage and confidence in the doing." ~ Paul Tillich

Falling in love with an addict was a blinding experience. Our life together never lacked drama, though it did eventually lack all else. We went through car accidents and a fire that destroyed everything I owned and everything he had brought to this country. He was arrested and jailed. Still, I felt fiercely loyal.

He had asked me to marry him within three weeks of our meeting. I attributed his hurry to his having "found the right one," and not wanting to lose a minute together. He pressed me incessantly to have a child. I did not understand at the time that this was his way of keeping me tied to him. This impetuous decision-making was a departure from my normally cautious nature and a sign that my own disease was active. As I allowed myself to become more dependent on him, I was getting sicker and sicker. I was not able to see that I was becoming obsessed with my husband. He became less and less dependable and I became more and more focused on how to help him so he could be more dependable for me. I was still in denial about my motives, so I told myself things such as, "If I were the one who had a terrible disease, I would want him to be there for me. How can I offer him less than that?"

I came to Nar-Anon when I was nine months pregnant, desperately in need of support, and finally convinced that I could not survive my life's insanity without help. The minute people started sharing, I felt as though I had come home. My crazy experiences were theirs. Nothing I said seemed to shock them as it had my friends, and they had a peace and acceptance in them that I wanted.

Thought for Today: I will listen to my own dreams and not throw myself into the dreams of others. I will grow stronger as I follow my Higher Power's will, as He does not give me burdens I am not strong enough to bear.

"A lie has speed, but truth has endurance." ~ Edgar J. Mohn

When faced with the absurd behavior and the resulting negative consequences of addiction, I still thought I could respond, in a mature way, with reason and dignity. You've gotta' be kidding!

At first, I found that I would rather retaliate for the hurt and pain by getting even. I took great pleasure in telling my war stories to anyone who would listen, even strangers.

I could never purge my hurts with enough self-pity. Other people stopped being interested. Even the police were not interested. They are interested in crime and in evidence, not in the blues. All I had was my own self-destructive behavior and it bored other people.

As I grew in Nar-Anon, I discovered the maturity I wanted through the shared experiences of others who are also affected by addiction. I am maturing through the practice of the Twelve Steps and Twelve Traditions. I am maturing by understanding such concepts as co-dependence, detachment, enabling, and denial, in myself and in the addict. I am maturing by learning about the nature of the illness of addiction, its progress and pitfalls, and most recently, recovery. I also mature by learning the nature of my own illness. I am growing more mature. I am recovering.

Thought for Today: There is a peace in knowing what I can and cannot do to influence outcomes. I can still be hurt and disappointed, but I do not have to react in the same old immature ways.

"Maturity doesn't come with age - it begins with the acceptance of responsibility." ~ Edwin Louis Cole

One of the first things that drew my attention when I came into the rooms of Nar-Anon was that the members who seemed to have the most serenity shared a lot about letting go. Even though there might be chaos all around them, they still talked about letting go and trusting in a Higher Power to maintain sanity and peace of mind.

I am learning that I have to let go of things as well as people. For instance, I have no control over the public transit train that I take to work. I have no control over whether the train gets me to work on time, just as I know I have no control over the addict in my life. A Nar-Anon member once said, "We have to let go of the elephants while the ants march up our legs."

Is it possible that there is a better plan for my life if I am willing to surrender?

Thought for Today: I have noticed that when I do allow myself to Let Go and Let God, there is peace and serenity. The outcome, in most cases, turns out much better when I let my Higher Power have control.

"We have found that the working of these steps will bring the solution to practically any problem." ~ Nar-Anon Blue Booklet

When I first came to the rooms of Nar-Anon, I could not understand or even grasp the idea of "surrender to win." I believed to surrender would mean I had failed, so I never gave up on anyone or anything. No matter how exhausted I was, I persisted. Living with an addicted husband taught me that if anything ever needed to be fixed or repaired, I had to do it.

One day when I arrived home from a long day at work, I found that my toilet had overflowed all the way into my bedroom. I immediately went to work. After three hours, the toilet was fixed and the rooms were cleaned. Filthy and exhausted, I washed up. After dinner, I went to start the dishwasher but it would not work. I brought out the schematic and started to tear it apart to fix it. Every time I turned the dishwasher on, a fuse blew. Four fuses later, I had a moment of clarity – surrender, let go and let God.

That day, a new ritual began in my household. I now look forward to that special time when my son and I do the dishes together. Today, I am grateful for the broken dishwasher and more grateful for the understanding that surrender is the path to serenity.

Thought for Today: I can choose how I react to the happenings of this day. I can look at them as problems or opportunities.

"The gift of opportunity does not always come with a beautiful wrapping."
~ Anonymous

When I first came to a Nar-Anon meeting, I had plenty of doubts about the program. I did not believe the program or its members could help me. How could they improve my situation, mindset, and overall feeling of despair? I was sure that the Nar-Anon meeting was just another group of people who could not understand my struggle. I figured that I would show up, prove to myself that my reasoning was right, and justify my point of view. As I listened to each person share, the opposite began to happen.

One by one, I heard them describe many of the same incidents, frustrations, confusions, and resentments that I was experiencing. I was so amazed to discover that I was not alone in this struggle. It had always seemed so very private, as if it belonged only to me. I experienced an awakening! I heard that others were suffering as I had been and that there was a process that could bring some sanity, peace and serenity into my life.

Thought for Today: The more I try to deal with another's problems, the more I realize how ineffective I am. The more I entangle myself, the more my anxieties prevail and my entire mood shifts into depression. When I practice my program, life is much less complicated. Today I will keep it simple and be happy in the knowledge that I am not alone.

"Keep an open mind and attend as many meetings as possible. Feel free to share and ask questions after the meeting. You will soon make new friends and will feel very much a part of the group." ~ Nar-Anon Blue Booklet

Self-pity is defined as "the self-indulgent belief that your life is harder and sadder than everyone else's." I spent many of my early Nar-Anon meetings overcome with self-pity. I was married to an addict. In my mind, my life was more difficult than anyone else's was and I was miserable. The addict was wasting our money on drugs and had even been arrested. I was living with huge problems and I had no answers. I had a right to feel hurt, sad and angry.

At a meeting, I heard a member share that she was grateful to be married to an addict. From an earlier sharing, I knew her life was not easy and her situation was not much different from my own. So I thought I must have misunderstood her.

She explained that if she were not married to an addict, she would never have considered coming to Nar-Anon. Without the Twelve Steps, she would still think the way she always had. No one would have suggested that she did not need to solve every problem. She would not have learned to turn to her Higher Power to handle those things she could not. She would not have learned about gratitude. Gratitude helped her change her perspective. With gratitude, she could look for the good things in her life and take the focus off the bad things. She understood she could love herself and be happy even if she did not have the perfect life.

I had not misunderstood. I was engaged in self-pity and it was self-indulgent. It was time to change my attitude to gratitude.

Thought for Today: If I see myself clearly and honestly in relation to my present circumstances, I will see that I can still choose to be happy and grateful and I do not have to become the victim of self-pity.

"Self-pity is our worst enemy and if we yield to it, we can never do anything good in the world." ~ Helen Keller

I am finding that Nar-Anon can help me in all areas of my life, not just with addiction. My work is stressful and my many appointments require a tight schedule. This past week I had twenty meetings scheduled. Even after my reminder calls, some did not show up and a few called to reschedule. Things were not going as planned. I had expected my week to go smoothly. Before going to Nar-Anon meetings, working the steps and using the other tools of the program, I would have obsessed about how inconsiderate these people were. How dare they make a commitment and not follow through.

I am learning that I cannot expect others to have the same priorities as me. I can take care of myself by planning what to do and to let go when I am disappointed. I can let go of my expectations. I can acknowledge my disappointment, but I can also decide how I want to feel. Instead of feeling resentful, I can be at peace with things the way they are. I can look at the positive and appreciate the people who did show up and understand why some needed to reschedule.

Thought for Today: I will take care of me – my schedule, my feelings and my needs. I do not have to be tossed aside and I can be free of resentment and anger and enjoy my life's moments.

"While transformation results in changes in thoughts, feelings and behaviors, the actual process of transformation does not involve changing these things directly but instead requires a change in perspective—altering one's core assumptions about the nature of things." ~ Marilyn Schlitz-Mandala, PhD

In Nar-Anon, we learn that each person is capable of solving his or her own problems. When we lose control of our lives, it is often because we are too busy trying to fix other people's lives and problems. For me, other people's problems felt much easier to fix than my own; it also made me feel useful.

I once took two days off from work to call the insurance company, and research and call rehabilitation centers to get my loved one into treatment. However, when I presented him with the list of rehabs and the possible times for admission, my loved one was ungrateful. He did not appreciate the time and effort I had spent to help him. Further, when I went back to work, I had missed an important deadline and my supervisor gave me a disciplinary warning.

Nar-Anon step work teaches me that I do not have the right or the responsibility to run someone else's life. If I continue to try to control the addict in my life, I not only lose control of my own life, but I also rob the addict of the opportunity to solve his or her own problems, in their own way and time.

Thought for Today: If I mind my own business and work on improving my self-control, I will be an example for others around me, possibly even someone I care about. Today, I am neither a controller nor a controlee.

"Relinquishing control is the ultimate challenge of the Spiritual Warrior."
~ The Book of Runes

If I indulge in negative thinking, I work myself into anxieties about things that may never materialize. This behavior results in wasted worries and possible ill effects on me. I know my peace and serenity certainly suffer. Why is it then that I still contemplate fearful thoughts? Can I not let go? Can I not begin to trust? So what if the addict relapses? Have I not relapsed in some of my own shortcomings?

When I find myself indulging in negative thinking, I use the tools of my Nar-Anon program. I call my sponsor or another member and talk about my worries to release my fear. I read my Nar-Anon literature. I remind myself that I cannot see the future and that worry never stopped or prevented something from happening. I then turn my worries over to my Higher Power and tell myself, it would be better if I stay in the here and now. I must let go of the future and the rest of the world.

Thought for Today: I must live one day at a time, as tomorrow is not promised to me. Therefore worrying about tomorrow and what-ifs will not bring peace and serenity to my life. Creating attitudes that show my sincerity towards others and trust in my Higher Power will bring me what I want, a balanced existence away from the fearful ups and downs of obsessive worry and fear.

"Do not anticipate trouble, or worry about what may never happen. Keep in the sunlight." ~ Benjamin Franklin

I did not realize that I was co-dependent. I took my boys to a concert, and I brought along a book on co-dependency. I bought a drink to relax and sat down in the corner to read. As I read, I began to realize that I had many co-dependent traits. I had been attending Nar-Anon meetings and I wondered why I was not getting better after the addict was out of my life. I thought I was working the steps, but I still had so much craziness, anxiety and insanity in my life. I reminded myself of a dog chasing its tail, going in mad crazy circles, chasing something I was never going to catch. All my focus was on that tail! When I did stop chasing it, I was too exhausted to do anything else. Mental and physical energy were things of the past. I did not know "what my tail was." I felt as though someone was sitting on my chest all the time. I was so wound up. I found relief in drinking until I fell asleep, or taking a drug to put me to sleep.

The drinking and pills were becoming a habit. I was craving them daily. At first, I only drank at weddings. If there were no weddings, then I did not drink, period. Sometimes it would be years between drinks, but now I was doing it almost every night.

Suddenly, it hit me like a ton of bricks: I needed someone or something to take care of. I had no clue how to live without being needed. I needed to be needed! I needed to take care of someone, not just me. I did not care about myself. I had no money and went without my insulin, and my health suffered. Now I see that this is classic co-dependent thinking. When I realized my insanity was caused by my need to care for others, it was as if the fog had lifted. The weight of the world was off my shoulders... It felt great! I feel great!

Thought for Today: Today I am thankful for my Higher Power. I am thankful for Nar-Anon and its Twelve Steps. With the help of my Nar-Anon program, I have learned that the only person I need to take care of is *me*.

"There is only one success—to be able to spend your life in your own way." ~ Christopher Morley

I started attending Nar-Anon meetings because everything that I had attempted to do in an effort to change my daughter had failed. My life was spinning out of control. During the past year, through Nar-Anon, I realized that I could not change the addict; the only person I could change was me! I had started to drop out of life, but now I know that is not the way to deal with her addiction. This year I am determined to get on with living my life.

Losing my daughter to drugs is similar to losing a loved one in a tragic accident. She is gone and I miss her, but I need to get a grip on myself and move on with my life. Listening to others share how they cope with having a loved one who is an addict, helps me to realize that I do have much to be thankful for in my life.

In the back of my mind, I do have hope that some day my daughter will see the light and get better. I also have hope that some day she will recover and come back into my life. I have learned from Nar-Anon that life is full of twists and turns. I have also learned that I need to have hope and not expectations, because having expectations is the source of the fear and anxiety that in the past had taken over my life. On the other hand, I also hope that I will have the courage to deal with the absence of my daughter, and not let those fears and doubts move back into my life. I have no idea what the future will bring. I will live just for today.

Thought for Today: I hope that just for today I will not let this situation destroy me. I will try to do something that will bring me some type of joy, however small, and I will ask God to make me a better person.

"Hope is great. And hope supported by faith creates an unbeatable duo."
~ *Meditations for People Who (May) Worry Too Much*

One of the greatest things about the Nar-Anon program is how it can change our lives. I think of the members in my group who share how they have grown and become happier. Some are taking on new challenges in their lives; some are doing service in the group. One member said he tries to think about what he would be doing if he did not have an addict in his life. That helps him to focus. I see growth – I see recovery. I have learned to have better relationships in my life by becoming more involved in Nar-Anon. I can contribute in so many ways by doing service work at the group level and above. I have confidence in myself from the love and support I have received in Nar-Anon. I can see the progress I have made, and I am finally getting my life back. I have learned to set boundaries, take care of myself and make changes with the help of my Higher Power. Today I am able to make decisions in my life that I had never dreamed would be possible.

When I came into the program, I felt I had a life-changing power available to me if I was willing to take it. Working the Nar-Anon program has brought recovery into my life. In order to keep my sanity, I must be serious about my recovery. I have the ability to think about my decisions and the outcome or consequences of my actions and reactions. Suddenly I see a new person emerge and changes are taking place in my life.

Thought for Today: "Keep coming back, it works if you work it, and it won't if you don't, so work it because you are worth it." This is the saying I repeat to myself to continue making the changes necessary in my life, and to share with the newcomers in the group so they can gain the hope and courage to return to our meetings.

"Be not afraid of going slowly; be afraid only of standing still." ~ Chinese Proverb

It would be so nice if I could take these Twelve Steps one at a time – in perfect order – and then never have to take them over again. If they were so ingrained in my spiritual, physical and emotional being that they were a total part of me, there would be no more worrying, no more anxiety, fear, or resentments.

The first three steps are the awareness and acceptance steps: I have admitted that I am powerless; I came to believe that there is a Power greater than myself; and I know that I need to turn my will and my life over to this Higher Power. I believe that my Higher Power can help me if I help myself. Next are the action steps four through nine: I have taken my inventory, admitted my shortcomings and I am entirely ready to have God remove them. My amends have been made. Finally, we come to the last three steps, the maintenance steps. Without these I would stop learning and growing. Without these last three steps, I could not pass the message of recovery on to others. That in itself is one of the most important aspects of the Nar-Anon program.

Recovery is a never-ending process. I will always have addicts in my life, whether they are clean or not. I have come to realize that this program offers me a way of life that I never imagined was possible.

Thought for Today: My happiness today does not depend on the happiness of others. I am grateful for the addicts in my life, which led me to this path of discovering myself.

"May the storms of life be gentle showers and the light of God's love shine brightly upon your pathway." ~ As We Understood

RESPONSIBILITY

Because of the drug use, the stealing and lying, and the chaos that goes along with active addiction, I asked the addict to leave our home. The chaos persisted, and in time, I changed the locks on the house and banned her from the premises. The sadness that followed my decision was intense. I was fraught with anxiety, and shed many tears. Many times, I contemplated allowing her to return home, even though she was still using. I was not prepared for the intense pain and anxiety that resulted from my decision. I felt worse than when the addict was at home.

Thankfully, a friend suggested that I attend a Nar-Anon meeting. In time, I began to realize that the addict had never been held accountable for her actions because I had always bailed her out of difficult situations. I realized that unless the addict was forced to accept responsibility for her actions, my home life would not improve. I longed for a normal life and I was desperate for relief from the agony and pain of living with her addiction. I had reached my bottom and knew that I was miserable and needed help.

Nar-Anon helped me to realize that I needed to take care of myself. I learned that I have choices and I can set boundaries that are good for me. I took responsibility for myself by not allowing her to come back home while she was still using drugs. I took responsibility for myself by seeking help in Nar-Anon.

Thought for Today: It can be very empowering to take responsibility for my own choices. I will act in my own best interest today.

"When we go through storms we ask where is God. I'll tell you where He is. He's backstage designing a rainbow." ~ Dr. Robert Schuler

As I practice the Twelve Steps of Nar-Anon, I learn to make healthier choices. I can now identify times in my life when I have made less than healthy choices. There is a slight sense of regret or loss that accompanies the overwhelming feelings of forgiveness and release. I could have handled relationships better. I regret the loss of a healthy relationship with myself. I have suffered the most devastating feelings of hurt from my own berating and scathing criticism. Instead of believing, I have stretched to try something new. My first instinct is to condemn myself for not seeing what was undetectable, and unpredictable.

The beautiful part of being a child of my Higher Power is forgiveness. What I can not do, I know my Higher Power can. Where I am weak, I know that my Higher Power is strong. When I cruelly belittle myself, my Higher Power is loving and compassionate. My Higher Power changes me from the inside out. Even as I habitually pursue chaos and perfection, I am being gently taught about contentment and peace.

Thought for Today: Today, I will thoughtfully bless and forgive myself. I will remove "if only" from my vocabulary and I will replace these words with "I did the best I could at the time." I made the right decision for that moment.

"When fear is in my relationships, I forget that it started in myself." ~ *Paul Ferrini, The Bridge to Reality*

Step Six is an action step. It teaches me it is time to slough off the old, to apply the new. I once heard someone use the illustration of buying a brand new leather coat and then slipping the old, worn, patched up corduroy blazer over the top, because it was familiar. I believe that I have to try to let go and let my Higher Power provide me with a new coat.

As I prepare and work the Sixth Step, I must remember to allow my old habits - perfectionism, chaos, self-doubt, and fear - to fall away. In this way, I allow my Higher Power to reveal new habits - forgiveness, acceptance, contentedness, and gratitude. I know that loneliness will not reign and depression will not get a foothold when I accept and use my new habits. Soon, I will know joy every day. It will come from within. It will not be tied up in external approval or recognition. I am not this person yet, and I accept that the process will take time and diligence, compassion and trust.

After years of practice, I still want things to be my way, but as I hand my life over to my Higher Power each day, I notice that changes are taking place within me.

It is why I recognize the loneliness now instead of being frustrated by it. It is why I know I can make a different choice next time, instead of wallowing in a mistake. It is how I know that I will not be in chaos forever. That is the only way to survive the discomfort of growth and the pain of change. I believe that the person my Higher Power is lovingly creating me to be is better than the person I am today.

Thought for Today: Hope exists even in the deepest valleys and caverns of despair. Its light guides me to higher ground. When I keep myself open to change, change happens. Slowly, a new person emerges... change is taking place.

"Suppose you wanted to talk to the stars, and you succeed, but it turned out the stars themselves are not on speaking terms." ~ John Brunner, The Infinitive of Go

My loved one suffers from the disease of addiction. By living with active addiction, I learned that I could not trust the addict. I could not trust that he would be honest about whether he was staying clean or using, how he was handling money, or if he was honoring any promises he made.

When I came into the Nar-Anon fellowship, I was afraid to trust a room full of strangers with my secrets. Then, I heard about sponsorship and decided I could trust one person. So I quickly chose a sponsor and shared my story.

I continue to attend meetings and call my sponsor when I need help. I use the tools of sponsorship, telephone calls and meetings, and slowly I am learning more about the Nar-Anon program. I am regaining my ability to trust in my Higher Power and others. As I continue to grow and experience the benefits of recovery, I am learning the importance of anonymity in the Nar-Anon program. I now know that I can trust the members, and today I share openly at meetings.

Other tools of the Nar-Anon program that helped me to learn to trust again, with the help of my Higher Power, are the literature, which helps me direct my thoughts to the positive; writing in my journal, which helps me understand myself; and service, which allows me to help others and appreciate my own recovery.

Thought for Today: When I begin to use the tools of the Nar-Anon program, I am able to trust again. I found a better way to live.

"Remember…You can do wonders if you keep trying. You can cope with anything; you really can. In-depth faith always wins over difficulties. Keep going strong with the excitement principle." ~ *Dr. Norman Vincent Peale*

I think that the message of Nar-Anon is taking hold in my brain. The first message - I have no control - is a great help. I have seen the addict on several occasions over these past few weeks. She looks terrible. I have no control over her, and I will continue to pray for her recovery.

Another new way of coping with this disease is that when I see my daughter, rather than getting angry, sad and upset, I will be grateful for the fact that she is still alive. I will be thankful that she is closer to getting some help. In talking with her, I have concluded that she does not want to be where she is. Her addiction does not mean that she does not love us. It means she is sick.

Several members in my meeting share how they deal with their addicted loved ones by turning them over to their Higher Power. I listen to the peacefulness in their voices when they describe how the Nar-Anon program helps them deal with the disease of addiction. This sharing of their experience gives me strength and hope. They have something that I want. Perhaps it is best if I do what they do.

Thought for Today: I know the tools that Nar-Anon has given me are working, and that is how I am able to find peace and serenity in my life.

"There are victories of the soul and spirit. Sometimes, even if you lose, you win." ~ Elie Wiesel

"E quindi uscimmo a riveder le stele" – (And so we emerged again to see the stars). This Latin phrase is the last line of <u>Dante's Inferno</u>. After attending Nar-Anon meetings for more than one year, I am beginning to feel as if I have emerged. Out of the darkness, I can once again see the twinkling of the stars, both literally and figuratively.

I spoke with one of the members about how the little things in life that used to make me angry just do not seem to be that important anymore. I have been thinking about this aspect of the Nar-Anon message since I am beginning to see the stars. When I was first dealing with the disease of addiction, I did not see any light. All that enveloped me was darkness and despair. I did not notice the stars at night. In fact, I did not see the light of day, even though I was outside.

The little things in life that used to upset me are still there, but by working the Twelve Steps of Nar-Anon, they are no longer a source of anger. I have been able to put those little irritants into perspective and realize that in the grand scheme of things, my anger was not warranted. I am amazed that I can truly see and appreciate the light of day and the peacefulness of looking at the stars at night.

Thought for Today: While the addict may still be out there using and hurting herself, my perspective about how I should be dealing with her has made all the difference in the world. I am learning that I have absolutely no control over her, and I need to concentrate on my survival.

"Just to be is a blessing. Just to live is holy." ~ Abraham Joshua Heschel

I was a spectator on the sidelines of life, never a participant marching in the joyous parade of the living. I lived in fear of losing the addict to the disease of addiction. Watching the addict self-destruct made me resentful, and I lost the joy life had to offer. I perceived my life as one continuous nightmare. Then, with the help of my Higher Power, I found Nar-Anon. After my first meeting, I felt better. I did not understand many things that were said, but I could see that there were others in my shoes. They had experienced addiction, understood my problem, and yet they seemed happy.

I kept attending meetings, and slowly I began to understand the program. I could see the part I played in the cycle of addiction and the parts that are out of my control. I am not responsible for the disease of addiction, whether it is my spouse, friend or child who is suffering. I now know that "I didn't cause it, I can't control it, and I can't cure it." I also know that I do not have to enable the addict or protect my addicted loved ones from the consequences of their using. I can heal and recover regardless of what the addict chooses to do. I can wish my addicted loved ones health, happiness, peace, and serenity, but they must choose how they will participate in the parade of life.

Today is a new day because I found Nar-Anon. In this program, I found the way to turn the focus from the addict to myself. I have chosen to step off the curb and participate in making my life a joyous one.

Thought for Today: I will choose to have love, laughter, serenity, peace, and joy in my life.

"The most important lesson that man can learn from his life is not that there is pain in this world, but that it depends upon him to turn it into good account, that it is possible for him to transmute it into joy."
~ Rabindranath Tagore

By watching my dysfunctional alcoholic parents, I had become familiar with unacceptable behavior. I chose men that were alcoholics and batterers. My last lover was an addict. When we met, all of my friends were afraid for me, and even her friends told me that she was a hopeless addict. When confronted, the addict cried and told me that with the love and help of the right person, the habit could be controlled. I loved the addict and wanted to help; I was hooked.

The addict and her teenage daughter moved in with me a month later. I remember thinking that all they needed was a safe place to be without stress. I felt that she was the one. I remember thinking that we could save each other, and it was us against the world. The honeymoon lasted about three months.

When I joined Nar-Anon, I was trying to control everything while the addict was doing more drugs, and the daughter hated us for being together. I had hit my bottom. I sat in the meetings and slowly learned that I could not save either of them. I learned that in order to love another person, I have to love myself first; that the only adult I can take care of is me.

I also learned that people from dysfunctional families bring others into their lives that make them feel as they did in their families of origin. And it did feel like home: the love-hate relationship, the feeling of disgust, pity, and shame. I worked the Nar-Anon program and went into counseling, learning to keep the focus on myself. I became ready to leave the relationship two times, and both times the addict went into a recovery program, only to be thrown out a few months later. I was amazed at how slippery those situations were for me, and how easily I let myself be manipulated.

Thought for Today: I see how I joined in the dance every step of the way, preventing the addict from hitting bottom. I will keep the focus on me and keep going to my meetings, and work on my recovery.

"People come into your life for a reason, a season, or a lifetime. When you figure out which it is, you'll know exactly what to do." ~ Michelle Ventor

Before I came to Nar-Anon, everything and everyone was my responsibility. I took pride in my ability to fix any bad situation and clean up other people's financial and legal troubles. I helped the addict in my life avoid the consequences of his actions. I went from treatment centers, to lawyers' offices, to courtrooms, and to the probation office. I drove two hours to see the addict in prison and I drove him to and from work when he was in a work release program. I was a one-person rescue squad. After many years of this, I was an emotional wreck. I was exhausted, resentful, physically unhealthy, and spiritually bankrupt. I was out of control and I was alone. I finally found Nar-Anon.

It was a pleasant surprise to realize that I am not responsible for others. I am only responsible for my own actions and emotional well-being. If I am not in a good mood, I can ponder the reasons why and determine my choices. I can choose to stay in a foul mood or take steps to change it. The option is mine. I cannot blame others, and I cannot depend on others to fix it for me. I learned that my entire obsession with others was my way of taking my attention off of me.

Thought for Today: When I become obsessed with other people's lives, I know it is time to look in the mirror and discover what I am hiding from.

"It's not our disadvantages or short-comings that are ridiculous, but rather the studious way we try to hide them, and our desire to act as if they did not exist." ~ Giacomo Leopardi

My spouse was using drugs when we met, but things started to change for the worse once we married. All we did was stay at home and all our money was spent on drugs. Our relationship deteriorated rapidly. I always felt as if I was at fault even though I vehemently defended myself in arguments. When I was alone, I felt responsible for all that went wrong. My self-esteem took a dive. I started to change by placing restrictions on myself, and I stopped talking to friends, going out and taking care of myself.

My spouse changed and became physically abusive. One night, we had decided to go out with friends (a rare occurrence). On the way, we started to argue, and without warning, I was slapped across the face. When we arrived at the party, I struggled to hide my swollen lip. I can still feel the humiliation, the shame and how stupid I felt when I tried to make excuses. The drug use and violence continued to increase and finally, I mustered the courage to ask my spouse to leave. That same night I received a call from a rehabilitation centre – the addict had checked in.

Our relationship is slowly starting to heal. My spouse has been clean for a few years and attends Narcotics Anonymous. I started going to Nar-Anon meetings and now I work my own program. Nar-Anon meetings are my safe haven. I feel accepted, and without the meetings, I would not have had the courage to change, grow and work on my issues. I am shifting the focus off our relationship and onto me. I have stopped playing the victim. I have met amazing people at my meetings. I no longer isolate when I am in a bad space. I reach out and call someone when I am in need. I feel comfortable with Nar-Anon members because I know they understand and will not judge me. I have changed so much. It has been a slow process but an exciting and sometimes daunting one.

Thought for Today: I am changing, learning to accept myself and love myself. This has not been a smooth transition. I know that I need to take care of myself before I can contribute to any relationship.

"You yourself, as much as anybody in the entire universe, deserve your love and affection." ~ Buddha

One day I met my husband at his office. He looked terrible, clutching his stomach, shaking and crying with pain. I asked what was wrong. He said, "I'm not sure; I need to get some medicine." I had seen him like this twice before. I was sure it was diabetes. Then the bombshell hit. He confessed that he had a heroin problem and was seeing a psychiatrist who has prescribed methadone. He was ill because he was all out. My husband continued on methadone for over a year and we lived in relative normality. Then slowly, subversively, things started getting wobbly. He was using again; anger, tears, and remorse. Then he went back on methadone, followed by a patch of excessive drinking, then heroin again, and on it went. This is the spiral, which I now know is not unusual in addiction. I became as sick as the user.

Finally, we both started going to meetings – him to Narcotics Anonymous and me to Nar-Anon. What a relief! I was not alone. There were people who understood. I remember feeling my anger and resentment lessen at my first meeting when I learned that addiction is a disease, like cancer or diabetes. I didn't cause it, I can't control it and I can't cure it. Today I am grateful that I am married to an addict because I have been given the opportunity to explore my spiritual nature and move out of my comfort zones. I have taken a good look at who I am, what I want and where I am going. I am facing my past, my faults and my fears. I am becoming a better person, a happier person, and a more serene person. I am slowly but surely learning not to suppress my emotions and fears, but to release them and grow.

Thought for Today: I am grateful that I live with an addict in recovery because it keeps me from settling into complacency. Working my program gives me the opportunity to look at myself and grow.

"No longer forward nor behind I look in hope or fear. But, grateful, take the good I find, the best of now and here." ~ John Greenleaf Whittier

My Nar-Anon group leader had finished a reading from the <u>Nar-Anon Blue Booklet</u>. It still rings in my ears, "...to release our addicts with love, and cease trying to change them." I wondered. I took another look at the reading and I was reminded that it actually says, "We only ask… for the grace to release our addicts with love and cease trying to change them."

I understand the word "grace" to mean a special favor or a privilege. Rudyard Kipling said, "Each in his place, by right, not grace, shall rule his heritage." Nar-Anon readings suggest that if I ask for a change in my thinking, versus a change in the addict, I am practicing the principle of release. What is stopping me from releasing my addicted loved one? Am I still seeing addiction as a moral issue, and am I obsessively holding the addict to my self-righteous standard of behavior?

Step Two suggests that there is a Power greater than myself that can restore me to sanity and allow me to accept the addict as he is. Step Six gives me the opportunity to become entirely ready to have my unforgiving and judgmental defects removed. I realize I will find no peace if all I find is fault.

Thought for Today: I ask my Higher Power for help in using the Twelve Steps to release the addict with love and cease trying to change him. I am freed from my feelings of anxiety and fear of the future.

"All truths are easy to understand once they are discovered; the point is to discover them." ~ Galileo Galilei

Whenever I am asked to speak at a meeting, I automatically feel panic. What could I possibly say that would help someone, especially a newcomer? How can I reveal my blunders and mistakes? How will doing this help anyone? Why do I still have so many character defects? All these questions run through my mind and the self-doubt starts to build. The committee in my head roars.

I take a deep breath to clear my head and I say a silent prayer, "Higher Power help me say something that will help someone and please do not let me sound desperate and crazy. Let me share my experience, strength and hope. Let me tell them how the Nar-Anon program has helped me bring peace and serenity into my life. Help me to get the message to those in need."

I remember I must turn my life over to the care of my Higher Power. Then I am confident that what I say and how I say it will be what someone needs to hear. I hear me give hope as I share my story and reveal the new strength I have found in the program. I trust that what I say is my Higher Power's will. I know I am being guided to carry the message.

Thought for Today: My recovery and my program are gifts I have received from other Nar-Anon members. When I am asked to speak, this is my chance to pass on some of the strength and rewards that I have received in the program.

"We cannot hold a torch to light another's path without brightening our own." ~ Ben Sweetland

The important phrase in the Sixth Tradition is "never endorse, finance or lend our name to any outside enterprise." As an individual who practices the Nar-Anon Program, I have the right to and am even encouraged to be involved in any enterprise that I feel is worthy, but not on behalf of Nar-Anon.

A Nar-Anon group should never engage in such practices, as it would take time away from the group's primary purpose. Our meetings usually last only an hour or two. If the group were involved in financial ventures, it would leave little time for our members to work our recovery program. Our recovery is the program's primary purpose and must come first.

The second concern is when a Nar-Anon group has much in common with an outside enterprise and lends our name to that enterprise. Even slight variances from the Nar-Anon program can cause confusion regarding the spiritual principles of our fellowship.

Finally, the Sixth Tradition also reminds us that although Narcotics Anonymous and Nar-Anon are closely related programs and often work together in the spirit of cooperation, we should always keep in mind that we are two separate entities. When working together on special functions, each group should be responsible for its own agenda and define it own responsibilities.

Thought for Today: Since many of us in Nar-Anon are prone to taking care of everyone else while ignoring our own needs, Tradition Six keeps the focus squarely where it belongs. By working in cooperation not affiliation with Narcotics Anonymous, we can learn from each other and celebrate our own recovery programs.

"Our Family Groups ought never to endorse, finance or lend our name to any outside enterprise, lest problems of money, property and prestige divert us from our primary spiritual aim; but although a separate entity, we should always cooperate with Narcotics Anonymous." ~ Nar-Anon Tradition Six

I had been in Nar-Anon for several years but I was still having a difficult time. I was still feeling hopeless and frustrated. I did not believe the program was working. I felt that my recovery was not happening fast enough and that my Higher Power was not helping me. I continued to make bad decisions, had a bad attitude, and lectured and argued with the addict in my life. The same character defects I listed in my fourth step inventory a year earlier were still plaguing me. I knew my character defects and had admitted them to anyone who would listen. Why wasn't God removing them?

A fellow member suggested that I needed to go back and study Step Six. He asked me if I was entirely ready for my Higher Power's help. He believed that his Higher Power removes only what he is entirely ready to let go. He suggested it might be possible that I still valued my old behaviors and was not ready to let them go.

With that suggestion, I was able to truly work the Sixth Step by examining the reasons that I was holding onto the defects. By trusting in my Higher Power, I found the courage to be entirely ready to move forward.

Thought for Today: I must be willing and open to change. If I am still focused on the past and the addict and am trying to control others, I am not open to allowing my Higher Power to remove my defects of character.

"Our dilemma is that we hate change and love it at the same time; what we really want is for things to remain the same but get better." ~ Sydney J. Harris

When I came to my first Nar-Anon meeting, I was overcome with pain and anger. I blamed the addict for my weight gain, but mostly I blamed him because I was unhappy. I knew I was not in the wrong, and I felt that what I said and did had nothing to do with my unhappiness.

I realized there was something terribly wrong and I did not want to go on living this way. I felt like running away from this awful life I led: being uncomfortable in my own home, being such a bitchy and ugly person, having this terrible heavy secret that my life was miserable, feeling such over-powering eternal guilt, and blaming myself for my son's drug use. I had to admit the unmanageability of my life.

When we went to family counseling, our counselor pointed her finger at me as the one who took care of and controlled our family. I was indignant, hurt and humiliated. How could she think I was the one who was to blame?

By attending Nar-Anon meetings, I learned what that counselor was trying to tell me. I began to get help in changing myself. Working the steps with a sponsor made me realize that I probably was as insane as the addict was. What an awakening!

Thought for Today: In Nar-Anon, I can look at myself, recognize my defects and work on them each day. I can let go today, realizing that my life is mine, and the addict's life is his. Today I can take care of myself and still be supportive of others, one day at a time.

"It is hardly possible to build anything if frustration, bitterness and a mood of helplessness prevail." ~ Lech Walesa

Over two years ago, I gave the addict in my life an ultimatum to stop using or get out. He chose to leave. We divorced, not over his using but because when he left, he found another woman who enabled him in his addiction. At a Nar-Anon meeting, I shared with the group my latest stunt to hurt and get even with them.

My group is always understanding and non-judgmental. One member suggested that there are only two emotions, love and fear. When someone is acting in a loving way, their behavior and attitude is positive, and when someone is acting based on fear, their behavior is negative. It is interesting how I will hear something at a meeting and it will roll around in my head, finally sinking in three days later.

I thought about all the things that I had been doing raging at the addict, insulting the girlfriend, and belittling them both. I realized my rage resulted from my fear for the addict and for myself. I was afraid he was going to die and there was nothing I could do to stop it. My behavior toward the girlfriend was also fear-based. I was afraid because I could not control what she was doing and that her enabling him was harming him. In my sick mind, I thought if I could hurt her, she would go away. He could then get better and perhaps we would have a chance. I finally understood that my rage and insane behavior were negative and hurting us all.

Thought for Today: Addiction is a disease and a disease does not fear or love, it just is. I can choose my reactions.

"So much of what I call my co-dependency is fear and panic because I spent so much of my life feeling abused, trapped, and not knowing how to take care of myself in relationships." ~ Anonymous

My son has been clean for four months and is faithfully going to NA meetings several times a week. Earlier in the week, he was trying to stop one of his friends from using. I thought about the times that I had tried to do the same thing with my son during his active addiction. This week he got a small taste of what I had been going through. We had a nice chat about this experience of being the friend of someone in active addiction. I shared with him two thoughts I heard from a Nar-Anon member.

The first one is "by keeping one foot in the past, and one foot in the future, you are pissing on today." Every time something did or did not happen, this is what I did. Now I try not to think about the past and what happened or how I felt. Nor do I think about what is going to happen. I try to think about myself today.

The other saying I love and apply is "Don't do something for someone that they can do for themselves." This has helped me greatly in dealing with the addict. I was consistently doing things for him to make sure no one would know about his active addiction or would talk badly about him or look down on him. I have learned to step back and let the addict take care of himself and to deal with the consequences of his actions.

Thought for Today: When I attend Nar-Anon meetings, I have the opportunity to learn a better way to live. I can take what I like and leave the rest – just for today. I also know that the addict can do the same.

"We are not what we know but what we are willing to learn." ~ Mary Catherine Bateson

I found that I was anxious, angry and out of control. The addicts in my life had become my main focus. I was lost most of the time in anger, resentment and self-doubt. I was consumed by sadness and hate. I kept track of all the hurt I was experiencing. Clearly, drugs seemed to have won.

I had fought the battle against addiction: I pointed out to my husband and son that they were doped up, that it was ruining our relationships and family and that I was tired of the lies and broken promises. I ranted about how this had gone on too long and I did not want it to happen anymore. I made sure they knew what losers they were becoming, how much they were hurting me, and how everything that was wrong would be right if they would only quit using drugs. I wanted them to do what I wanted. If they didn't, I was not going to be happy! They didn't and, sure enough, I was not happy.

I sought help from doctors and a therapist who referred me to Nar-Anon. I thought Nar-Anon was going to help me change the addicts. I had new hope! If I kept coming back, surely some wise member could tell me what to do to make them stop using. So I did come back and I did my best to apply the program.

Looking back, I see how the program worked as I worked it by changing me. What a relief! I have new hope. I no longer have to scream and holler.

Thought for Today: My focus is to detach my emotions from their disease of addiction. I know that I cannot control the disease or those affected by it, including myself. I can, however, decide to surrender and be free.

"When anger rises, think of the consequences." ~ Confucius

I heard it said in a meeting that family members also behave like addicts. How can that be? Reflecting, I took a look at myself. I found I am addicted to food. I eat when I am full. I eat everything I see as if it were the last bit of food in the world. Yet when I discovered my loved one was using, I could not eat for months. Other times, I have been addicted to keeping everything clean and neat in my life. Everything had to be orderly all the time or I constantly cleaned late into the night. I was always tired. I wanted all those bills that were created by the addict to be paid off right now. I thought that if I worked overtime I would be able to do it. I was killing myself daily; thinking I alone could take care of everything. Compulsive eating, obsessive cleaning and being overly responsible are symptoms of my disease.

Now I am open to the truth of my greatest addiction: the need for change in my addicted loved one. The addict has the obsession that one more pill or fix will make him or her feel better. My obsession is that the addict needs to change and with that change in the addict, I will feel better. The drug addict uses because the addict cannot not use. I obsess and worry about the addict because I cannot not worry. In Nar-Anon, I too learn a different way to live and with the tools of the program; I too have a daily reprieve from my addictions.

Thought for Today: Today, I will go to meetings, be of service, and work my steps to keep my life in balance. I choose not to be an active addict by taking one day at a time.

"We are all of the same cloth, though of a different cut." ~ Nar-Anon Blue Booklet

Anxiety is defined as "the strong wish to do a particular thing, especially if the wish is unnecessarily or unhealthily strong." This certainly describes the way I feel and how I approach the addict in my life. I have an unhealthy wish to make him stop using. I want him to love me and treat me the way I want to be treated. Before Nar-Anon, I thought this was a necessary and normal thing, even though it dominated my thinking and resulted in extremely high levels of anxiety.

In Nar-Anon, I am learning that this way of thinking is not only unhealthy but also unnecessary. Control over others is not my job; it is an obsession. I am learning I can reduce my level of anxiety by releasing my unhealthy wish to control. No matter how good my intentions or how pure my desires, I need to understand and accept that it is not within my power, not my responsibility, and therefore, not a healthy thought.

So what can I do? I can establish healthy boundaries for myself. I can treat others, and myself, the way I wish to be treated. I can turn over the things that I cannot control; I can accept my Higher Power's plan.

Thought for Today: When I feel anxiety, I need to examine my thoughts and wishes. Is my desire related to my own well-being or to someone else's? If I see that my thoughts are related to control, I need to let go, trust in my Higher Power, and enjoy the day.

"As a single footstep will not make a path on the earth, so a single thought will not make a pathway in the mind. To make a deep physical path, we walk again and again. To make a deep mental path, we must think over and over the kind of thoughts we wish to dominate our lives."
~ Henry David Thoreau

Today I express my fears and know that my Higher Power will control the outcome. I am where I need to be. When I feel anxiety, I can focus on the slogan THINK, which reminds me how to react differently.

        T - Thoughtful
        H - Honest
        I - Intelligent
        N - Necessary
        K – Kind

THOUGHTFUL – Before I act, I consider other people; I remind myself that everyone has the right to be treated in a kind and considerate way. I will try to anticipate only my needs and leave others to their own.

HONEST- This is one of the most important things I can do to change myself. I have come to know that honesty will help me get well and I trust my Higher Power to take care of the rest.

INTELLIGENT - I believe that intelligence has been a hindrance for me in this program. I have the need to understand why, how, when, where. My mind works with facts. With the disease of addiction, I keep trying to figure it out, read more about it, and listen to another expert. I now accept that there are no answers, that every addict's bottom is different and none of it is my business.

NECESSARY - It is necessary for me to understand why the Nar-Anon program is about my recovery and me. When I finally accepted that Nar-Anon is about me, not about the addict, about my reactions, my feelings and my behaviors, I was able to begin the recovery process.

KIND - I have always felt that I was a kind, loving, caring, giving individual. I am now learning the difference between real kindness and enabling. It has been my experience that what I called kindness was for me, not for the addict.

Thought for Today: By using the slogan "THINK: Thoughtful, Honest, Intelligent, Necessary, & Kind," I can change with the help of my Higher Power.

"Never be afraid to sit awhile and think." ~ Lorraine Hansberry, A Raisin in the Sun

Some of the lessons I am learning at my Nar-Anon meetings are that I cannot control someone else, feel their emotions, hear their thoughts, or change them. These have not been easy lessons for me.

All my life, I have been easygoing in order to please other people, especially the addict in my life. I will listen to the addict give his opinions and usually allow him to have his way. It was so much easier not to argue. I felt that I did not matter and that it was important for him to get his way. It seemed that it made him feel good when he thought he had the upper hand and letting him get it would make him happier.

The truth is that deep down inside I was annoyed by the addict's choices, so I would turn to sarcasm, cause an argument, start yelling and swearing, and then apply the silent treatment for hours, even days if necessary. We were both good at arguing and had learned to use sarcasm as weapons from our families. Eventually this seemed to be the only way that we could communicate. It became harder to have a conversation without hurting each other.

Not until I came to the rooms of Nar-Anon, did I realize that I was hurting and that the addict and I never had any peace. We never took the time to say what we truly had on our minds or listen to each other.

Changing my thoughts and behavior was not easy for me. My growth has been slow. Now when the addict and I touch base and talk with each other, I try to work my program. I am learning to overlook his sarcasm and not feel disgust and anger, but to honestly listen to what he is saying.

Thought for Today: I am realizing it is my thoughts that affect me, not the addict's, and that I can be at peace and happy today, if I choose.

"Our willingness to do the work to become more conscious is what paves the way for us to recognize the unmistakable touch of grace." ~ Cheryl Richardson

I tried to manipulate the affairs of my life to reduce the pain of others. That eventually caused me pain. I could not stand to watch other people make mistakes and choices that I thought were wrong for them, when I knew I could show them a better way. I have learned that at some level I will always have a compulsion to do this. I have also learned that this is okay, this is my process. I know that when I need to be reminded of this, my Higher Power will gently tap me on the shoulder with reminders such as, "Does this have your name on it?" "Are you in control?" Sometimes I will ignore the gentle reminders and meddle in other people's lives and choices anyway. I would like to say that I could not remember too many times that those reminders had worked. In reality, I do not remember *any* times that they had worked. Things only became worse and my interference delayed other people from learning the helpful lessons that their life had for them.

Now as a member of Nar-Anon, even though my old survival techniques still sometimes surface during a crisis, I can rely on the tools of the program to help me realize what I can do. I can choose instead to not react. I can see these problems as part of the solution. I can let go and allow the process to work in ways that I cannot understand. Sometimes, as a problem continues for years, I want to jump in and fix it, because I haven't the patience to wait. I cannot understand why it has to take so long, but I do not have to understand it. I just have to accept it.

Thought for Today: Nar-Anon reminds me to use the tools of the program to change the things I can, and to depend on my Higher Power for acceptance of the things that I cannot change. The serenity and support that come from the Nar-Anon Family Groups are unbelievable. It works!

"A little kingdom I possess, where thoughts and feelings dwell; And very hard the task I find of governing it well." ~ Louisa May Alcott

Before I came to the Nar-Anon program, I named myself "Pitiful Pearl." I was so obsessed by worry, fear, obligation, guilt, and coping with the addict's behavior that I could not focus on me. I wondered what I was doing wrong.

There are nights when I do not feel like going to a meeting but I have found those are the times when I get the most from my meeting. One saying I heard early on really hit me. Someone was speaking about getting off the "pity pot." I knew from experience what that meant.

At every Nar-Anon meeting, I was encouraged to listen so that I could learn a new way of life. I learned that my worry and fear never stopped anything from happening, nor did it cause anything to happen. My guilt only hurt me; it had no affect on the addict. I learned that my obligation was to my own recovery and me. I learned to "let go" as a way of coping with the addict's behavior.

Thought for Today: If I live in the here and now, if I live one day at a time, I will no longer be stuck in the past and I will not project the future. I am so grateful for these blessings! I continue to contribute my experience, strength and hope to others at meetings and my service to Nar-Anon. I have faith and experience fantastic adventures by trusting in a Power greater than me. Now I call myself "Potential Pearl."

"Self-pity is easily the most destructive of the non-pharmaceutical narcotics; it is addictive, gives momentary pleasure and separates the victim from reality." ~ John W. Gardner

My need to be in control had caused me to obsess with worry about the future and to have regrets of the past. When the addict was out using, I would mistakenly fixate on what I had done that had caused the addict to use, and what I could do to make sure that it did not happen again. I would be consumed with worry over what was going to happen next. Would he end up in jail, in a hospital? Would the chaos of him being out again be more than I could fix this time? What was I going to do? What *was* I going to do?

Nar-Anon offers slogans such as "One Day at a Time" that allow me to remove myself from regrets of the past and worries over the future. This particular slogan reminds me that I need to accept the past then let it go. I have no control over the future. Worrying about what might happen will not change the course of events. I am not in charge. I have a Higher Power who will take care of me if I ask and get out of the way.

Thought for Today: I have been given the gift of today by my Higher Power. I have a choice to accept this gift and follow my Higher Power's will or to stay obsessed in the past and future and try to exert my will. Through many futile attempts at pushing my will to no avail, I can now receive the gift of today and take pleasure in the time that I have.

"Do not dwell in the past, do not dream of the future, concentrate the mind on the present moment." ~ Buddha

When I get angry, I feel as though I have to justify my actions and defend why I feel the way I do. This started long before my children began using drugs.

When my children were small and I established a rule, they would always ask why. I felt that I owed them a detailed explanation, which I thought would make me feel better. I believed, "No" should never mean just "No." I felt I had to find the right words and the gentlest way to tell them why I had to say "No." I believe I did this because I did not want them to be hurt or make them upset. I felt that this was the right and loving way to parent, and once they understood me then they would obey.

I discovered, with the help of the Nar-Anon program and therapy, that I was reversing roles and putting myself in the child's role of explaining to an unhappy parent. I was reliving and trying to correct the frustration and anger I felt when my parents told me "No." I am beginning to understand that it was me who needed the long logical explanations. Today, I understand that as a parent and as an adult, I do not need to explain my every action to anyone, but rather I am choosing to do so. I was doing this so others would be pleased and happy with me.

Thought for Today: I need to be okay with myself. I will remember that my power is to know what is right for me. It is okay to be myself; I do not always need to justify my decisions.

"Learning emerges from discovery, not directives; reflection, not rules; possibilities, not prescriptions; diversity, not dogma; creativity and curiosity, not conformity and certainty; and meaning, not mandates." ~ Stephanie Pace Marshall, PhD

I remember coming into the Nar-Anon program and thinking that I was going to get help. I did not know what kind of help, but I was hoping that my life would get better, the addicts would get clean, and my family would be happy again. I am so amazed at this journey I am taking and how the experiences of other members in my group have changed my life and the way I think. I am grateful for every person in Nar-Anon, as they have all had an impact on my spiritual, emotional and physical well-being. I am grateful for the meetings, the readings, the literature, the service work, and all those who have so willingly shared their thoughts and feelings that helped me to grow. I am grateful for the addicts because without them, I would not have come into Nar-Anon and I would not be the person that I am today.

Today the addicts are not clean and sober, they are not in a program, nor are they interested in recovery. However, I have come to believe that my happiness does not depend on the behavior or happiness of another person. I do not have to carry the burdens of anyone else along with my own. I have had a spiritual awakening and I have learned that I am not God. I have a Higher Power who I can trust to take care of the addicts. I can only trust and have faith that my God has a plan for me and for the addicts, and this plan can best be carried out if I get out of the way.

Thought for Today: With the help of my Higher Power, I can change myself – others I can only love.

"The great awareness comes slowly, piece by piece. The path of spiritual growth is a path of lifelong learning. The experience of spiritual power is basically a joyful one." ~ M. Scott Peck

- **God** – my Higher Power, the one I petition to help me through the darkness that envelopes me;
- **Grant me the Serenity** – allow me to have serenity, a disposition free of tension and anxiety or negative emotions, the shining light that relieves me of my stress;
- **To accept the things I cannot change** – to tolerate with dignity the things I cannot change: that addiction is a disease which makes the addict lie and steal, that she is killing herself and she is still refusing to seek help;
- **Courage** – allows me to face the difficulties in my life without showing fear, having faith and hope;
- **To change the things I can** – my own anger and anguish, my impatience, my controlling nature, to stop enabling and set boundaries;
- **And the wisdom to know the difference** – the knowledge with common sense and insight to know what I can change and what I cannot change. I can change the way I react to adversity with patience and understanding. I cannot change another's behavior. I can change my anger into acceptance. I cannot change the addict.

True serenity will come when I realize that I must take care of myself. I can only change myself. I can control only my actions and reactions with the help of my Higher Power.

Thought for Today: Now I know that if I am angry, then it is me who is allowing myself to be angry. If I have the serene feeling that I seek, then it is me who is allowing me to be serene.

"With the help of my Higher Power I shall accept what I cannot change with courage, dignity and good humor." ~ One Day at a Time in Al-Anon

I believe that I have always been a perfectionist. If there was problem lurking somewhere in my family, I found it and worked on it until it was solved. My husband is an alcoholic and was when I married him; I thought he just liked to drink. Since I considered alcoholics to be people who lived on the street and ate out of trashcans, he was not a problem. However, when my son became an out-of-control addict, I spun into action. I decided that since problem solving was what I do best, this would be a breeze. I tried my best to stop the addiction, but it continued to get worse. As his using increased, I tried harder until I was no longer able to function at home or at work. I hid from my friends and my family because I did not want them to ask me how I was.

At some point, I had to abandon this way of thinking and admit that there were problems that I could not solve. This is when I came to Nar-Anon. I learned that I was living in chaos and thriving on a way of life that only helped me survive the disease of addiction.

Even though my old survival techniques will sometimes surface during a crisis, I can now rely on the tools of the Nar-Anon program to help me realize what I need to do, and how I need to act instead of react. I need to see these problems as part of the solution. I need to let go and allow God to work in ways that I cannot understand. Sometimes, I still want to jump in and fix it, because my old habit of impatience returns, but I understand that I must wait on my Higher Power.

Thought for Today: Nar-Anon helps me remember to use the tools, depend on my Higher Power and trust the process. The serenity and support that comes from this program is unbelievable. It Works!

"The art of living lies not in eliminating but in growing with troubles." ~ *Bernard Baruch*

I am living in a period full of hope: I feel hope without any basis for expecting obtainment. This is how I have been feeling for the last several weeks since the addict said she has had enough and wants to re-enter normal society. I told her I wanted to help her and I was hopeful she would succeed.

Nar-Anon has taught me that loving and positive attitudes are more productive than the ones I used in the past. I have come to realize that I have to stop insisting she go into a rehab program because this is more a hindrance than a help in her life. I have come to believe that expectations were the source of all the anger and anxiety that had taken over my life. She could still leave the program before finishing and continue her self-destruction. Or, she could finish the program and I would choose to make adjustments to have her back into my life. I have learned that life can be full of twists and turns and I can face them one by one, as they come, using the slogan "Easy Does It."

Thought for Today: Today I am hopeful the addict will complete her recovery program. If this does not happen, I still have my own program that teaches me I am powerless over her. I have a Higher Power to take care of me, and she has her own Higher Power to take care of her.

"We need to learn to give up our expectations about outcomes and catch ourselves when we are trying to fix anyone. We look to find a balance between taking care of ourselves and helping others; we can be available to those we want to help without taking on all their burdens." – <u>*Paths to Recovery*</u>

Recently I was having lunch on the veranda of a condo with a wonderful view of a beautiful beach. I was peacefully watching the pelican fish, and a pair of seals playing down by the ferry dock. As I was enjoying the serenity of the moment, a boat came down the channel, perhaps a bit faster than it should have. I watched the ripples of its wake disturb first the marker buoys in the channel, and then the boats at anchor nearby. The ripples continued toward the shore, raising then dropping, all in their path. I noticed that the closer an object was to the path of the boat, the more profound the disturbance. The buoys bobbed wildly since they were closest, but by the time the ripples arrived at the shore, the sea gulls barely noticed. It occurred to me that my proximity to the addict has a similar effect on the impact I feel on my life from her using. I realize that I can control that impact by managing the distance at which I keep her problems.

Detaching is not always easy, but it seems that when I view the addict's problems at a distance, I feel able to objectively assess my own situation. Once I keep myself out of the problem, I can more easily see a solution, even if that only means minding my own business.

Thought for Today: Today I know that detachment is essential to any healthy relationship. Each of us is a free individual, with neither one in control of the other.

"The higher one climbs on the spiritual ladder, the more they will grant others their own freedom, and give less interference to another's state of consciousness." ~ Paul Twitchell

When I started in Nar-Anon, I knew my life was out of control. Before I went to my first meeting, I had exhausted every resource I could think of and nothing had worked. The addict was still using and I did not know what to do for him or myself. I was physically, emotionally, and intellectually spent. I had no answers and nowhere else to go.

In Nar-Anon, I found a group of people who understood my experience, weakness, and hopelessness. I did not have to expend energy explaining or defending myself. The readings at the beginning of the meeting provided pearls of wisdom that gave me tools to deal with my life one step at a time. One of the first pearls I received was that I only had control over my own life, and in order to find serenity, I must cease trying to control the lives of other people. I learned that the control that I thought I had over the addict was merely an illusion. I only needed to recognize that I did not have control in the first place.

When I finally realized that I could not change the choices of the addict, it was as though a weight was lifted from my shoulders. I realized that I was wasting a lot of time and energy, and, eventually learned to give that time and energy to myself. I felt guilty at first, but soon began to feel stronger and hopeful that I could have peace in my life, even if the loved ones in my life chose chaos.

Thought for Today: I have now been in the program long enough to share my newfound experience, strength, and hope with others within the Nar-Anon group. Taking my eyes off the addict and putting them on myself was an essential first step for me.

"You don't need strength to let go of something. What you really need is understanding." ~ Guy Finley

Step Seven suggests that I can do away with my character defects by humbly asking my Higher Power for help. One such defect I have asked for help with is my negative thoughts. I have been shown how my thoughts have affected me. If my thoughts are negative and critical, I feel a churning and uneasiness. If I continue in my negative thinking, I harm myself and the people around me. When I am critical, I am prevented from experiencing the serenity that my Higher Power offers me.

When I ask my Higher Power to remove my faults, the result is similar to the magic of sitting in the chair at a Nar-Anon meeting. Simply being willing allows changes to occur and gives my Higher Power time to open my eyes, my heart, my spirit, and my mind to the answers that are there for me. Sometimes, I need to be still, quiet, and listen for that small voice inside. Other times, I need to take action. I am learning the wisdom to know the difference.

Thought for Today: I will become more spirit-controlled and less mind-controlled. My Higher Power leads me to feelings and places that are wonderful and serene when I trust enough to ask for help with my shortcomings. All that I need to do is offer my willingness.

"To be nobody but yourself in a world which is doing its best, night and day, to make you everybody else means to fight the hardest battle which any human being can fight; and never stop fighting." ~ e. e. cummings

The benefit of having no expectations is that I will rarely be disappointed. I heard this the other day and started to think about the addict. I started to think about the situation in which I find my family in regarding the addict and her drug addiction. I wondered how much of my anxiety is due to my expectations for her; expecting her to give up drugs and to lead a "normal" life, because that is what I want for her!

I know that as a parent I expect nothing but the best for my children. It pains me to see my once lovely daughter killing herself, and it saddens me to think that soon she might be in the penal system because of her behavior. Her drug addiction has led to her stealing and committing fraud to support her habit. My expectations for her are not fairing well in the grand scheme of things. I cannot honestly say that I had any expectations of her while she was growing up. I guess I thought that like me she would turn out to be a productive member of society.

I do love her so much, and I am beginning to realize there is more to life than love. My mother used to say, "Every mother monkey loves her baby monkey, but love does not make the world go around." Does this mean that I have given up on my daughter? No, but I have given up on trying to control her through my expectations. Does this mean that I will stop loving her? I do not think so. It is putting some perspective to my situation.

Thought for Today: When I feel there is nothing I can do, I remember that a Power greater than myself can change what I cannot. Then I release the addict and my expectations to my Higher Power and find peace and serenity.

"And in the end, it's not the years in your life that count. It's the life in your years." ~ Abraham Lincoln

Lately, I want the luxury of being able to miss the addict. I want to think about her, her beautiful smile and infectious laugh. I want to be able to sit and laugh for hours on end with her. My wife is also having a hard time. She is pensive and sad. When I tell her that we have no control and that we need to turn this all over, she replies that she knows all of this, but she cannot seem to shake the loss. I know from past experience that if I try to control the addict, I will not be able to function in my own life. Last year there was an example. I started to attend Nar-Anon meetings because everything that I had attempted in an effort to change the addict had failed. I was out of control and had started to drop out of life. I came to realize through Nar-Anon, that I could not change the addict, and the only thing that I can change is the way I think about the addict and her addiction! I have started this year determined to get on with my own life.

I now realize that I have much to be grateful for today. We still have our oldest daughter and our grandson. Both of us have our health, family and friends. In the back of my mind - way, way back there - I do have hope that some day the addict will see the light and get clean. Today, I have hope that I will have the courage to deal with her absence and not have those dark days move back into my life.

When we begin recovery in Nar-Anon, we learn: Just for today, I will not let this destroy me. Just for today, I will try to do something that will bring me some type of joy – however small. Just for today, I will ask to know God's will for me and for the power to carry it out.

Thought for Today: The message of Nar-Anon is "One Day at a Time." I have learned the message! As one member shared last night, "I have no clue how I will react to something that the future will bring that might be devastating, I will live just for today."

"Perfection is reached, not when there is no longer anything to add, but when there is no longer anything to take away." ~ Antoine de Saint-Exupery

I was on the freeway recently when the interchange between freeways came up suddenly. I realized I was in the wrong lane and I missed my exit. I would have been able to change lanes in plenty of time but I missed the signs.

Signs are all around me, but it is easy to miss them. When my daughter's life began to unravel, I started seeking the reasons, but I did not know what to look for. I could not believe that she would ever get involved with drugs, and so I missed the signs. It was not until I found an envelope of white powder that I realized there was a drug problem. A few weeks after my discovery, she wound up in jail.

A friend told me about Nar-Anon, and my husband and I went to our first meeting. We had begun to recognize the fact that we had missed some important signs and thus some opportunities for change. I began to see how I had become so wrapped up in her addiction, and how necessary it was to begin to change my life. I needed to let her run her own life, make her own mistakes, and suffer her own consequences. I am learning to turn her over to her Higher Power, so we all can get on with our own lives.

Thought for Today: My life deserves my attention. I can watch for the signs that will let me know that I am focusing on another's life and their problems while neglecting my own. Focusing on me is similar to driving in the appropriate lane for the turns I must make to find serenity and peace of mind.

"The world is round and the place which may seem like the end may also be only the beginning." ~ Ivy Baker Priest

When I take Step Seven, I become humble and willing to accept my Higher Power's help. I come to believe that everything is happening, as it should be. I trust in my Higher Power's plan and ask that my shortcomings and doubts be removed. Below is the meditation that helps me achieve acceptance, peace and serenity:

Beyond my mind's ability to grasp,
may my soul know and remind me
that those things that are beautiful or ugly,
the addict's sensitivity and his crazy drug addiction,
are all part of my Higher Power's world.

That life is precious and fleeting and I can look beyond what bothers me, and that everybody has the potential to learn and change in their own way and at their own pace.

May I be my Higher Power's instrument of peace –
More open and supportive, helping others and myself to realize our potential.

May I be healthy and creative, free from danger and sorrow.
If sorrow comes, may I turn my suffering to compassion.
May my compassion for others go beyond the sympathetic self-pity that makes me lose myself.

May compassion for myself turn my mistakes into lessons, pushing me beyond my fears and limitations always considering my limitations wisely.

May I be kind and considerate towards difficult people
giving them time and space, honoring their humanity.

May I learn to receive well even if it is not exactly what I want.
May I rejoice wholeheartedly in others' happiness.
May I accept things as they are.
May I be open and balanced.
May I find serenity, equanimity and peace

Thought for Today: I will accept things as they are, recognize my shortcomings and humbly ask for my Higher Power's help.

"Humility is the only true wisdom by which we prepare our minds for all the possible changes of life." ~ George Arliss

I am learning in Nar-Anon that before I can make changes that are best for me, I have to accept the reality of my situation. Then I need the willingness to make the changes that would be in my best interest. My feelings of fear, rejection, upheaval, and embarrassment can only stand in the way of my recovery if I am willing to let them. By accepting my power and my limits, where I was and who I am today, I am then able to open the door to positive change. My acceptance and willingness are the keys to my recovery.

When I was finally willing to accept that I was powerless over the addict and could not change him, I was ready to make a decision. I no longer wanted to live with active addiction. I accepted the fact that I had to move because the addict refused to leave. I became willing to give up my apartment and take the necessary steps needed to change my life for the better. I saved my money, made my plans and found a new apartment.

With the help of my Higher Power, the Nar-Anon Program, these rooms, and the support of the fellowship, I found the courage I needed. I am still willing to pray for my addicted loved one and hope that he can find the acceptance and willingness to begin his own journey of recovery.

Thought for Today: The gifts of the program – peace, freedom and serenity – are mine today because I was willing to put my well-being first. My recovery is worth taking the necessary steps.

"The most dependable quality in the universe is that of change. A willingness to change eliminates the word failure from our vocabulary." ~ Tom Crum

I am learning: Don't get too Hungry, Angry, Lonely, or Tired.

When I lose it with anyone at work or at home, I am usually one of the above. As soon as I eat, calm down, rest, or make a phone call, my life gets more manageable. This is one of the many important concepts I heard as a newcomer.

I believe that sometimes the same thing applies to the addict. When she was in a rage over nothing, I would think it was my fault and I needed to do something to fix it. Now I think that maybe she was hungry, angry, lonely, or tired. However, I have also learned that she can take care of herself. So I ask the addict only one time how she feels, hoping she focuses on herself. If she does not respond, I remind myself that I cannot take care of the addict's needs and I will find something else to do until she figures it out herself.

I thought for a long time that it was my job to take care of everything in the addict's life. I thought I should work as much as I could to pay all the bills, come home, cook, and feed everyone. I would stay at home when I was not working. I thought that I did not need friends because they would get in my business or use up my valuable work time. Thanks to Nar-Anon, I am learning to take care of myself and understand that others can do the same.

Thought for Today: I know that I have to take care of myself and remember my limitations. It is okay to HALT when I am overwhelmed. If I do not take care of myself, who will?

"Only one thing has to change for us to know happiness in our lives: where we focus our attention." ~ Greg Anderson

Just because I do not use drugs does not make me perfect. I came to Nar-Anon because of the addict, the imperfect one. There was nothing wrong with me. I thought I was perfect. It did not take me long to see that I had some shortcomings and character defects. I was not perfect after all!

Nar-Anon introduced me to the Twelve Steps. The steps provided me with a guide, a map for self-discovery and healing. By practicing the principles of the program, I was encouraged to make changes in my life. I discovered a relationship with a Higher Power of my understanding that I could turn to for guidance, help and healing.

The program talks about accepting life one day at a time and letting go of things and people that are not my responsibility. It also talks about taking my own inventory and having the courage to change. I can take the necessary actions to do the things that are my responsibility. In the program, I learn what it takes to improve my life and my relationships with others. I learn how important it is to put the focus on myself. I realize that I am also imperfect, but today I finally understand that it is okay not to be perfect. It is progress not perfection that is important.

Thought for Today: Nar-Anon has shown me that I may not be perfect and it is okay. I am the only one I can change with the help of a Higher Power, and if I keep coming back, things will get better.

"I, not events, have the power to make me happy or unhappy today. I can choose which it shall be. Yesterday is dead, tomorrow hasn't arrived yet. I have just one day, today, and I'm going to be happy in it." ~ Groucho Marx

When we open our meetings, we do a series of readings. Our group felt it would be helpful to not only read one tradition at the start of each meeting but, also, to briefly discuss its meaning, purpose and importance. Before discussing Tradition Seven, I thought it only applied to monetary contributions from the members so our group could pay the rent and buy literature for the newcomers.

However, as I became more involved in the Nar-Anon program, I learned we have financial obligations to Nar-Anon in other ways. Other financial obligations are contributing to our World Service Office or to starting a new group. Our local region should finance sending a delegate to the World Service Conferences to ensure our group's thoughts are heard at the world level. This is another way of being self-supporting.

Another way to contribute to the program is to give of our time. I can contribute by making coffee, cleaning-up after a meeting, helping on a convention committee, or taking a service position in my home group, area or region. My contribution can be as simple as staying after the meeting to give comfort to a troubled newcomer.

The second part of this tradition tells us we should "decline outside contributions," as they may be offered with expectations attached. In order for our program to remain true to its spiritual principles, we must remain true to our sole purpose. To do this, we must remain politically independent from other organizations and be self-governing. Contributions from outside entities, no matter how noble their purposes may be, could tempt us to make concessions or promote that outside organization.

Thought for Today: When I was desperate, the Nar-Anon program was there for me because members gave their support of time and money. I will now do the same. By giving back, I support the program so that it is there to help others in need.

"The best things in life must come by effort from within, not by gifts from the outside." ~ Fred Corson

There are times when I think I hate the Twelve Steps. When I am angry, sad, tired, and deep in grief, I know I am trying to exercise control over something or someone other than myself. Sometimes it is all I can do to get out of bed and walk through the day without remembering which step I should apply to a difficult situation or how I might work a step to make me feel better. I know this is the time when I need the steps more than ever, but somehow, I am too intent on wearing my pain to think about them. I do not want to read a book or pamphlet, repeat a saying, call upon my Higher Power, or even contact my sponsor. I would rather fold into myself and just feel. I have spent so many years denying and blocking my emotions that to actually connect with what I am feeling seems more important to me than handing them over at this time.

Through my years in Nar-Anon, I have learned the signs that tell me when I am being the guest of honor at my own "pity party." This feels different. It is not denial; it is not self-pity. It is recognizing and owning my feelings and emotions. I know I have the Twelve Steps to follow when I feel ready to work through these emotions. I know I have Nar-Anon family members to call upon who will listen with compassion when I need them. Then for a short time, I will let myself feel my feelings. Because of the work I have done and sharing at meetings, I am confident that I will know when it is time to snap out of it and pick up some literature and start Twelve Stepping once again.

The steps remind me of a dear friend of mine. We see each other far too seldom, but when we do, it is as if no time has passed at all. It seems neither time nor distance separates us for we are linked heart and soul. We would be there for one another in a heartbeat, with no questions asked. I feel the same way about the Twelve Steps.

Thought for Today: The Twelve Steps have become a part of me, heart and soul. They will always be there for me when I need them – no questions asked, with answers ready to be given.

"Although the steps are simple in concept, living with them takes courage, honesty, humility, dedication and tears." ~ The Nar-Anon Twelve Step Program

Humility was a tough concept for me to understand. I confused it with humiliation. I learned that humility is the quality of being modest or respectful. I learned that humiliation is the feeling or condition of being lessened in dignity or pride, the act of damaging somebody's dignity or pride.

Before Nar-Anon, I tried to control and manipulate others through humiliation. I was not respectful of others. I foolishly saw myself as smarter and more capable than others. I felt that I had all the answers and therefore others should listen to me. These attitudes led me to more self-defeating behaviors. When my attempts to control others failed, I became angry and hurtful.

By practicing humility, I realize that I am not above others in a position of power, nor are others above me. I have no right to control, judge or hurt those that do not agree with me. Humility also frees me to be respectful of myself. Now that I understand humility, I no longer sit in judgment of others or allow others to judge me. I am kinder to myself as well as more accepting of my shortcomings. When I encounter a problem I cannot solve, I humbly ask for guidance from my Higher Power. I do this with respect. I do not beg and think of myself as inferior because I cannot solve this problem. I merely ask and wait for the answer.

In Nar-Anon, I have learned that humility is freeing. When I practice humility and turn my will over to the care of a Power greater than myself, I open myself to great possibilities. I accept that my Higher Power is in charge. I let it be my guiding force. I respect that others can do the same, and that decision is between them and their Higher Power. I remove myself from the need to compare myself to others and to judge. I can respect all.

Thought for Today: GOD is a great acronym for Good Orderly Direction. Today I will humbly turn my will over to a Power greater than myself and follow that direction.

"Prayer is not asking for what you think you want, but asking to be changed in ways you can't imagine." ~ Kathleen Norris

How do I feel today? Not so good. I am alone. The addict has been out using for days, my phone has been cut off, the addict has our car, and I cannot get to a meeting. My thinking is racing to "what if" or "what next." I realize that I am letting fear run the show and control my choices. I can read my Nar-Anon literature.

Reading Nar-Anon literature will probably change my mind about how I am feeling. As I read from <u>Sharing Experience, Strength, and Hope</u> written by other Nar-Anon members, I am reminded that I am not alone in facing whatever it is that I perceive as a problem. Others have been where I am today and they have found the solution with serenity and peace of mind. I need only look through my literature to find an answer. I am reminded that worry never prevents or causes anything to happen. I am not that powerful. I am reminded what I can do and what I cannot do. I am reminded that I can let go and let God. Slowly, I get grounded; peace and serenity return. Literature is one way I can stay connected to the Nar-Anon fellowship and program.

Thought for Today: Reading literature is one of the tools that I can use to work my Nar-Anon program. It is always available when I cannot get to a meeting or find a Nar-Anon sponsor or friend to talk with. I need only go to my books and find the help that the program offers.

"The daily reading of Nar-Anon literature will help us move out of the problem and into the solution. Aided by a Higher Power, we can have our thoughts directed from negative thinking to a positive outlook. Nar-Anon literature is a readily available tool that keeps us in touch with our new way of thinking." ~ <u>The Nar-Anon Twelve Tools of Recovery</u>

When I have a difficult time distinguishing between my unhealthy, controlling behavior and the healthy behavior of setting boundaries, I look at my feelings and motives about what I am doing.

Who am I focusing on? Whose behavior am I trying to change – mine or someone else's? I become controlling when my actions are motivated by fear. If I fear what will happen in my absence and therefore do not take a trip or go to a show with my friends, I am trying to control. I have lost focus if I allow others to control me simply to win their favor. I am trying to control if I set up ultimatums and threats that I have no intention of following through on. In Nar-Anon, I have learned that the idea of controlling someone is an illusion.

So what are boundaries? Boundaries are healthy, personal limits I set for myself. It is important to set boundaries I can live with. When I set a boundary and do not keep it, I risk diminishing my self-esteem and lessening my credibility with others. Boundaries should be a reflection of healthy self-love. When I set my limits, I make a decision about what I will and will not accept. In this process, I decide ahead of time what my actions should be. Then when faced with a difficult situation, I already know how I want to behave. A personal boundary is for me only. Boundaries are healthy, loving limits I set for myself.

Thought for Today: I will set limits for myself because they are good for me and help me be the person I want to be.

"God, grant me the serenity to accept the people I cannot change, the courage to change the one I can, and the Wisdom to know it's me." ~ Anonymous

I came to an open Nar-Anon meeting today although I wanted to go shopping. I knew I needed a dose of Nar-Anon recovery: Steps One, Two and Three. Because I have been around the program for a long time, it is easy for me to think I know it all. However, from my years in Nar-Anon, I also have learned the value of being humble and recognized the importance of being open and respectful. So I sat in the back of the room, listened and learned. By being open, without judgment, I create the opportunity to receive. I allow my Higher Power to fill me up with what I need to hear. Humility allows me to be open to learn something new and remember something I may have forgotten.

What I love about the Nar-Anon program is how it gives me the opportunity to learn. I can learn from each member of the fellowship, both long time members and newcomers. It is also a two way street and they can learn from me if they choose to do so. Yes, I admitted I am powerless over my "know it all-ism" and when I humble myself, I allow my Higher Power to send me the words that I need to hear from other members.

I am scheduled to give an open talk in two days. I will be sharing before others and I will need to ask my Higher Power to help me to find the thoughts, words and feelings that I need to share. It is hard for me, Miss Know It All, to practice humility, but I am glad I came today. I am reminded of what I need to do instead of listening to Miss Know It All.

Thought for Today: True humility is the opposite of arrogance. It is not submissive behavior but modest willingness to surrender to a Power greater than myself for guidance.

"Humility leads to strength and not to weakness. It is the highest form of self-respect to admit mistakes and to make amends for them." ~ John (Jay) McCloy

The addict in my life called and asked for a ride. I told her that I had an appointment and did not have the time. She asked if I could drop her off, and I agreed. When I saw my addicted loved one, I was immediately worried and I asked her if she ever thought about going to rehab - to which she replied, "No, I never do!" Okay, I had a slip, but instead of arguing I remembered my program and that her recovery is not my business.

However, this little display of concern seemed to make her panic. When I turned left instead of turning right, I reminded her that I had an appointment and she asked me to drop her off - not drop her off and take her back. She apologized and said she forgot. I wanted to scream "Forgot! I spoke to you less than ten minutes ago on the phone and you forgot!" I wanted to tell her how the drugs are really having an effect on her – and not a good one! Instead, I dropped her off and went on to my appointment.

While driving I began to think about how I would have reacted before I sought help in Nar-Anon. The addict is my drug. I needed to be helping her to make me feel better, when in fact it never does. Actually, I am destroying our relationship and hurting myself with my obsession to help. Just like an addict who takes drugs to feel better, the more I help, the more harm I do.

Thought for Today: I realize that my need to control the addict is my drug. Before Nar-Anon, this drug was killing me, but thanks to my program, I now can detach and release her with love, and for today, that is enough.

"Just for today I will adjust myself to what is, and not try to adjust everything to my own desires." ~ Nar-Anon Blue Booklet

I admit that I am powerless over my life's situation, that my life is unmanageable. My friends do not want to be around me when I am out of control. I do not want to be around me! I am learning to take my pain to my Higher Power and let that power handle it, while I go out and play.

By not acknowledging my powerlessness, I am lying to myself. Recovery is not easy, that is why we are here, why we go to meetings and why we work on ourselves. The Steps are written in a specific order for a reason, to bring us to a healthy, sane and serene life, learning to live life on life's terms. Because of this program, life can once again be good for us. This is the hope of recovery. I remember that as a child I was powerless over my alcoholic father, and his physical abuse of my mother and me. It was frightening growing up in abuse. But you know what? I survived, and I believe I can move forward. If we stay in denial about our situation, we cannot begin to hear the message of recovery. When recovery begins, there is a completely new life out there waiting for us.

Thought for Today: Once we accept our powerlessness, we can learn to live a better life. However, just because we have recovery, does not mean there will be no more problems. It means that now we have the tools to help us recover without being crushed or broken.

"The very experiences that you have resented or regretted most in life-the ones you've wanted to hide and forget-are the experiences God wants you to use to help others." ~ Rick Warren

The Nar-Anon slogan "Think" is simple but profound. It is easy for those of us who live with an addict to be carried away with our feelings and emotions. We tend to get angry and frustrated with them, because we love them so much. We want to protect them from themselves and the world of addiction. Why can we see so clearly what is going on around them and the impact that addiction has on their lives and others? They are on a road to self-destruction!

It is not our role to make the addict see what they are doing. If we rant and rave about their behavior to them and others, it only strains our relationship and accomplishes nothing. Fortunately, we do not have to wait for them to change to maintain our serenity and peace of mind. We only need to stop and shift the focus back to ourselves and take responsibility for our actions as our way is not working and we must seek another.

If we step aside, the addict may reach his or her own breaking point. Our interference is our own form of blindness. We must be aware of this and *think first* before saying what is on our minds. We can do more damage than good with our words.

Thought for Today: Reminding myself to think first before speaking allows me to focus on the intent as well as the potential feelings and impact my words may convey.

"Take no thought for the future actions of others. Neither expect them to be better or worse as time goes on, for in such expectations you are really trying to create. This is God's job, not yours. Love alone can create. Love and let be." ~ Nar-Anon Blue Booklet

My minor son, who is the addict in my life, has been in recovery for several months now. As his father, I am legally responsible for him. For the first months of his recovery, I watched (with some amount of wonder) the positive changes, a transformation really, in a boy who had been everything that an addict can be. I remember where we were. I see where we are and I again look with anticipation at where we might be going.

However, always lurking under the surface is the thought that the possibility of relapse is real. I sometimes live in fear of the addict's relapse. He is still subject to mood swings, self-centered demands, and irrational thoughts. I still become resentful of what he has put my wife and me through - the money we have spent, the visits to juvenile hall and juvenile court, therapy and, of course, all the time at Nar-Anon meetings and activities.

The addict has disrupted our lives and I have moments when these angry resentments and fears boil over into words and actions. My resentment turns to gratitude when I remember that recovery does not return one to the time before addiction. Recovery does not automatically bring an end to the pain of the past or to the fear of the future. Recovery is a new opportunity at a new peaceful way to live.

Thought for Today: Nar-Anon gives me the opportunity to safely share my feelings, both of gratitude and resentment. My Nar-Anon friends help me through the angry moments. They help me to look for the good, help me to deal with the pain, and help me to focus on gratitude. I can view my life and the life of my addicted son, as I choose. I choose to be grateful.

If you concentrate on finding whatever is good in every situation, you will discover that your life will suddenly be filled with gratitude, a feeling that nurtures the soul." ~ Rabbi Harold Kushner

The addict in my life was redecorating his bedroom and picked a color for the walls. I questioned, "Since he's always stoned, how would he know what color to choose?" I stepped in, chose and bought a different, lighter color that I considered more appropriate for his room.

Arrogance makes me think not only that my decorating color scheme is superior, but that my thoughts and beliefs are more important than the thoughts and beliefs of others, that my life has more credence than the lives of others.

In the past, my arrogance made me think that my way was the best way and the only way for everyone. Now, when I start thinking this way, I practice Step Seven and humbly ask for my arrogance to be removed. Without arrogance, I can accept others' thoughts and beliefs and know that ultimately their feelings are their own. Humility allows me to respect the thoughts, beliefs and feelings of others, especially those of the addict.

Thought for Today: This newly found relationship with myself has opened up a whole new world of joy for me that had been previously overshadowed. My priorities are finally in line. I am humbly human.

"It is what we learn after we know it all that really counts." ~ *Unknown*

Shortly after my son was born, his father was arrested for violence while under the influence of cocaine and alcohol. His bail and attorneys were expensive. We could not pay our monthly bills and had to file for bankruptcy. We worked part-time on top of full-time jobs to legally free him before and after he was convicted.

During our children's growing up years, our family spent the weekends visiting the addict in prison. We had to wait in line, follow prison rules, and be searched, in order to visit him. We hoped that our visiting him would make his time go faster and easier. We thought it was important for our children to be with their father. I did not think to ask at what cost.

For almost twenty years in my denial and magical thinking, it never occurred to me that drug use was the issue. I had been thankful our family's challenge was only a legal issue and not a serious illness. It also never occurred to me that drug use was an illness.

I learned that the life threatening disease of addiction plagued my family, and that my partner was a severe addict. With the help of Nar-Anon meetings, slogans, program calls, literature, sponsors, steps, conventions and service work in Nar-Anon, I slowly detached. I decided not to do prisons anymore. Even when, as a young adult, my son's addiction took him to prison, I chose not to go there although I will always love him.

Thought for Today: Although it has been a tough concept for me to accept, detaching with love means that I focus on myself and my recovery rather than spending all my time worrying about the addict's business. With this, serenity slowly returns to my life.

"If I put a small value on myself, I can rest assured the world will not raise my price." ~ Unknown

While preparing to speak at a Nar-Anon convention, I was asked, when I introduced myself, to also mention who was my "qualifier." The word "qualifier" reminded me of how often I hear that word used by Nar-Anon members. The dictionary defines qualifier as "somebody who meets the requirements of or has the qualifications for something." To qualify for the Nar-Anon program, I only need a family member, friend or loved one who has a problem with addiction. Simply put, Nar-Anon is for those who love an addict.

When I share at meetings, I say my son is the addict in my family and the reason I came to the program. Someone often would share after me and comment on my preference for using the word "qualifier," also not liking to use the word "addict." I remembered feeling that way, too, until I realized admitting that my son is an addict, and always will be, whether he is a recovering one or not, is part of my acceptance. When I accept him and his disease, then I can let go, turn my attention onto my own recovery, and go on with my life. I am not sure I can do these things if I cannot say the word, "addict," admit that my son is one and, more importantly, admit that I am the parent of an addict for the rest of my natural life.

Thought for Today: My loved one will always be an addict, a member of my family and a part of my life. Acceptance does not mean submission to a sad situation beyond my control. It means having the wisdom to accept the facts, become aware of my options, and then decide what I will or will not do. I will keep coming back!

"We cannot change anything until we accept it. Condemnation does not liberate, it oppresses." ~ Carl G. Jung

Every morning before getting out of bed, I would remind myself to keep my day running smoothly, to see that I was not carried away with doing a million things and end up completing nothing. After I reminded myself, I turned to my Higher Power and prayed for help to have a peaceful, undisturbed day, so I could get my projects done.

It has taken a long time for me to recognize that I have made a huge error in my morning ritual. Yes, I asked and I prayed, but I did not erase all the activity that was going through my mind. My mental lists were unbelievable. Lately, I have realized that I am a big hindrance to my progress. I always thought that to get something done, I had to take charge, help, make corrections, and see that everything was a-okay, my way. What actually happened was that by the end of the day I was exhausted, felt inept, and wondered why I ran around in circles. Not long ago, I was invited to a series of open talks. The last speaker hit a nerve; he was talking about me! That talk left me with reminders: "Errors! Mistaken thinking! Let go! Give it up! Do nothing!"

The speaker had realized that his Higher Power could do what he had not succeeded in doing. I thought it was worth a try since he had many achievements. I am in training now, sitting still, clearing my mind and giving up my day to my Higher Power. If I begin to falter, I know that the Twelve Steps of Nar-Anon will remind me that my Higher Power is willing to take over and bring balance to my life.

Thought for Today: By listening to other members, we are able to discover ways to improve the balance in our lives. Each of us has so much to give in this program, from the newcomer to the seasoned member. Each of us has our own experience to share to help others learn more about themselves.

"The change of one simple behavior can affect other behaviors and thus change many things." ~ *Jean Baer*

Many of us came to our first Nar-Anon meeting desperate for answers. I wanted to hear some magic words or be given exact instructions on how to fix the addict. The addict is an intelligent person but I could not understand why he made such poor choices. I feared that he was going to die. I wondered if he would ever get help in time. The addict's behaviors, which included lying, breaking promises and stealing, were out of control. My life had become unmanageable as I tried to control his behavior.

At first, I did not understand what the Nar-Anon program and meetings were about. No one gave me any advice or solutions. I needed instant answers. They just said, "Keep coming back." After attending many meetings, I began to face some of my fears, which previously I could not even identify. I learned slogans, such as "Let Go and Let God" and "One Day at a Time" to help me cope.

When I attend meetings regularly, I am reminded that every day my Higher Power offers me a new way to face my challenges. As I listen to my group share their experience, strength and hope, I begin to believe that I too can change. I am learning that I can change my fear to faith, my panic to serenity, my self-centered false hope to God-centered, real hope. I can do this in my own time and my own way. All I have to do is stay connected by attending my meetings.

Thought for Today: I have choices in how I will deal with my fear. I can choose to face everything and recover, or to forget everything and run.

"Fear is like fire. If controlled it will help you; if uncontrolled, it will rise up and destroy you. People's actions depend to a great extent upon fear. We do things either because we enjoy doing them or because we are afraid not to do them." ~ John F. Milburn

Nar-Anon has many slogans. The purpose of these slogans is to remind us that we can respond differently and improve our situation as we face the problems caused by the disease of addiction. Many times my sponsor and several Nar-Anon friends have told me to let go and let God. This was not an easy concept for me to grasp. During a discussion of letting go, I was reminded of a real example of where my stubbornness and willfulness had caused me unnecessary pain and suffering.

I was learning how to water-ski and I had fallen several times. I was determined to ski and did not want to be seen as a quitter or failure, so when I fell, I hung onto the towrope trying to pull myself back upright. It should have been obvious that it could not be done, but I continued to try and was dragged by the powerboat. After several failed attempts, I swam back to the boat. As I climbed into the boat, full of lake water, bruised and sore from being dragged, the spotter looked at me bewildered and said, "Why didn't you let go?"

Thought for Today: In some situations, I find the more I struggle, the more difficult the situation becomes. Nar-Anon has taught me that letting go is one course of action I can choose. I can let go of my problems and turn them over to a Power greater than myself. My Higher Power has the ability to solve the problems that I cannot.

"There is an art to facing difficulties in ways that lead to effective solutions and to inner peace and harmony." ~ Jon Kabat-Zinn

All of the Nar-Anon tools help me live day by day. The one that helps me the most is sponsorship. When I choose a sponsor, I slowly make a bond with that person, little by little establishing trust. My sponsor is there to help me use the Twelve Steps. My sponsor is there when I have a crisis. I can call my sponsor at anytime and talk about what is happening. My sponsor knows my story so I do not have to start from the beginning. My sponsor shares her experience, strength and hope or sometimes a suggestion. My sponsor has become much more than a friend; I can tell my sponsor anything. My sponsor is like family, someone I can trust.

The other tools that help me are all my Nar-Anon friends, other members I have come to know from my meetings. They, too, have become like family to me. When I cannot get to a meeting or get in touch with my sponsor, I have the Nar-Anon literature that I read every morning. Many times, these readings help me through my day. Each page has a lesson of recovery for me if I choose to use it. Sometimes, all I need is a thought or slogan to get me through a rough spot.

Thought for Today: I cannot share my thoughts with most people, but as soon as I walk into the Nar-Anon rooms, I can feel the love and know that I will never be judged, just loved for who I am. When I use any or all of the Nar-Anon tools available to me, I can find the peace and serenity that seemed so elusive in the past.

"Chance makes our relatives, but choice makes our friends." ~ *Jacques Delille*

I was so desperate, frustrated and full of anger when I walked into my first Nar-Anon meeting. I felt so much relief when I left. Caring fellow members spent time explaining the Nar-Anon basics and how the program helped them. They said it might take several meetings for me to understand what Nar-Anon was all about and how it was going to help me regain my serenity.

I remember the group leader who directed some of his attention and encouragement directly to the newcomers that evening. I purchased the daily reading book and read every page on anger that night. I also read every page of my newcomer's packet. I attended other meetings in the area that first week. It was not long before I felt less desperate and less angry. I was beginning to apply the first three steps of Nar-Anon. I was beginning to understand my son's disease and the common behaviors of addicts.

Within a few months, I began to encourage newcomers. After four months, I lead my first meeting. I made new friends who understood what I was going through and they became family. I was willing to give back what Nar-Anon had given to me – peace, serenity and comfort to those who were once newcomers like me.

Thought for Today: "Each Nar-Anon Family Group has but one purpose: to help families of addicts. We do this by practicing the Twelve Steps of Nar-Anon, by encouraging and understanding our addicted relatives, and by welcoming and giving comfort to families of addicts." ~ Nar-Anon Blue Booklet

"I am not a quitter. I will fight until I drop. It is just a matter of having some faith in the fact that as long as you are able to draw breath in this universe, you have a chance." ~ Cicely Tyson

How can I find serenity and peace in my life when my son is killing himself with drugs and his life is a mess? This was the first question I asked when I started attending Nar-Anon meetings. I am a good mother and good mothers care about and nurture their children. The concept of detachment was beyond my comprehension.

I have since learned that my concept of being a good mother actually enabled my son to continue using drugs. I had to realize that an addict does not think or respond to kindness as non-using people do. Once I realized that my attempts to help my son were only making the situation worse, I knew I needed to learn to detach.

For me detachment meant emotionally disconnecting from the addiction so I could deal with my son in a rational way. When I was attached to the addiction, my mood depended on how my son was doing. If he was doing well, I was happy. If he was high, I was depressed. If he stole my possessions, I was in despair. If he fell into a pit, I was at the bottom to protect him. I had an emotional investment in how my son was performing which gave his addiction control over me.

When I learned to detach, I cut the cord that connected us. Now when the addict relapses, I am able to stand and not end up at the bottom with him. I am at the top and ready to help when he is ready to receive it, being fully aware that it is much easier for the addiction to pull me in than for me to pull my son out.

Thought for Today: Detachment does not mean that I do not care; it means I allow myself emotional health so that when the addict is ready for help, I am ready to give it.

"Today I will apply the concept of detachment, to the best of my ability, in my relationships. If I can't let go completely, I'll try to "hang on loose." ~ *Melody Beattie*

"Nar-Anon Twelfth Step work should remain forever non-professional," meant to me that I was not walking into a room with people I had paid to 'fix me.' I was among equals who wanted to help me because they understood what it was like to be in my situation and how to deal with addiction. I had spent a lot of money on plenty of professionals. They had read the right books and gone to the right schools, but they had never been where I was and, as such, could never 'fix me.' That is not what I needed so I stayed broken.

When I started going to Nar-Anon meetings, I began to feel whole. The members that support me in meetings may or may not have read the right books or gone to the right schools. Nevertheless, they have lived the horror of another person's addiction. From their sharing of experience, strength, and hope, I gain courage and faith. I do not need a degree in communication to lead a meeting, nor do I need to be a journalist to write out my story for a Nar-Anon book. A sponsor does not have to have a degree in psychology. We need only to have lived through the problems of addiction and have the desire to share our experience with others with the same problems.

Nar-Anon, as an organization, may require professionals to deal with the business end of the organization. However, those of us who have been in the trenches, whose only compensation is our own recovery, must do Twelfth Step work – carrying the message, being a sponsor, leading meetings, and working at various levels of service.

Thought for Today: Today, I will carry the message to others with the help and guidance of my Higher Power.

"Nar-Anon Twelfth Step work should remain forever non-professional, but our service centers may employ special workers." ~ Nar-Anon Tradition Eight

I remember when I ran around doing crazy things in a desperate attempt to change the addicts in my life, and hoping to get rid of this disease called addiction. I called it concern; I called it helping; I called it necessary, and I did it with the best of intentions and in the name of love. But the disease called it enabling and it would not go away. I can look back now and see my mistakes and I am grateful that I can see my growth.

When I come into the rooms of Nar-Anon, I listen; I open my mind and eventually my heart. The program helps me to make decisions that are best for me. I listen, I share, I learn, and I accept. Finally, I surrender. I cling to the slogans, the literature and the sharing of the other members. I form a bond with my Nar-Anon family, the people I meet and come to love. Slowly, I become stronger, I begin to change and grow. Just like the addicts, I am ready and willing in my own time.

Thought for Today: Life is precious. I want to make every day count and not let mistakes become excuses. I can share now because I have been there. I know the pain; I know what it is like to have a broken heart. When I look back, that pain is not as strong. I remember the good times. I have the memory of the pain, but not the pain itself.

"My advice is: Go outside…enjoy nature and the sunshine, and try to recapture the happiness in yourself and in God. Think of all the beauty that is still left in you and around you and be happy." ~ Anne Frank

My Higher Power did not answer my prayer for patience with a lightning bolt from above to give it to me instantly. Instead, my Higher Power has given me multiple learning opportunities, chances and trying situations such as an addicted loved one to develop my patience.

By living with active addiction, I have been placed in situations that have required me to dig deep down inside, to find the patience within me and apply it to my current crisis and my daily life. I am thankful I have the Nar-Anon program. It has given me the opportunity to look at my problems and learn to react differently. I am learning that challenges happen in most people's lives. I am also learning that I cannot hurt others with harsh words without hurting myself.

In Nar-Anon, I have heard members say that their Higher Power has a wicked sense of humor and "beware of what you ask for because you may get it." Before Nar-Anon, I had no self-control and little regard for other people or circumstances that came my way. Working my program has taught me to be kinder and gentler to my surroundings. I have learned to stop and think before my feelings take hold and I count to ten before I speak. I am able to deal with people in a new and different way by giving them the chance to express their opinions without judging them. I am learning to listen and to be open minded when dealing with others and the decisions they make. I know that these are their choices and not mine. This has given me time to sit quietly and enjoy my own growth. I am a work in progress!

Thought for Today: I feel free from my own self-absorbed, narrow opinions. I think before I act or speak. I am no longer on remote control. I am learning the value of patience.

"Have patience with all things, but first of all with yourself." ~ St. Francis de Sales

When I was new in the Nar-Anon program, I thought that taking a searching and fearless moral inventory of myself, making a list of all the people I have harmed, and being willing to make amends would be intimidating. I had been attending meetings and working with my sponsor for several months when she suggested that I write a list of all the people I had harmed and those people who had harmed me. She suggested that I start with my earliest childhood memories and stop at today. The list was very long. Next, she encouraged me to make a list of my fears, starting again at childhood.

When I looked at these two lists, I was able to see how my fears, shortcomings and character defects were related to my relationships. Once I saw this connection, I knew the value of making amends and letting go of the past. I had been playing perceived wrongs repeatedly in my head for years, staying stuck in the past. As I forgave those who had harmed me and made amends to those I had harmed, I was letting go of not only the past but also the pain that was associated with those resentments. I felt better as if a weight had been lifted from my shoulders.

Many of my fears began as a child, fear of the dark, fear of being alone and fear of failing. Once I wrote them down, they were less scary. As I let go of the past, I no longer needed to be stuck in relationships that were not meeting my needs. I saw why I kept reliving bad experiences, trying to make them right instead of letting them go and moving forward to a new life. Taking Steps Four and Eight allowed me to see my weaknesses and to discover my strengths.

Thought for Today: Recognizing my fears and shortcomings, forgiving others and myself with the help of my Higher Power, has given me hope and the ability to recognize my strengths.

"To have your attention in the Now is not a denial of what is needed in your life. It is recognition of what is primary." ~ Eckhart Tolle

DOUBLE WINNER PRACTICES DETACHMENT August 9

I am a double winner, an addict and a grateful member of Nar-Anon. I trust today when I end up somewhere by accident that I am right where I need to be. I still struggle with my fierce desire to control. It proves to me that my disease is alive and well, even if I am not using.

I was at a Narcotics Anonymous and Nar-Anon convention with my sister who has been teetering on the edge of recovery after being court-ordered to the program. The first night, we walked to a meeting where there were three hundred recovering addicts. My sister decided that it was too much for her and went to a bar and got trashed. She spent her first day at the convention hung-over in our hotel room with the curtains drawn shut. I called my sponsor and my support group and they all agreed that I did not need to bring her bacon & eggs as she requested, but could enjoy my day as I had planned.

The next day, I told her about my plans and invited her to an open meeting. To my surprise, she wanted to go. The speaker was funny and I could see my sister laughing and relating. I could also see that I needed to continue to let her go and turn her over to her Higher Power. I know any control from me, positive or negative, would get in the way. I have to trust that her Higher Power is watching over her and that she has her own bottoms to hit. It is all a learning process.

Thought for Today: Recovery is a journey we can share, but each person must make their own decision on whether they want to take the trip.

"There is guidance for each of us, and by lowly listening we shall hear the right word." ~ Ralph Waldo Emerson

I have often wondered if this is going to be me for the rest of my life. Who would have thought that I would be attending meetings on how to overcome the darkness that an addict brings to my life and to have the courage and determination to continue with the meetings week after week, month after month and for some, year after year.

Recently, the addict came to our house with a look of desperation; she looked physically terrible. Here I was with my drug-induced daughter who cannot force herself to get some help, even though I know she does not want to be controlled by this disease of addiction. This time the old feelings of desperation and darkness did not take hold of my soul and being. Prior to Nar-Anon, I would not have believed this was possible. Prior to Nar-Anon, I would have been angry, upset, shaking, physically sick and much more.

I think of yesterday and thank my Higher Power for guiding me to Nar-Anon. No longer do I have the thought that "this is me for the rest of my life" when I think about attending Nar-Anon meetings. I would be dishonest to myself if I said that I would rather be doing something else such as sitting back resting after a long day or enjoying some time with family. I have come to realize that my life could be a lot worse than attending Nar-Anon meetings.

Thought for Today: I have come to enjoy the company of others who are in the same boat as me. I also enjoy the feeling that maybe something I say can make a difference in another person's journey through his or her darkness and desperation.

"The fragrance always stays in the hand that gives the rose." ~ *Hada Bejar*

I decided that I was sick and tired of feeling sick and tired. I came to realize that the addict and I were killing ourselves - she by using drugs and me with my worry, anger and fear. I realized that the First Step of the Nar-Anon message was indeed true. I have no control over the addict and my life was out of control. What a difference this one simple concept began to make in my life. I did not have to continue down this path of destruction.

I began to realize that it is useful to write down my thoughts, feelings, desires, and my sadness in dealing with addiction, and my victories over it. I am learning not to have expectations of others; that way disappointments will not follow. The changes that I see in myself and others who regularly attend the meetings are huge. I marvel at the transformation that has taken place in my outlook on life.

Thought for Today: Steadily, I listen, soul search, and realize the meaning of each step, apply it and then go to the next step. If I slip, I go back and start over. I have found that going back and starting over gets easier each time.

"By working the steps, following the traditions and using the tools of the program, we begin, with the love and help of our Higher Power and others, to change ourselves." ~ Nar-Anon Blue Booklet

Before I joined Nar-Anon and learned about the slogan "Think," I was at the beck and call of the addict. Whatever he asked: Fix the car, go to the store, lend him money, pay his lawyer, post his bail, visitations to hospitals and jails, I was there without a thought. I did not understand I had a choice. I felt victimized and resentful, and my life was out of control and unmanageable. I did not realize that I was reacting and being too sensitive to every situation.

At my Nar-Anon meetings, I am learning a better way to live. I hear others share how they have changed and how they react to their addicted loved ones. I now understand that I do not have to fix what the addict broke. It is not my job; it is not my responsibility; and this unhealthy behavior only results in unnecessary pain. I am learning that I could stop and think. Now I think before I act or speak. I stop for a moment, look at the situation and listen to what is being asked of me.

I am not helping the addict when I try to fix the problems he has created, but only enabling him. When I allow the addict to deal with his own problems and suffer the consequences of his actions, I find that these consequences may aid him to seek recovery. When I stop, think and choose my reactions, I remember the addict has choices too. I can put the focus on me and take care of myself. In doing so, I am taking control of my own life.

Thought for Today: I will not let someone else's crisis overtake my thoughts or dictate my actions. I will think before I act, and when necessary choose detachment.

"We also often add to our pain and suffering by being overly sensitive, over-reacting to minor things, and sometimes taking things too personally." ~ Dalai Lama

I never realized I was lonely and isolated before coming to Nar-Anon. I spent days by myself because I did not think anyone would understand me or the problems I was living with. I started working the Nar-Anon program, applying the steps to my problems and things started to improve. I became involved in service work and stopped isolating. I now realize that I was never really alone. I always had a Higher Power. With this knowledge I now can be physically alone, but not lonely. I can always share my thoughts, troubles, and joys with my Higher Power.

I was at the bottom of a mountain recently and as I looked up, I began to cry. I realized something inside me was changing. I was becoming more outgoing, more accepting and laid back. Today, not much robs me of my serenity. I continue to stay involved in the Nar-Anon program and do service work. People from Nar-Anon have become very special to me. I can receive and give love more freely today and I laugh more than I did in years past.

Thought for Today: Once I accepted that I had a Power greater than myself, I realized that I was never truly alone. Recognizing my powerlessness freed me from believing everything was my responsibility. It is funny how my kids are now the parents and I am the free spirit.

"And when I do get lonely, I have the comfort and support of a Higher Power who never leaves me." ~ Courage to Change

The reality that my loved one is an addict and has a disease is a tough reality to face. It is hard for me to have much hope, when the addict is always causing problems for others, as well as himself. The addict's refusal to seek help, stop lying, and be responsible is very frustrating!

I can see the answers easily, so I ask myself, "Why can't the addict?" "Does the addict walk around with rose-colored glasses convincing himself that everything is fine?" When disaster strikes, my addicted loved one acts bewildered and unable to understand what has happened. Then, I want to shake him and say, "Face reality. It is as plain as the nose on your face! You are hooked on drugs and that is the problem."

Of course, trying to get the addict to face reality is not easy. He is in denial about anything being wrong, and definitely does not see the situation the same as I see it. Many times the addict does not even think he has a drug problem. Rose-colored glasses seem to be forever glued to his face. However, there are times when I am also in denial. I allow myself to wear those same rose-colored glasses and convince myself that I can fix him. At times, reality is a tough thing to face and the struggle for growth can be overwhelming. As someone who loves an addict, I must face the reality that I have no control over his disease of addiction or the problems it causes. I must leave the addict alone to discover this on his own. I cannot do it for him.

Thought for Today: I must have the strength to allow the addict to make progress in his own time. Living in denial only hinders the recovery process for me and for the addict.

"The reasonable man adapts himself to the world; the unreasonable one persists in trying to adapt the world to himself." ~ George Bernard Shaw

I came to Nar-Anon confused and anxious to get my addict into recovery. This, I had decided, was the answer to all our problems. I listened to the readings and heard there were steps we needed to take in order to "work this program." That sounded simple enough – I needed to admit that my addict had a problem and then I would have my spiritual awakening. Then after having this spiritual awakening, our family would be back to normal.

The world today seems to be in fast forward. That is how I lived my life before coming to Nar-Anon. Always in a hurry to get things done, always in a hurry to solve everyone's problems, never wanting anyone to have to suffer any consequences. I soon learned that consequences teach us lessons, and that I needed to learn those lessons right along with the addict. I embraced the program and worked the steps according to my Higher Power's plan for my life. I found that I could not skip from Step One to Step Twelve without working all the steps in between. I am a work-in-progress and even though I have had my spiritual awakening, I will never be finished with my Nar-Anon program. For me, change can only come slowly.

Thought for Today: Because of the addict, I now have a program for helping me to become a healthier person. "I may not follow it exactly, but I will have it."

"When I slow down long enough to smell the roses, I usually see the beauty and all else that is ours to share." ~ Morgan Jennings

Live and Let Live is a two-part slogan. Because of my experience with addiction, I had to work the second part of this slogan "let live" first. Before I came to Nar-Anon and began practicing the principles of the program, I instantly had an opinion of those I met. I was "judging the book by its cover." I now use this slogan to grant others the dignity to make their own choices. I am learning not to be so quick to judge others.

Since attending Nar-Anon, I know there is more to people than I can see at first glance. I can listen and learn from everyone, if I keep an open mind. I have a common experience with the members of my Nar-Anon fellowship, because everyone in these rooms loves an addict. Today I make an effort to let each person, even my addicted loved one, be the person they choose to be. I am learning everyone has a right to live their life as they choose to live it and deal with the results.

I am also learning to practice the first part of this slogan – the "live." I too suffered from the effects of my loved one's addiction. I was neglecting my own needs and not living my own life. This part of the slogan reminds me that I can and should make a life for myself regardless of what others do. Their lives are not my responsibility and I must let go of this false sense of responsibility.

Thought for Today: This new awareness and acceptance has taught me to focus on changing myself. When I practice this principle, I can relax and enjoy my newfound friends and my life. I have a full time job taking care of me.

"Slogans serve as gentle, calming reminders that our circumstances might not be as impossible or as desperate as they at first appear. These concise expressions of wisdom offer quick reassurances that we really are able to cope with whatever life brings, prompting us to take constructive action and to treat ourselves and others with compassion and respect." ~ How Al-Anon Works

Looking back on my life, I do not think there was ever a time that I did not live with active addiction. My father was an addict who my mother threw out when I was four years old. When I was eight years old, my mother married another addict. The only thing that I remember clearly was the never-ending cycle of fights, accusations, verbal abuse, and chilled withdrawals. Unfortunately, I did not learn from my mother's mistakes and I also married an addict. For some reason, my blinders were on and I truly shut out his using.

The situation became critical when I had my third child, a mere fifteen months after my second. The stress of having two children so close together (both born premature and very ill) resulted in my husband using more until he could not hold a job. He was fired from two jobs consecutively. This all came to a head one day after a fight of all fights. He became physical and I was knocked unconscious. After being admitted to the hospital with a fractured skull, my doctor sat down and had a heart to heart talk with me. I divorced my husband but still sought help for me.

I joined Nar-Anon. I found love, support, comfort, and understanding. I found a program where I could learn the skills I had been lacking my entire life. Slowly, I learned to take life one day at a time, to let go, to realize I am not responsible for the actions of those I love, to face myself honestly, and to understand that I need to nurture and love myself. In finding my own self, I recovered my self-esteem. I adopted the Twelve Steps of the program and I have put my life back together.

Thought for Today: I am in a better position to offer love and support because I have learned to separate the things that addicts do from who they are. Through this, even though I do not always approve of what they do, I am still able to love them.

"We can only learn to love by loving." ~ Iris Murdoch

I divorced my husband of eight years after he broke my arm in a drunken rage. He received jail time for domestic violence and I was sentenced to a Twelve Step program. I was not ready. I thought that everyone at the meeting was completely dippy. How on earth could I condone anyone's using? Were these people mad or what? I must say, looking back, I had a serious case of selective hearing. I lived in denial and I was incapable of taking an honest look at myself.

Sometime later, I started having problems with my teenage daughter. She crashed my car, cleaned out my bank account twice and pawned most of my appliances. I threw her out. That is when she broke down and confessed that she was an addict. I immediately jumped into action. I was going to fix my child, so super-mom found a treatment center. I started moving mountains to get the money I needed. I begged and even convinced the bank to increase my mortgage. Never mind that I could not afford it and I had no idea how I was going to pay it back. It was my duty to fix my child's problems.

My daughter completed her treatment, came out and was doing well. The treatment center recommended that I go to Nar-Anon meetings. I ignored that advice. Of course, I did not have a problem. I was, after all, this loving and devoted mom. Six months later, my fall came when my daughter relapsed.

My world fell apart. In desperation, I finally sought help in Nar-Anon. I cannot stress this enough - it was my salvation! Not long afterwards, I discovered that my youngest daughter was also an addict. With the program's support, and what I have learned, I handled the situation in a much more positive way.

Thought for Today: I have a better perspective now so that I can detach, let go and accept that nothing I do will ever change the choices the addicts make.

"We do recover. Slowly, new persons emerge. Change is taking place."
~ *Nar-Anon Blue Booklet*

I believe that someone with an active addict in his or her life must have invented Caller ID.

Before attending Nar-Anon, I did not know I had a choice. I thought I had to do whatever was asked of me. Not to do so was being self-centered and selfish. I was in graduate school receiving collect calls from my brother who was active in his disease. He was supporting his drug habit by robbing banks. He was caught and went to prison. I thought I had to take all of his calls, no matter the time of day or night, no matter what was going on in my life.

I started attending Nar-Anon and I learned that I had choices. I could take care of myself and not feel responsible for my brother's circumstances. One of the ways I started taking care of myself was to get Caller ID. I did this so I could screen my calls and decide whether to accept the addict's calls or not. I did this for me, and it is unimportant whether the addict knew or knows that I am screening my calls. The Nar-Anon program teaches me that I have choices. I can decide to continue to help the addict or I can decide not to help the addict.

Thought for Today: I have choices. I can take responsibility for my actions and well-being. I am not obligated to do things for others that I do not want to do or are harmful to me in any way. Taking care of me is not selfish. Today I choose to live my life by putting my Higher Power first, then me, then others.

"Our most important focus during times of stress is taking care of ourselves. We are better able to cope with the most irregular circumstances; we are better able to be there for others, if we're caring for ourselves." ~ Melody Beattie

I think I am finally beginning to realize an important goal of the Nar-Anon message, to accept I have no control over the drugs or over the addict, and to accept the fact that my life is spinning out of control. My question is: "What do I do next?"

By using the tools of the program, I have learned new ways to deal with these problems. One of them is detachment. Just let go! It sounds so simple. I have come to realize that addiction makes the addict a very manipulative person, full of empty promises with no goals in life. The thought of this sends chills down my spine. Today I know there is absolutely nothing I can do or say to change that. It was a relief to have this burden taken off my back.

With the message of the program, my group and the Nar-Anon tools, I have learned to detach with love from the addict by allowing her to control her own life. She needs to make her own decisions and suffer her own consequences. I can detach with love by setting boundaries that are good for me. I can love the addict, but detach from her addiction. I can keep coming back and work the steps until they work for me.

Thought for Today: Now I allow other people to accept their own responsibilities, valuing the importance of detaching with love.

"Your success and happiness lies in you. Resolve to keep happy, and your joy and you shall form an invincible host against difficulties." ~ *Helen Keller*

My life experiences taught me to suspect and question the kindness of others. I thought there would always be a price to pay when someone was kind to me or loved me. I grew up with active addiction in my family, and the price I paid for kindness and closeness was steep. I could not afford to become close to others, as I did not want to pay that price. When I tried relationships outside the family, I picked the same type of people as my family members, and the relationships failed.

I then protected myself from being hurt by avoiding a commitment in any kind of relationship. In time, I recognized that this strategy was becoming dangerous to my health and I was not really living. Self-imposed isolation had become my commitment. I was alone because that was the only way I felt safe to live. I decided no one was going to hurt me again. After some time, I realized that this way of living was also wrong.

As I turned further into myself, I could see I needed help. I took a chance and began attending Nar-Anon meetings. I had a wait-and-see attitude. I would wait to see if the Nar-Anon principles of recovery were true, and more importantly, what they would cost me. I needed a new life; the old one did not work anymore. I needed freedom from my fear of rejection and abandonment.

In the Nar-Anon program, I have a new, loving family that offers unconditional kindness. I am learning to receive this kindness with an open heart. I am also learning to give. I believe that real love and kindness are gifts that will only grow when given freely.

Thought for Today: I have a need to interact with others to live a full, happy and healthy life. The Nar-Anon program has shown me that real kindness and love do not always have a price attached.

"Real love is selfless love. It expects nothing in return. It is not conditional. It doesn't keep score. It is too seldom given. Many of us came into the program hurting, feeling unloved, looking desperately for love, unable to love selflessly. But we are learning." ~ Each Day a New Beginning - Daily Meditations for Women

When I went to my first Nar-Anon meeting, I was confused and I was looking for answers. I did not know how much to do for the addict. I wanted to understand the difference between caretaking and care giving. I continued to attend meetings and I learned from the sharing and experiences of my fellow Nar-Anon members.

I am learning that one way of enabling is doing for the addict what she can do for herself. I decided that I would stop enabling her. I would ask myself each time I thought I was enabling her, if this was something that the addict was capable of doing for herself. Was I going to do something for her that will not help her growth?

Helping the addict to avoid the natural consequences of her action was another enabling action, so I made another change. As I made these important changes, I no longer tried to intervene when I saw that her using landed her in trouble.

I learned, as I continued going to meetings, that I could be flexible without becoming a doormat. To me, that meant I had choices, and I could change my mind when I felt it was necessary. This thought and this growth is comforting to me because it shows me I can control my life. I am making changes that are good for me.

I can help the addict when I think it is the right thing to do, and when I feel that I want to do it. I learned that I could love the addict without smothering her. It is nice to learn that I do not have to live with everybody I love, nor feel guilty when I am not doing for them what they can do for themselves.

Thought for Today: I wanted to know how much footwork I needed to do before I could turn the addict over to my Higher Power. What I finally came to understand is that I can let go and the answers that I am looking for will be here when I am ready to receive them.

"Sometimes the way is not clear. ....That is the time to stop, ask for guidance, and rest. That is the time to let go of fear. Wait. Feel the confusion and chaos, then let it go. The path will show itself. The next step shall be revealed." ~ Melody Beattie

Step Eight does not ask that I list the harm others have done to me. It asks that I list the harm I have done to others and be willing to admit and correct my past errors. The first time I read Step Eight, my reaction was who have I harmed? To whom do I owe amends? I came to my first Nar-Anon meeting thinking I was the victim. The addict in my life was cruel, insensitive and self-centered. I was not the one who needed to make amends, I was owed amends.

It is a slow process but I am learning that I chose my role in our relationship. I was the person primarily responsible for allowing myself to be a victim. I willingly stayed in a situation I found unacceptable, with a person who I loved but found lacking. Therefore, the first person I needed to list was me.

Because of my negative attitude toward the addict, I thought it was necessary for me to take care of everything. In my mind, the addict was not capable; he could not cope with life and its problems.

As I continued to grow in the Nar-Anon program, I realized my attitude toward my addicted loved one was disrespectful and condescending. My controlling behavior toward the addict showed him that I considered myself socially and intellectually superior to him. I was passing judgment on him and finding him inferior. I was also standing in the way of his recovery. The second person on my list was the addict.

Thought for Today: Step Eight gives me the opportunity to examine my behavior towards others and myself. Step Eight is a healing Step. It helps me to unburden myself from a distorted perception of reality and guilt from past behavior. By practicing Step Eight I have learned a better way to live.

"To be aware of a single shortcoming within oneself is more useful than to be aware of a thousand in somebody else." ~ Dalai Lama

I was sitting at a meeting one evening and the topic of childhood abuse came up. By listening to others share, I was reminded of my own childhood abuse, which started in grade school. I realized that the abuse I suffered as a child affected my adult relationships. It also played a part in how I dealt with the addicts in my life. I had learned to be a victim.

I had been abused since I was five years old, physically, emotionally and mentally. It is no wonder that at times I still react in fear when someone confronts me. I do not make a choice whether it is or is not in my best interest to stand my ground. I react without thought, run in fear and then wallow in pain and desperation for days.

Nar-Anon helps me heal. During the times that it is difficult to get through the fear, I can use the tools of the program. The more I practice my program, come to meetings, apply the steps to my problems, share and listen, the smoother my transition from fear to faith. I am becoming a stronger, healthier person and can now carry the message to others.

The more I pray, meditate and ask for guidance, the more I receive the help I need. It is now easier for me to achieve serenity in times of despair and pain, thanks to the Twelve Steps of Nar-Anon and thanks to the members of my Nar-Anon family, who with their unconditional love, help me to recover.

Thought for Today: I will not let the ghosts of past abuse rule my life. With the help of my Higher Power and the support of my Nar-Anon program, I will choose serenity and peace over fear.

"It might be that a newcomer feels victimized by persons and events beyond her control, but as hard as she might try, she cannot regain control over them. These Steps have helped many in similar circumstances learn how to stop being victims and take responsibility for the part of their lives they can and should manage, while finding ways to stop being hurt by those parts they cannot, or should not, control." ~ The Nar-Anon Twelve Step Program

My father had a terrible temper. My mother often told me that I had my father's temper. The day I hit my father over the head with his dinner plate, when he was cursing in my face, I believed her. When my boys were little, I was afraid to punish them in anger. I would send them to their rooms until I could cool down.

However, when my addicted son was using, there were many times he picked a fight as an excuse to leave and use. Many times, I obliged him by ranting, raving, screaming, and crying as he slammed doors and walked out of the house.

Today, even though I am in recovery, I still know how to push the anger buttons of the addict and others. I realize that others know how to push my anger buttons as well. Today, I take responsibility for what I am doing and where I am headed. Today, I try to choose my reactions. Today, I stop and think before I react with anger. Today, I will say something humorous or say things in a kind way. Today, I do not want my anger to give the addict an excuse to use.

Thought for Today: Recognizing and owning my feelings is an important step in my recovery. Learning to choose my reactions to my feelings is a priceless gift. Another's behavior is not about me. I didn't cause it. I can't control it. I can't cure it. My thoughts, however, are the cause of my behavior. Only I can control my thoughts. Only I can change my behavior. I can choose to let go of the negative. I can choose to embrace peace.

"God help me learn to accept my own and others' anger as a normal part of achieving acceptance and peace. Within that framework, help me strive for personal accountability." ~ Melody Beattie

At my Nar-Anon meeting, there was a discussion on enabling. One member asked, "How can I give food, clothing, money, and shelter to a perfect stranger and not help my addicted love one? It is not right if I give to strangers and not to my family. If I love the addict, who is suffering from a disease, why deny him the basics?" Another member stated, "I think giving money, food, shelter, or clothing to the addict in my life is helping to dig his grave. I am not allowing him to experience the consequences of his actions. I am contributing to the prevention of his hitting bottom and seeking recovery."

Do I love unconditionally when I enable the addict's using? Am I standing in the way of natural consequences of addictive behavior? Am I acting to eliminate my own fear and guilt? Am I acting to make myself feel better or needed? To release with love does not mean to deny the addict, but to allow free choice to the addict. When I am enabling, I am not allowing the addict to find the dignity and the self-esteem that come from taking responsibility and solving problems.

Thought for Today: I have choices. First, I can consider my motives, and then the consequences of my actions. Once a choice has been made, such as setting limits on my giving or protecting my safety, I try to be consistent. With the help of my Higher Power, I make decisions. I remind myself that things change, even though I may not see it.

"If I stay in the problem, I am not working on the solutions." ~ *Anonymous*

"A breakdown paves the way to a breakthrough" is a quote shared by a Nar-Anon member from her therapist, which sums up my journey toward detachment with love and respect. My learning curve of many, many lessons, not mistakes, bruised my ego enough that I could finally understand and accept emotional detachment. It was not a happy time, although in retrospect, I can see it as my breakdown and an honest beginning of my breakthrough recovery in Nar-Anon.

I often hear the comment, "the addict has to reach bottom" and I can relate this to my own bottom, my own breakdown. Once I could understand, believe, and accept that I had to change, I could truly find enlightenment. For me, detachment is the key to success as it says in one of our Nar-Anon pamphlets. I continue to find new meaning in every word, phrase, and sentence of our literature and in the open sharing at the Nar-Anon weekly meetings.

Thought for Today: A Power greater than me has responded to my willingness by giving me the motivation to keep coming back and to keep learning.

"Be on the lookout for mercies. The more we look for them, the more of them we will see... Better to lose count while naming your blessings than to lose your blessings to counting your troubles." ~ Maltbie D. Babcock

Nar-Anon meetings begin with the reading of several pages from our Nar-Anon literature. One night, a newcomer asked, "What does, 'To watch is not to love' mean?" I could not give her a clear answer. I knew that I constantly watched the addict in my life. Therefore, if 'to watch is not to love,' what was I feeling for the addict?

Being the logical type, I looked up the definition of love: "Love is an intense feeling of tender affection and compassion." I examined the feelings I have for the addict. I had to agree that they are intense, but many of them are neither affectionate nor compassionate. I must love him; he is all I think about. I had heard before that many of us are obsessed with our addicts, so I went back to the dictionary again to find the definition of "obsession." "Obsession is an idea or feeling that completely occupies the mind." That certainly described the feelings that ruled my behavior when it came to the addict.

I remembered another reading that states, "We have learned that addiction is an illness… It is a two-fold disease: a physical allergy coupled with an obsession of the mind." I then looked up the definition of "addiction." There were two; one explained a physical dependence on drugs, and the second was more general…"great interest in something to which a lot of time is devoted."

Thought for Today: When all I can think of is the addict in my life, I remind myself that the meaning of addiction is much closer to the meaning of obsession than to that of love. Today, I will choose love.

"To watch is not to love." ~ Carl G. Jung

I have learned in Nar-Anon that feelings just are. One day I decided it was time for me to start thawing out. I was ready to feel the feelings I had frozen for so many years. It was time to face the reality of drug addiction and confront it head on. I realized that having someone I love seriously addicted to drugs was like feeling the death of that person. At the very least, it feels like the death of my dreams for that person and me. All the feelings of sadness and pain came to the surface. I knew I had been stuffing them for too long. It was time to grieve this loss and start living the only life I have to live, my own. I was ready to start my journey of recovery.

If others choose to avoid help and let addiction ruin their lives, then so be it. It will make me sad; it may anger me, disgust me, and make my heart ache. It is okay to feel these feelings today, as long as I do not stay there very long. With the support of the Nar-Anon fellowship, I will keep my grace and dignity and I will hold on to some kind of happiness. My contentment will not come from things I cannot control; it will come from my inner self.

Thought for Today: I am willing to try, even though at times I will fail. I will also succeed and try some more. Through it all, I will make progress. This is the time I need to be patient with myself. Soon I will grow stronger and wiser because of my willingness to work a good program and attend meetings on a consistent basis.

"Let no feeling of discouragement prey upon you, and in the end you are sure to succeed." ~ Abraham Lincoln

I experienced great sadness when I lost my husband after a long illness. I grieved for a long time and I often thought I would never be able to get beyond my sorrow, and feel peace and happiness again. However, the healing process was working even when I was unaware of it. I was able to release my grief by journaling, meditation and with the support of my Nar-Anon group. Someone said that they had used the Nar-Anon program to help them through their grief when they had lost their loved one to addiction. They allowed me to share my feelings of loss and I began to recover.

On a recent camping trip in the mountains, I had a great day writing and meditating. Later, as I walked in the woods, I came upon a deer. She was so beautiful and so close I could have touched her. There were no pine trees or flowers in this particular area, and it was not a place where you would normally see a hummingbird, yet one flew right up to me. I cannot explain the feeling of peace I had at that moment. My daughter always said her father would come back as a hummingbird! I took this particular bird as a sign from him that it was okay to let go and get on with my life. Since that day, I have had happiness and peace in my life.

Thought for Today: My Higher Power has given me the gift of healing. Through prayer and meditation, I find that I can heal the wounds of losing a loved one and the effects of addiction. I can find peace and serenity.

"We hope to give you the assurance that no situation is too difficult and no unhappiness is too great to be overcome." ~ Nar-Anon Blue Booklet

Addiction is like a chain reaction. It is a disease that affects the user and their family members, friends and co-workers. I tried to control, cover up, and take on the responsibilities for the addict. The addict's illness affects me because I care for him and love him. Eventually I feel used and unhappy. I worry, lose trust, and become angry. The addict blames others, and me, and tries to make me feel guilty. If only I could change something.

When I discovered Nar-Anon, I found other people with the same feelings and problems I was experiencing. I learned that I cannot control the addict. I cannot change him, or anyone else but me. I became so addicted to the addict that it was difficult to shift the focus back on myself. I found that first I must admit that I am powerless. I must put my faith in my Higher Power to begin my journey and release the addict with love and cease trying to change him. By working the Twelve Steps, following the traditions, and using the tools of my Nar-Anon program, I find that I can receive the grace to release the addict with love.

Thought for Today: I can help stop the chain reaction of addiction by breaking the chain. I will no longer be a link that supports the disease of addiction.

"The important thing is to learn which interactions are destructive and which might be creative and then have the courage to attempt a creative approach. The change must begin with the non-user. The drug dependent person will not seek help in recovery as long as his immature needs are met and his problems solved by his family and friends." ~ A Guide for the Family of the Addict and Drug Abuser

Attending Nar-Anon meetings has become a way of life for me. Whether I just show up and fill a seat, contribute by sharing, or just listen, I learn a lot at my meetings. I learn to not judge and to be tolerant. I learn from those I least expect to learn from, sometimes even a newcomer.

Once a newcomer was sharing in great length and detail, all of the enabling things that she was doing for her addicted loved one. She said she was mystified that in the end, it made no difference; there was no change in the addict. For me, it was easy to see that the addict was just doing the things that an addict does, and that she was doing the things that an enabler does. It was clear to me that it was a mistake on her part to expect that her behavior was going to change the addict's behavior.

Suddenly, I remembered that earlier that day, I had rationalized my way into thinking that I would do this special something for the addict in my life so that he would not have to hurt so much from the consequences of his behavior. I thought I had figured a way to help him out that would not be enabling. Listening to this newcomer talk about doing the same thing that I was planning to do helped me to see how clearly insane my thinking was. I was about to compulsively "pick up" my old behavior.

Thought for Today: The time that I do not feel like attending a meeting is the time when I need to be there the most. When I think I am not hearing anything of value is when I will pay close attention. When I feel I have nothing to contribute is when I will share. By attending meetings, I learn, teach, and sometimes just practice, being.

"Everyone needs help from everyone." ~ Bertolt Brecht

When I first began coming to Nar-Anon meetings, a fellow with many years in a Twelve Step program would constantly remind me, "It's about the steps. Use the steps." I felt similar to a young Jedi Warrior who was trying to blow away someone else's evil empire of addiction, being told to "Use the Steps, Luke. Use the Steps."

I can try the steps and prove to myself that the Nar-Anon Family Groups program, as outlined in the Nar-Anon Blue Booklet, can work for me. It means what it says. I can find serenity and peace of mind. My fellow member suggested to me that his experience could be my experience if I were willing to try it for myself. He was telling me I could learn from my own experience that this is true. The suggestion was that I follow the steps, and test them out for myself.

I know that my confidence in the steps has increased over the years as I continue to practice them. Step Nine helps me to change the way I think about everyone and everything in the world. It affords me peace of mind and releases me from guilt. What I am finding is that as I make a sincere effort to do what it tells me to do, I do experience what it says; in short, it works when I work it.

Thought for Today: I can sit around judging the steps and discussing whether the steps will work as the program says they will until I am blue in the face, and I will learn nothing. However, if I try it, if I test it out, if I practice what the program says, I will inevitably find out that the steps do work, and my conviction of their value as a spiritual practice will become unshakeable.

"Start by doing what's necessary, then what's possible, and suddenly you are doing the impossible." ~ Saint Francis

Last night I read a newsletter published by Nar-Anon. The article listed some ways to get the most out of the Nar-Anon message. One that jumped out at me was that I should keep a journal about my thoughts and concerns. This would help me get my emotions and feelings out so that I could move on. When I started keeping a journal on the events that had dominated my life for over a year, I mainly kept a running log of events that occurred in the addict's life. As I was growing in the program, the journal started to reflect *my thoughts* on the message of Nar-Anon – not so much on her problems. My writing now reflects how I deal with addiction, not what the addict is doing.

During the previous trials in my life, I did not think they would be going on for years on end. I now realize, thanks to Nar-Anon, that addiction will be there for the rest of my life, whether the addict is in recovery or still using. I am reminded of those who do not attend the meetings on a regular basis, but only when things get tough. The Nar-Anon readings tell me that if I want to learn how to deal with addiction, I must attend the meetings to share and to help others, and to hear something that might make a difference in my life. Selfishly, I attend the meetings for me. I want relief. I want healing. I want to move on. This is where I need to be.

Thought for Today: Without the experience, strength and hope of the program, I easily become a victim of denial. I want to believe that the problem has solved itself, even though at gut level I know that this is not so.

"The only limit to our realization of tomorrow will be our doubts of today. Let us move forward with strong and active faith." ~ Franklin Roosevelt

The topic of discussion at my meeting last night was "turning the corner." I immediately thought of turning the corner in the future. In other words, what will the disease of addiction bring into my life? What trials will I be dealing with? How will I respond to whatever is just around the corner? Will I be able to handle a crisis?

I heard from a member that this topic elicited thoughts on the corners he had turned since attending meetings. Another member said that after listening to others, she realized that when she finally set boundaries and enforced them, the weight of the world was lifted from her shoulders. I can empathize with her as I, too, have felt that the weight of the world was lifted from my shoulders when I began to get a grip on my anger.

I realized that our meetings are a safe haven for me, because despite the best intentions of family and friends, they do not understand the disease of addiction as well as the members of Nar-Anon. The topic last night made me realize that I have turned many corners since attending meetings. To me, future corners are not a concern anymore because I am learning the simple slogan *Just for Today*.

Thought for Today: Nar-Anon meetings are a safe place where I can come and share about my fears and sorrows without feeling ashamed of them. I believe this is a powerful healing tool! Everyday I thank my Higher Power for the wonderful program of Nar-Anon.

"If you don't run your own life, somebody else will." ~ John Atkinson

I have learned that addiction is a disease. It may never go away, but with the help of my Higher Power, I can learn to accept it and then try to live with it.

I once heard that addicts needed special help when they were ready for recovery. Immediately, I agreed because this was what I wanted to hear, so I enabled, paid her debts, and manipulated her through her crises, thinking that this would keep her clean. What I did not realize is that I was doing this with expectations. When it did not work, I became angry.

Going to Nar-Anon meetings, I learned about the effects of manipulating and enabling. Thanks to the program, I am able to make decisions and set boundaries in my own way, and in my own time. I believe that by dealing with the suffering and challenges in my life, with dignity and courage, ultimately good will come from it, even though it may not always be apparent to me. I think of this often, and it helps me get through the day. I know that I am getting better and that there is still a long way to go, but the slogan *One Day at a Time* gives me courage, strength and hope.

Thought for Today: By working the program of Nar-Anon, I am able to live with the disease of addiction without it destroying me. I am able to move on with my life. My life now consists of living with an addict and her problems, but I can choose to not allow her problems to affect me. My dark anger and condescending attitude is no longer present.

"The shortest way to do many things is to do only one at a time." ~ *Sydney Smiles*

Addiction is a family disease. My children have suffered from the effects of another's addiction. In Nar-Anon, I am learning this suffering can manifest itself in many ways. Some children become obsessive about doing schoolwork. Others are compulsive about outside sports and activities. Still others avoid assignments and do nothing. My daughter's grades in high school took a nosedive when she discovered that her father was an addict. Other members of my Nar-Anon group have shared that their children became obsessed with schoolwork, sports or activities. Unfortunately, others shared that their children became addicts.

Just as the disease of addiction affects the addict's self-esteem, addiction affects the self-esteem of family members. Some children stop feeling good about themselves because they mistakenly think they are responsible in some way. My children thought that because they had an addict in their family their lives were ruined. They appeared unmotivated and spiraled downward.

As a parent in recovery, I believe my job is to lead by example, so I practice the Twelve Steps to the best of my ability. I have learned when I put my children in the care of a Higher Power, I can set personal boundaries and let go to allow them to learn from the consequences of their behavior. In Nar-Anon, I have learned to quit rescuing and blaming everyone else, including the addict. I have become ready to do something useful and constructive with my own life. Then, and only then, can I be of any help to others.

Thought for Today: I will try not to take it personally when my children show the effects of the disease of addiction. I will love them and give them over to a Higher Power. I can hope they get healthy as they see me work my program in Nar-Anon.

"I am only one, but I am one. I cannot do everything, but I can do something. And I will not let what I cannot do interfere with what I can do." ~ Edward Everett Hale

Nar-Anon has many slogans. Many of them are clichés that I have heard before I even knew about the program. Before I was in Nar-Anon, I never took them seriously. Today I am finding these simple slogans can help me deal with difficult situations. They are simple but powerful phrases that help me to remember some very important Nar-Anon principles. As one member expresses in the following poem:

Calm my spirit, calm my mind,
Know my Higher Power will lead the way,
Remember "Easy Does It,"
I can do it "Just for Today."

"Let Go and Let God,"
"One Day at a Time,"
I can "Listen and Learn,"
If I "Keep an Open Mind."

When I put "First Things First,"
I can "Live and Let Live,"
Don't forget to "Keep it Simple,"
Slogans have so much to give.

Just "Think," "How Important is It?"
As I seek serenity,
Although my Higher Power will lead me through this,
"Let it Begin With Me."

Thought for Today: I will try to remember and practice the slogans of the Nar-Anon program. They serve as gentle guides that help me choose new reactions to old problems and situations. They are helping me make better choices. They also help me deal with fear that can often cloud my judgment and prevent me from having the courage to change myself for the better.

"Slogans are the railings we hold onto as we climb the steps." ~ Unknown

I am trying to deal with my daughter and her drug abuse. She has changed so drastically from the light-hearted, loving child she once was. Like mine, her life became unmanageable. When I began attending Nar-Anon meetings, I asked myself, "Just what are these meetings supposed to be doing for me?" The pain of seeing my daughter on drugs will never go away, but attending Nar-Anon meetings has truly helped me learn to deal with that pain. My program helps me to get my life back. My life no longer depends upon my daughter's recovery from drug abuse, or the insanity that comes along with active addiction.

Nar-Anon has shown me that I am not alone. When members share at a meeting, I learn that others have similar and worse problems with addiction and their loved ones.

My situation could be much worse. I see the strength the program gives to everyone who works the steps. There are members living with many different situations involving addiction. I am learning to be grateful for what I have today and to have faith that I too can gain the strength to deal with my problems.

Thought for Today: I see more sunshine than darkness every day.

"Keep your faith in all beautiful things; in the sun when it is hidden, in the spring when it is gone." ~ Roy Gilson

I am practicing detachment with love, and it is helpful to me. I no longer stay up nights worrying about my daughter sleeping in alleys. I no longer obsess about where she is at any given time. I no longer worry about my phone ringing at three in the morning, advising me she is in jail again. My heart goes out to my daughter when she calls to tell me she is hungry, but because of my Nar-Anon program, I no longer have to drop everything and rush out to buy her a meal. All of this is painful to me but I am learning how to deal with it. I know that when I detach from the addict's drama, I improve my life, as well as hers.

While my heart still aches, I no longer am in constant pain. My stomach is no longer in knots 24/7. While I think of her often, I try to concentrate more on my needs than hers. I am concentrating on my career more. I am learning how to deal with pain so I can experience peace and serenity in my life.

I am far from perfect. I have faults to address. I know my impatience requires considerable attention. As I work on this and other defects, I feel better, not only about myself, but in general.

Thought for Today: As I lovingly detach from the addict's problems, I can take the time to look at my own defects. I am working on the only person I can change – myself.

"Everyone has heard the expression, 'what you sow is what you reap.' Obviously if we want to create happiness in our lives, we must learn to sow the seeds of happiness. Therefore karma implies the action of conscious choice-making." ~ Deepak Chopra

I could never figure out why I always bit off more than I could chew. I always brought home stray animals. Once they grew out of babyhood, I looked for another baby who needed me. I thought I would go insane without a needy thing to fill my life. My need to be needed also got me involved with an addict. I used to think this was accidental, but then I realized it had become a pattern. I was attracted to needy people and they were attracted to me. That is why I found my addicted loved one and how I eventually found Nar-Anon.

My relationship with the addict brought me to my first Nar-Anon meeting because, of course, the addict needed to get off drugs and I was going to find out how to get him to stop using. I had been attending meetings for some time, and one night I was pouring my heart and soul out to what I believed were deaf ears. I felt so bad because I felt that I was not getting better. I felt lost and hopeless. When I left the meeting, I was a basket case. However, as I was leaving, a woman came up to me, hugged me, and told me that she did not know why she came to the meeting that night, but something was pulling her there. She told me she was feeling badly, until she heard me speak. She then said that it all came to her: that she was meant to be there to hear my words, and now knew what she needed to do to get healthy again. She felt her Higher Power was speaking to her through me. I then understood why I had gone there that night.

I realized my Higher Power brought us together. We were both at our bottoms and we both needed to hear healing words.

Thought for Today: I lose nothing when I share love and healing thoughts with others. By sharing, I only increase the benefits to both.

"Today and every day, I will pray for the wisdom to choose wise counselors and the strength to love and heal myself." ~ Each Day a New Beginning – Daily Meditations for Women

Step Nine was the topic of a recent meeting. At first, I thought that my daughter had to apologize to me for what she had put me through these past several years, and what she is still putting me through. I also thought that I should forgive her, but when I listened to the Nar-Anon message, I realized she did not do anything to me, but rather she did it to herself. What has happened to me is that I let myself be affected by her actions.

Studying Step Four, I found out that I was not a victim. On the contrary, I had many reasons to ask my daughter for forgiveness. Before Nar-Anon, I was full of anger. That anger led me to deride, belittle, try to shame, and generally try to make the addict feel like a worthless person. I did not know that addiction was a disease and I thought my daughter's attitude was an attempt to attack me and make me suffer. I now fully realize that this way of thinking was wrong and useless, and that my initial reactions did more to alienate the addict than to help her. My reactions harmed my daughter and me. My anger did little to alleviate the suffering I was feeling. It only made things worse.

Thought for Today: I first came to Nar-Anon because I was hurting, but after learning the messages of Nar-Anon, I realize that to make the hurt go away, I must make amends first to myself, second to the people I hurt, whenever possible, including my addicted daughter. Forgiveness is a step to freedom.

"When I am able to resist the temptation to judge others, I can see them as teachers of forgiveness in my life, reminding me that I can only have peace of mind when I forgive rather than judge." ~ Gerald G. Jampolsky

BOUNDARIES September 12

Boundaries are frequently discussed at meetings. I do not know if I have ever enforced my boundaries. I have tried by saying what I would not allow, but then, many times, I gave in and allowed the addict to disregard the limits I set.

Now, with time, distance and a lot of prayer, I feel that when my son returns home I will be able to set my boundaries and keep them. There will be behaviors and activities that will not be allowed in my home. I will tell him calmly what I will and will not accept in order for him to be welcome there.

In the Nar-Anon program, I am learning that I cannot change another person. The only person I can change is me. When I think back on all of the attempts I made to change the addict's behavior, I see that nothing worked. It may have lasted for a few days, but it was never permanent. In order for boundaries to work, they must be kept.

I have found that prayer and reading of Nar-Anon literature has helped me to focus on my behavior and needs. Sometimes I think having the courage to accept the things I cannot change is difficult, but the reality is, I cannot change the addict. Once I can get to that place of acceptance, there is a sense of calmness. This is where I believe I need to be before I can set meaningful boundaries.

Thought for Today: I will not worry so much about someone else's behavior but will focus on my own.

"He that respects himself is safe from others; he wears a coat of mail that none can pierce." ~ Henry Wadsworth Longfellow

256

In our local Nar-Anon region, we have an annual event called a Narathon, which is similar to a convention. At the Narathon, members from several meetings gather to hear speakers share their experience, strength and hope. It is always a wonderful way for me to connect with other Nar-Anon members outside my regular group. I have attended Narathons for the past three years, and each time I experienced exactly what I needed. This year was no exception, but I did receive a blessing in an unfamiliar form.

I was asked if I would speak at the Narathon. My immediate answer was, "Yes." Shortly after confirming I would speak, I was surprised that doubt crept into my mind. Could I do it? Could I get up there and share my story? I know I always heard what I needed from the speakers, so why did I worry? I am so grateful for the program. I reminded myself how far I had come and that talking about the past and the reason I came to Nar-Anon would not magically turn me back into the old me, the person without the program. I turned to my Higher Power's wisdom and asked for the courage to let the outcome be as it may. I knew that regardless of what I said, or how I said it, it would be exactly as it should be.

After it was all said and done, I was so encouraged to find that others did indeed identify with my story. The Narathon is a great event and I am so grateful to those in service who lend their help to ensure it happens every year.

Thought for Today: Just speak up. Someone will get value from your experience, strength and hope.

"One's pain is one's own creation." ~ Dalai Lama

When I discovered my loved ones were addicted to drugs, I felt great sadness. I felt as though I would never be happy again. The joy was gone from my life. Then I started to attend Nar-Anon meetings. In these rooms, I found others in similar situations and they still had joy in their lives. As I practiced my program, keeping the focus on my recovery and myself, I began trusting my Higher Power, and once again began experiencing joy.

I enjoy sitting in my backyard watching the butterflies. It is peaceful, and it always seems that I see the same brown and white butterfly. When it came today, I felt calm, as though it was playing with me. It would flutter and swoop around the yard, come towards me, then fly up and back again three or four times. I was giggling like an eight year old.

Next time you see a butterfly, take a moment to think about your Higher Power. Feel the love, thank a Power greater than yourself for something, and acknowledge this gift was from that power. It might bring a smile to your soul.

Thought for Today: I am grateful for the peace and serenity I am finding as I learn to release the addicts with love, one day at a time, and cease trying to change them. I am grateful for the guidance that helped me to find my way here. I pray for those still alone and in pain because of the addiction of a friend or loved one. Please help them to find their way to these rooms, so that I may give back the gifts I have been so freely given as well as a chance to share my experience, strength and hope with those suffering the isolation caused by living with an addict. As I try to reach out to others, may I be ever mindful of our traditions. I am trusting in my Higher Power's love and concern for me and the addicts.

"Nothing can bring you peace but yourself." ~ Ralph Waldo Emerson

I am familiar with the decision-making process of organizations such as government, corporations and schools. In those organizations, there are different levels of authority, a power structure. However, as a newcomer, I did not understand how the Nar-Anon fellowship worked. The Nar-Anon fellowship is made up of individual members who are all equals. In Nar-Anon, no one has the right to give orders. The whole Nar-Anon program is merely suggested. I can work my program in my own way and in my own time.

Nar-Anon meetings are conducted according to the wishes of the group, and decisions are made through discussions and the agreement of the members. This is called a group conscience. Each group can elect group officers. Officers are not paid; they are given the opportunity to perform a service for their group, such as chairing a meeting, making coffee, greeting newcomers, or representing the group at other levels of service. Members who act as leaders are reminded in our literature and Tradition Two that they are "trusted servants: they do not govern." This structure works well at the group, area and regional levels.

The Nar-Anon world organization requires a more business-like structure to perform business functions that support the program and help it grow. These functions include public relations campaigns, telephone help lines, development, approval and sales of program literature, organizing conventions, and conferences. At this level, the Ninth Tradition allows us to hire the necessary professionals to perform these functions efficiently. The Ninth Tradition also reminds these paid professionals that their sole purpose is to serve the Nar-Anon Family Groups. The area, region and world level employees have no authority to direct or to interfere with the structure, the decision-making authority, or the activities of the individual Nar-Anon Family Groups.

Thought for Today: My responsibility is to serve the members, whether my work is voluntary or professional; the only authority in Nar-Anon is a loving Higher Power as expressed through our group conscience.

"At the beginning, mankind and the obligation of selfless service were created together. 'Through selfless service, you will always be fruitful and find the fulfillment of your desires': this is the promise of the Creator..." ~ *Bhagavad Gita*

I am a fifteen-year-old member of Nar-Anon. When drugs and alcohol first reared their ugly heads, I was in denial. I ignored the bottles in the fridge, the hours my mother slept away, and the depression pills in her purse. I felt overwhelmed and helpless, so I ignored it all.

My mother ran away one day. She abandoned my little brother and me. At that time, my grandmother who is very important to me, informed me about my mother's disease of addiction. The thing that scared me the most had happened. My mother chose to run away from her problems and her life. She was using drugs to escape reality.

Today, I can sincerely say that Nar-Anon has changed my outlook and my life. Today, I know that my mother is a sick person and I can forgive her for the hurt that I felt because she ran away. I have learned that I am powerless over her disease and have to let go and let God. By doing this, I have found peace and joy over despair and distress. I miss my mother dearly and hope some day she will get better and come back to see me and share in my life. As I continue my high school education, I also continue to work my program and today I have hope for a better future.

Thought for Today: In Nar-Anon, I learn to forgive, release and move forward with my life.

"Today I will move forward with my life, despite what others are doing or not doing. I will know it is right to cross the bridge to a better life even if I must leave others behind to do that, I will not feel guilty, I will not feel ashamed. I know that where I am now is a better place and where I'm meant to be." ~ Melody Beattie

To me, manipulation is an art — a learned skill. When manipulating, I used a wealth of negative and self-serving behaviors to influence others, trying to make them act, think, and behave as I saw fit. I believed a master manipulator was someone who had practiced this art for many years. I was a master manipulator. I used negative behaviors, always trying, however, not always getting, all of the hoped for results. Manipulation was my main survival skill. That behavior was further honed during the crazy-making years of active addiction.

After being in the Nar-Anon program for several months, regularly attending meetings and working the steps with a sponsor, I have found that manipulating others is a negative and selfish behavior. I have lost the pleasure that I once derived from practicing it. In Nar-Anon, I have learned to speak my truth, to ask for what I want and need without an expectation in return. I no longer feel the need to manipulate others to get my way. Now, when I become defensive and react with manipulation, I catch it sooner and stop it, realizing that I am reverting to my old behavior. My pleasure is derived from attaining the gifts of the program honestly and naturally. By working on myself, I am letting go of the illusion that I should and could control others.

Thought for Today: In Nar-Anon, I am learning a better way to live. I can ask for what I need. If I do not get it, I can change my attitude and turn that desire over to my Higher Power, who I believe will give me what I need when I need it.

"If you don't like something, change it. If you can't change it, change your attitude." ~ Maya Angelou

I heard the birds sing today! I cannot remember the last time I heard the birds sing. Oh, the birds sing every day in my yard, but when addiction entered my life, it seemed that I had lost my direction and ability to appreciate life and the world around me. I have not heard the birds sing for a while, but today I did!

I am amazed at how wonderful hearing the birds sing made me feel. Yes, made me feel. Not think, but *feel*. The song was crisp and constant. I imagined a mother bird trying to get her baby bird out of the nest. I imagined a mother bird encouraging her baby bird to flap her wings.

It was a beautiful sound, one that I now realize I have missed dearly for these past few years. But today, I heard the birds sing.

Thought for Today: The disease of addiction had taken away my ability to enjoy the simple things in life. I did not notice the beauty all around me. Now, with the help of Nar-Anon, I can stop and enjoy the world as it is and take pleasure in the gifts given to me so freely.

"Happiness cannot be traveled to, owned, earned, worn or consumed. Happiness is the spiritual experience of living every minute with love, grace and gratitude." ~ Dennis Waitley

One night at a meeting, the topic of discussion was "courage." The person who chaired the meeting said that they thought coming to the meetings over and over again represented courage. I agree, but also feel that there is another factor: determination. Courage and determination are needed. When I first attended Nar-Anon meetings, I tried everything in an effort to get the addict in my life to change. Nothing worked! Indeed, I believe courage and determination were needed as I had a particular dislike for "therapy" in any form.

When I first attended Nar-Anon meetings, others said things such as - addiction is an illness, not a moral issue – and human nature tends to put up barriers of denial. The total and complete disillusion that I was experiencing was physically and emotionally debilitating to the point that I could not think straight.

As I continued to attend the meetings and listen to others, I heard situations that are sometimes much worse than my own. I began to replace my denial with a willingness to accept change. I heard members share their stories about the horrors of addiction, and yet they were able to laugh about simple things. They were able to sit there with a measure of contentment that comes from working the Twelve Steps.

Thought for Today: The desire to have the serenity that others have achieved became so strong that I kept coming back to the meetings over and over again. That desire for serenity began to replace my feelings of anger, grief, and desperation. Slowly a new person was starting to emerge. The change was taking place.

"Courage and perseverance have a magical talisman, before which difficulties disappear and obstacles vanish into air." ~ John Quincy Adams

As a teenager in my small hometown, I felt like a square peg trying to fit into a round hole. At summer camp and conferences, I felt more accepted. This contributed enormously to my sense of who I am.

By the time I found a Twelve Step program, I had lost myself. I did not know who I was, what mattered to me, or even which movie I wanted to see. I was consumed by my loved one. I wanted what he wanted, did what he did, spent my energy trying to solve his problems, handled his moods and tried to make him happy.

Weekly Nar-Anon meetings helped me focus on myself. After I had been coming to meetings for a while, I took a whole day to myself for an area workshop. I did not say where I was going. I let my husband think it was work, because I still could not stand up for myself. I found a lot of strength and hope that day, and after that, I started doing local and area service work.

As I gathered strength and found more serenity at my weekly meetings, I wanted more. I remembered how retreats and conferences had helped me before adulthood, and I tried them again. I joined a women's Twelve Step group, which had quarterly retreats. They helped me in working my program, and weekends away gave me perspective. I learned to think more on my own.

During my young adult son's active addiction years, I was so afraid he would die or spend long years in prison. It was so hard to let go and let him live his own life. When I could not help him, I helped other teens as a group sponsor. I did service work at a treatment facility and found a sponsor whose children had been to prison.

Thought for Today: Service work brings clarity, strength and depth to my recovery. In service, I have learned the importance of making time for myself and for my recovery.

"Service is a way to carry the message to others." ~ *The Nar-Anon Twelve Step Program*

One day a devastating awareness changed my life. I was working and my children were in school when I became aware of the drug abuse within my family. Addiction crept into my life and there it has remained. Abuse of marijuana allowed my loved one a delusional escape from reality. The heroin abuser was in a motionless stupor, sleeping the hours away. The crack addict displayed violent behavior. Drug abuse among my family members remains a painful, sad reality for me.

I was stuck focusing on the past and my addicted loved ones until I found Nar-Anon. I wished for the loving, kind people my addicted family members once were. I also missed the trust, laughter and fun we had enjoyed.

As I listened to others share at my first Nar-Anon meeting, I realized that I was not alone in my sad and confusing reality. I learned in Nar-Anon that I cannot change the past, other people or things, but I can change myself. I had a joyful awakening and renewed hope! As I continue to work my program, I learn to share my sadness and my joy. Daily, I work at letting go of old resentments. Daily, I keep my focus on me and on the positive things in my life.

The most helpful therapy available for me is the Nar-Anon program. No longer am I in constant turmoil with worry and regret. By working the Twelve Steps and attending meetings, I have learned to accept each new day with peace and serenity in my heart.

Thought for Today: Awareness is the first step in recognizing a problem and thus the first step towards positive change. Until I become aware of a problem, I cannot take appropriate action. I need to remember that I can do only what is right for me and allow others to do the same.

"Today I will be grateful for any awareness I encounter. I will display gratitude, peace, and dignity when life gets my attention." ~ Melody Beattie

When living in the chaos of addiction, I find that I have trouble making decisions from the simplest to the biggest issues that life throws at me; the issues that will affect my family's well-being and my own. Recently, my eighteen-year-old daughter, who is an addict, found herself in a crisis situation. This caused her addiction to escalate and her attitude and actions to become unbearable. Before coming to Nar-Anon, I would have found myself being drawn into the confusion, allowing her unacceptable behavior to continue. I was afraid to make a decision, afraid to ask her to leave, afraid of the outcome and how she would react.

From Nar-Anon, I am learning that my Higher Power will take care of things. I will wait for direction. I believe my Higher Power will put me where I should be. I believe I can ask my Higher Power to lead me, and I believe I will be shown if I am going the wrong way. I wait for a clear answer because sometimes no decision is better than the wrong decision.

Thought for Today: Addiction is a family disease. It takes many forms and affects not only the addict. I can make a decision on how to handle these problems with the help of my Higher Power and my Nar-Anon program.

"At the start of each day I can make the decision to turn my will and my life over to the care of God." ~ Courage to Change

I wanted and prayed for something good to happen for me, and Nar-Anon was where I found it. The old adage "let the addicts hit their bottom" is difficult for me to practice. Things can get bad before the addict realizes he needs help, if he ever does. I found that my idea of bad might be different from his. My wishes, desires, wants, and the hoped-for future for the addict are likely not his.

When I start determining what the addict's wants and needs are, then I am trying once again to control his life and take the place of his Higher Power. Once again, I recognize I have fallen into the same old trap, doing things for the addict that he should do for himself. When my focus is on him and what he desires or wants, I am making him responsible for my wants and needs as well. Today, when I make a decision on what to do about the addict, I do it for me.

I have come to believe that a Power greater than me can fulfill my wishes, desires and wants. Just as my Higher Power led me to Nar-Anon for help, this same Higher Power will lead the addict to help when he wants recovery. I can take responsibility for myself and have choices in my life, *not* in the lives of others. I accept my past choices by making amends to myself and others. This process has opened the door for a new and different life path for me. I am trying something different by not living in a repetitive past.

Thought for Today: Today I pray to my Higher Power to remind me that all I want and desire for myself is within me.

"Courage is not afraid to weep, and she is not afraid to pray, even when she is not sure who she is praying to." ~ J Ruth Gendler

I was really angry and confused when I heard I had to make amends. Why would I have to say I am sorry for anything I have done? It was all necessary. When I shouted, cried and said hateful things, it was because I was unhappy, made unhappy by the addict. I always felt right. I did not feel good, but what could I do? I only knew how to react crazy to the crazy things that were going on. When I thought of apologizing for the way I acted or the things I did, I wondered why I should apologize since the addict caused it.

When I read Step Nine from *The Nar-Anon Twelve Step Program*, I learned I could make amends by changing my behavior. I did not know that! I then understood why reading and using the literature is so important.

I have changed over the last two years. My reactions have changed, my attitude has changed; and I have found how this can affect relationships. Last week, reality was sad because I did not think my husband was there for me when he looked high and unavailable. While that was true, I did not react by telling him what a loser he was. I realized my expectation that he should take me into his arms and make everything all right was not reality.

A day later, he was there. He was attentive, caring, loving, thoughtful, and selfless. I was in heaven. I felt truly loved and cared for. What had changed? Only my attitude was different. I think if I had reacted in my old way, he would not have been able to come to an angry, hateful me and show love. I have changed my view of him. I treat him with respect and love. He is free to show his love for me, not because I expect it, but because he feels it.

Thought for Today: Amends sometimes just happen when I am working the program for me.

"When there are no walls of contempt we can keep giving and receiving forgiveness and understanding." ~ Anonymous

It is easy for me to blame the addicts in my life for all my problems; but blaming them does not improve my situation, and it certainly does not improve theirs. In fact, focusing on the addicts' problems, shortcomings, and behaviors allows me to avoid looking at my own, and prevents me from being a healthier and happier person.

When I put the focus on me, I can make choices that allow me to improve my life. I can say no when the addicts ask for money or my car. I can refuse to participate in a circular argument, by leaving the house. I can stop arguing and call my sponsor. I can even let the addicts have the right to their own opinions. I do not have to pay for collect calls from jail or for attorneys' fees. I do not have to get involved in any rescue missions. I can let the addicts suffer the consequences of their actions.

I do not even need to blame myself. I can forgive myself for past mistakes and do the best that I can just for today. The Nar-Anon program teaches me that I do not need to be perfect. It is a program of progress not perfection.

Thought for Today: Blaming others, including myself, is not progress; it keeps me stuck. When I am blaming, I am not growing and my recovery suffers.

"There are really only two ways to approach life -- as victim or as gallant fighter -- and you must decide if you want to act or react, deal your own cards or play with a stacked deck. And if you don't decide which way to play with life, it always plays with you." ~ Merle Shain

ACCEPTANCE WITH PATIENCE

Patience is the ability to endure waiting or a delay without becoming annoyed or upset. I am living in a dysfunctional situation with an active addict whose lifestyle is unacceptable to me. I find it difficult to have patience with the addict, other family members, friends, or co-workers.

My lack of patience is closely tied to my false sense of control over the lives of those around me. When others are not acting as I wish, according to my timetable, I feel I have lost control. Then I am apt to lose my patience by yelling and verbally abusing those around me, believing this show of emotions will help me gain control.

"Let Go and Let God" is one slogan I use to find comfort when I am faced with a difficult situation and find myself annoyed with someone else. By letting go, I am releasing them to a Higher Power. It allows me to look at them without a sense of responsibility. I find that when I recognize my false sense of control and let go, I can release my expectations and experience patience.

Thought for Today: Patience is not a matter of having things my way. It is a matter of surrendering and accepting what is and trusting in a Higher Power to give me what I need when I need it.

"You cannot create a statue by smashing the marble with a hammer; you also cannot by force of arms release the spirit of the soul." ~ Confucius

I used to feel that forgiveness was something I did for someone else. In reality, I need to forgive for myself. My past perception of forgiveness was to forget the hurtful offense caused by the addict. This exposed me to be hurt again. So what does it mean to say, "I forgive you"? Am I releasing this person from accountability? Am I giving in to smooth things over or to get self-satisfaction?

If I am willing to say, "You don't owe me anything," I can forgive and let go of the resentments that keep me sick. I can get off the roller coaster that tosses me up and down. For without forgiveness, there is hatred, resentment, guilt, and shame. I can forgive the addict and myself.

My resentments will hold me captive as long as I hold onto them. We can compare this to a monkey trap: the monkey sees a piece of candy in a hole, then reaches in and grabs the candy. Holding the candy, the monkey cannot pull his hand out. He is trapped, as I am when there is no forgiveness.

Thought for Today: I forgive as an act of love and not as an act of power, control or judgment over another. Through forgiveness, I free myself by freeing others from judgment and condemnation.

"Inner peace can be reached only when we practice forgiveness. Forgiveness is letting go of the past, and is therefore the means for correcting our misperceptions." ~ Gerald G. Jampolsky

I tried to find a metaphor to describe how I view your life on drugs. It finally came to me as I sat at the ocean's edge. I now realize that you have been riding riptides! For a long, long time, I have not known you or known where you have been. I could hear you but I could not see you. Now that I have this perception of where you have been, I cannot imagine why you have cravings to return to that deadly behavior.

I imagine that a person who swims ashore and survives the deadly sucking-under action of a riptide would count his or her blessings and never return. Yet, in your recovery, you describe a longing to try it again! My anger swells within my throat as I stifle the words on my tongue: "Are you out of your mind?" Of course you are. That is the insanity of addiction speaking. I know what it is, I cannot bear to hear it; but it is your truth and I must accept it.

Those who have ridden riptides are the only ones who know how to survive them. You must find a sponsor to be your lifeguard. I have tried to rescue you from your insanity almost to the point of my own destruction, but have learned through Nar-Anon that I must wait on the shore. I will pray for the serenity I need while waiting for you to stop riding riptides.

Thought for Today: I will not risk being sucked into the riptide of addiction. I will go to a meeting or call a Nar-Anon friend, but I will not ride the riptide with you.

"Acceptance of what is does not mean liking it as it is." ~ Iyanla Van Zant

I am a recovering doormat, and a grateful member of Nar-Anon. I was married to an addict for a number of years and went through more suffering than was necessary because I brought it on myself. I blamed him for all my troubles and refused to take on my own responsibilities just as he refused to take on his. That is why I am here.

At first, I did not want to come to Nar-Anon. When I started attending meetings, I did not even listen. I just sat there and vegetated, but somehow I felt better afterwards, so I kept coming back. I started to read the literature. Finally, I shared and that is when I started to get better. That is when I realized that I was where I needed to be and that others understood what I was feeling. Eventually, I was even able to listen to other people's stories and I started to care about them.

In Nar-Anon, I learned that I am only human. It is comforting to me to realize that the reason I had so many failures in my life is not that I was such a loser, but that I was trying to do things that were physically, mentally and emotionally impossible for mere mortals. When I confine myself to the things I can do and have the right to do, I do just fine. Even if I don't do just fine, I know that it is because I am only human, and therefore not perfect - just like everyone else.

Thought for Today: The greatest gift I have ever received from Nar-Anon is self-respect. I now know that I deserve love, peaceful surroundings, and respect from myself.

"Having committed our lives to change through these Twelve Steps, we recognize that change is a process and that we will use each of these steps again and again. Like the slogan, "Progress not Perfection," we are able to gain a deeper understanding of each step each time we focus on our progress." ~ The Nar-Anon Twelve Step Program

It is easy to let anxiety consume every waking moment when we live with an active addict. I felt a false sense of control and became anxious when I thought the addict in my life was going to use.

I was so consumed with living my life for the addict that I started neglecting my own responsibilities. I began to stay home so that I could watch her every move, as if this was going to fix the situation. I thought I could prevent her from using, spending so much money, or doing more damage to our lives. If I could make her see what she was doing to herself, her family, her life, all our lives, then everything would be okay. We could all live a happy, loving, healthy, stress-free life. It was only when I had reached my breaking point that I realized I could not continue and finally saw that this was insanity.

This monster, addiction, consumed my every thought, action, and emotion to the point where I became physically, mentally, and emotionally ill. I had to stop it now! I learned to let go. I realized I had no other choice. I finally got it! I have no control over the addict and I never did or will.

Thought for Today: We are free to make our own choices, as the addicts are free to make theirs. We cannot control another and trying to do so will only bring anxiety.

"We must cultivate our garden." ~ Voltaire

The Nar-Anon program has changed my world. Well really, the world has not changed; it is my thinking that has changed. I have learned to look at how and why I think certain ways. I have also learned that there is more than one meaning to the same word. I can now view situations and see the different ways that I can react to them. This way of living gives me choices. I do not have to react as I have always done in the past. Today, I have found a new way to look at life and cope with my problems.

I can remember in childish games, it meant you lost if you surrendered. I grew up feeling that surrender was not a way to go. However, since I have been attending Nar-Anon meetings, I have discovered surrender can have a completely different meaning. Today, I can surrender my will to my Higher Power. That does not mean I have lost. It means relinquishing control and putting my Higher Power in charge. I have determined I cannot do it myself but that does not mean that I am quitting. I am making a decision to turn my will over to the care of a Power greater than me, the God of my understanding.

Thought for Today: When I feel overwhelmed and unable to cope with my problems, I can surrender and let the God of my understanding take control. This is not the act of a quitter; it is an act of faith.

"The world we have created is a product of our thinking; it cannot be changed without changing our thinking." ~ Albert Einstein

In my wallet, I have a pair of golden earrings. They are small and not of much value. I keep them there hoping that one day I can give them back to the owner, my daughter, when she is clean and on the right path. I have had them in my wallet for over a year now. I wonder if some day I will be able to take them out of my wallet. I hope so. Since coming to Nar-Anon, I am not as obsessive with my thoughts about my daughter's addiction as I was one year ago, but I still think of her and want the daughter I used to know back in my life.

One day my daughter called me asking for a blanket. I thought, "Why not?" Even if she has it only for a night or two before it is stolen by some other addict that is okay. While buying the blanket, I encouraged her to get some help. I told her that I had long ago given up trying to understand why she was using drugs, and that I could not believe she had been living on the streets for over a year already. She replied she did not need help but wanted to come back home. While it broke my heart, I told her I could not allow her to come home until she gets some help. I was only able to set this boundary because of what I have learned in Nar-Anon. Before she left the car, she wanted to know if I still had the earrings. I drove off certain I had made the right decision. I am okay, although I miss my daughter very much.

Thought for Today: I am learning the message of Nar-Anon that I must go on with my life. Nar-Anon teaches me I have to make my own choices and make my own decisions. I am the one responsible for the consequences.

"You must do the thing you think you cannot do." ~ Eleanor Roosevelt

Someone recently shared at a meeting that he had started coming to Nar-Anon because he was tired of feeling bad. I remember, some time ago, when I was sick and tired of feeling sick and tired. I wanted my pain to cease. I wanted to get on with my life. I wanted to be strong for those around me who I love. To accomplish this, I started to work the Nar-Anon program, stopped thinking about the addict and began to think about myself. For some who have not experienced addiction in their lives, this may sound selfish. That is why our meetings are a safe place to be. We share these experiences with others who are going through the same situations we are, and we know that they will understand.

I can share the painful things I am going through with my sponsor, and then share my experience, strength and hope at my meetings. Knowing that I have a process to deal with my pain gives me a calm feeling. I know that total absence of this pain would be ideal but not realistic. I need to find serenity in my life by accepting the things I cannot change. This is what I have learned in my meetings. This is not to say that my life will be easy and pain free. Indeed, this process will probably take some time and much effort. The slogan "Easy Does It" teaches me patience.

Thought for Today: I will keep the focus on me and live my life by having faith in my Higher Power. I will have peace and serenity knowing that God is in control. I will be grateful for all the things I have in my life today, knowing that gratitude changes attitude.

"Progress is impossible without change, and those who cannot change their minds cannot change anything." ~ George Bernard Shaw

The other day I was speaking with a friend about addiction. He asked me if I believed in a Higher Power. I replied that I did. I also stated that since addiction came into my life, I have become closer to my Higher Power than ever before. I said that addiction is too big for just me to handle. I had tried for six years to deal with my son's addiction and when I could not conquer it, I sought help. I had reached my bottom and I wanted to hurt no longer.

Nar-Anon was the help I needed, and I believe God pointed me in the right direction. Now I am no longer alone. In one meeting, a member was so distraught over her son's actions that she broke down while telling us about his latest episodes of destructive behavior. She specifically stated that she waited until she came to the meeting to let it all out, as we would understand what she was experiencing. This is what I mean when I say I am no longer alone.

By attending Nar-Anon meetings, I have learned to see my Higher Power in every fellow member. I have found a better way to live by reading Nar-Anon literature, listening to members share at meetings, working with a sponsor who has helped me to better understand the Nar-Anon program and with whom I can confide my suffering, tell my secrets, and hear comforting words.

Thought for Today: Because I am no longer alone, I am better able to handle the hurt and all that goes along with it.

"We do not so much need the help of our friends as the confidence of their help in need." ~ Epicurus

Once upon a time, there was a desert nomad with a camel. When night fell, the nomad pitched his tent near an oasis, tied his camel to a stake and snuggled down. After a few hours, the camel poked his head into the tent. "Excuse me, Master," he said, "but I am so cold out here. May I please put my head into your tent to keep it warm?" The nomad, tired but agreeable, said, "Yes, but only your head. There is barely enough room for me in here." The nomad returned to sleep. Another hour passed and the camel woke him up again. "Oh, Master, my front legs are so cold. Please, may I put them into your tent?" the camel pleaded. The nomad, exhausted and annoyed, said, "Yes, but that is all! No more! I am pushed against the side of the tent already." The nomad yawned and returned to sleep. An hour later, the camel woke him once more: "Master, my hump is so cold. I can't stop shivering. May I bring in my hump?" he begged. "For God's sake!" cried the nomad. "Bring in your blasted hump! Let me sleep! I cannot bear these constant awakenings." He grabbed his blanket, rolled over and returned to sleep.

A few hours later, the nomad awoke and was freezing. He was outside of his tent and the camel was completely inside of it, toasty and warm. I am that nomad, the tent is my recovery, and the camel is my disease. The moment I begin to obsess about the addict, I am letting in the head of my disease. When I tell the addict how to run his life, I am letting in the front legs of the disease. When I do things for the addict that he can do for himself, I am letting in the hump of my disease.

Thought for Today: Now I know if I do not draw my boundaries tightly and keep my disease firmly outside the tent of my recovery, I may be on the way to relapse.

"Good fences make good neighbors." ~ Robert Frost

I have wondered if a mother bear mourns as she chases her cubs up a tree on her last day as a provider for them. After loving them, fighting for their survival and teaching them survival skills, their mother has disappeared and they are left on their own. I had to acknowledge that my days of instruction had ended when the addict was a young teen, but I am not sure that I had taught him all he needs to survive in the world.

I mourned for the loss of my parenting role as the addict and I each moved in our own directions. Nar-Anon has taught me the importance of my Higher Power in the process of letting go of my parenting job. I left the addict on the streets, and when I heard from him or saw him, I congratulated him on the baby steps he took toward his survival. As he went in and out of recovery, I maintained my distance, looking to the mother bear's brevity.

Perhaps the mother bear mourns like me. Her animal instinct protects her from suffering as she walks away from her cubs. As she continues her own survival, however, she must have no thoughts of taking care of her mature cubs any longer. To do so would put her life in jeopardy.

Thought for Today: I now take care of my own needs and myself. As I do so, the addict can learn silently as he is ready. He has been given my example and the example of others who his Higher Power has sent into his life. I hope his self-respect is coming from his accomplishments of independent daily living. I know that my serenity is coming from my own joy of living.

"Selfishness is not living as one wishes to live; it is asking others to live as one wishes to live. And unselfishness is letting other people's lives alone, not interfering with them. Selfishness always aims at uniformity of type. Unselfishness recognizes infinite variety of type as a delightful thing, accepts it, acquiesces in it, enjoys it." ~ Oscar Wilde

When I first came to Nar-Anon, I spent most of my time thinking and worrying about the addict. At particularly troubling times, I decided to say a new prayer I had learned called the Serenity Prayer. I would say it over and over, not knowing what else to do. I could not figure out what things I could change, and what things I could not change. One day at a meeting, a fellow member said that if she drew a circle around her feet, the things she could change were inside that circle and everything outside that circle were the things she could not change. It was a relief to realize that I do not have to carry other people on my back that each one of them has his own choices to make and his own responsibility to take.

I have been learning to let go of trying to change others and have found a place of serenity inside myself. That place is precious to me and staying serene is now a top priority in my life.

Thought for Today: My recovery is very important to me. I will look to myself for the changes I can make that will promote my growth in Nar-Anon.

"When we create peace and harmony and balance in our minds, we will find it in our lives." ~ Louise Hay

I cannot imagine what would have happened if I had come to a Nar-Anon meeting and no one was there to help me. Not only are the meetings there to give me experience, strength and hope and to help me through my difficult situations, but they are there for me to help others when they are hurting. This cannot happen if I stop working the program and stop attending meetings. So many people have come into my group and then never came back, or left after their crisis passed.

Without Nar-Anon members who continue with their program even when times are good, there would be no meetings. One of the best feelings I have experienced is helping another person through a crisis, or knowing that they appreciate the fact that I was there to listen. The help and support of a sponsor or other member who is there for me when I am hurting is immeasurable. I remember these things and choose to be there to greet new members, and to remember what it was like when I first came into these rooms.

Thought for Today: That is what Nar-Anon is all about – one person helping another, giving back what was so freely given to us. In order to keep what we have, we must give it away.

"Life is easy to chronicle, but bewildering to practice." ~ Louise Erdrich

The topic of our meeting last night was "advice." I have been in the Nar-Anon program for several years and the word "advice" reminds me of conversations with the addict in my life. He considers my advice to be lecturing. I could see others nodding in agreement when I shared about that. The addict and I are at a point in our recovery where I have asked him to let me know when he feels I am lecturing him so I can continue to work on that character defect.

I know what I have to do, but I also know that I can allow myself the time to be able to do it. I have no magic answers. I cannot let go of old habits in an instant no matter how much I wish I could. The Twelve Steps are there for me when I am ready to take them. I cannot force them to take me. I accept that one day I will be ready to work each step, and that my Higher Power will be right there with me. I am grateful that my program helps me to realize this.

Thought for Today: I do not have all the answers and that is okay. Today I will work my program and only when asked will I offer my opinions and suggestions. I do not want to fall into my old habit of lecturing.

"Advice is seldom welcome, and those who need it the most, like it the least." ~ Lord Chesterfield

I see Step Ten as a tool to use daily to help me keep the benefits of my recovery. It allows me to keep my life free of the emotional garbage and enjoy the treasures. When I look at my life daily, I admit I am not perfect, I am reminded of my humanity, and I let go of the guilt of my mistakes so I can enjoy my accomplishments. I had been attending Nar-Anon for many years before I finally experienced peace and serenity, and now I want to maintain it.

During the early years of my recovery, I repeated Step One often. I was still focusing on the addict. When I finally surrendered and accepted my powerlessness over the addict, I began to experience my own recovery. I am now able to recognize my own insanity and turn to my Higher Power for help. I received the courage to take my own inventory and I saw more improvements in my life as I worked on my shortcomings and character defects. I started dealing with the junk and clutter of my past, fixing it, or letting it go.

Step Ten is important because I do not want my life to fill-up with that junk again. I believe if I take a few minutes every day to look at my activities, good and bad, I can either make amends or enjoy them or let them go. I do not have to punish myself with obsessive worry. Daily inventory allows me to free myself from a false sense of guilt and maintain the progress I have made. I do not have to hang onto the rubbish of the past, even for one day. I can deal with it daily and maintain my peace and serenity.

Thought for Today: I will deal with my mistakes and achievements daily. I will make amends immediately, where necessary, and enjoy my accomplishments. In this way, I will maintain my peace and serenity.

"Nothing is a waste of time if you use the experience wisely." ~ *Auguste Rodin*

One of the three destructive forces that can destroy the group is gossip. When I first came to Nar-Anon, I was in fear of being judged. I had isolated myself from my family and friends, and I was ashamed to admit that there was a problem in my family. I did not want to be the center of discussion, and I certainly did not want my family to think of me as the black sheep with the loser relationship.

To this day, I believe that fear was justified because my family and friends are not in recovery. They do not understand that addiction is a disease. They believe that addiction is a moral issue, which in turn causes them to react in a negative manner. Their answer to the problem is simple – get rid of the addict, and all will be well. However, the truth is I also suffer from the effects of addiction, because I am replaying sick co-dependent behaviors that I learned from my family. I was trying to correct my sick dysfunctional relationships from my past while in my current relationships.

If it was not for the comfort level I found in Nar-Anon, that feeling of safety and non-judgment, I would not have continued to go to meetings, and I would not have gotten better. When I indulge in gossip, I remember that gossip is the by-product of low self-esteem. It is something I do to make myself feel better than others. I stop focusing on my own recovery and begin to judge others.

Thought for Today: I cannot recover from the disease of addiction when I am focusing on and judging others. I will not gossip and judge but keep the focus on me so I can experience the gifts of recovery.

"Abandoning gossip, he abstains from gossip; he speaks at the right time, speaks what is fact, speaks on what is good, speaks on the Dhamma and the Discipline; at the right time he speaks such words as are worth recording, reasonable, moderate, and beneficial." ~ Majjhima-Nikaya

A member of another twelve step program who is a newcomer employs my son. Because he was a financial success I mistakenly had a higher opinion of him than I would have for an addict who has lost it all. He came into my life at a time when I was establishing strong boundaries for myself and was reclaiming my own life. I was learning to keep the focus on me. I was making decisions regarding the behaviors I would not tolerate from the addicts in my life.

I allowed my son's boss to take me for a two-hour ride and found myself defending my principles! I had only known him a week, yet he was telling me what to do and because of my insecurities, I was accepting his advice. Finally, when he said that I was responsible for my son's recovery, the red light came on. I know that I didn't cause and can't control or cure the disease of addiction. I am responsible for my own recovery. My program tells me that I cannot control the behavior of others.

The Nar-Anon program and the Twelve Steps of Nar-Anon work! I can see my growth as a result of practicing this program. I am not the same person who walked into these rooms four years ago. The doormat is now at the door. Today I have the wisdom to let people and their advice in or keep them out. It is my choice. Neither guilt nor resentment rule over the relationships I have today. It took someone trying to lay a guilt trip on me to remind me that I am only responsible for my own recovery.

Thought for Today: I am thankful for all the people in the Nar-Anon program and most thankful to my Higher Power for the growth and recovery that I am experiencing today.

"Never mistake knowledge for wisdom. One helps you make a living, the other helps you make a life." ~ Sandra Carey

I feel as though I have been dabbling in my recovery. I have let the addict go, but have I done it with love? I feel calm, serene even, over longer and longer passages of time. I am not calling the addict nor trying to make up with the addict. I am not obsessing about the addict, but have I detached with love? I wonder if the nasty kernels of my anger are going to show themselves at the least desirable time, leaving me feeling crazy and out of control. I am suspicious of myself.

I am learning that I can take my inventory anytime I need to. It has been suggested that there are three types of inventories I can use:

1) Spot Check – Stopping momentarily each day to assess my attitude and behavior.
2) Daily Inventory – Stopping at the end of the day and reviewing what happened and how I reacted.
3) Long-Term Periodic Inventory – Special days I set aside for reflection on my life. Usually done in a special place such as a retreat.

By studying Nar-Anon literature, I am learning that I can do what I need to do. I have this right. I do not need to always look after someone else. I can focus on what I need. I can decide what is best for me at the time. If I want and need to reach out, I have that choice when I feel it is the right time for me to do so. I can decide I have choices and I like it.

Thought for Today: I am realizing that when I practice my program I remain serene.

"The greatest of faults, I should say, is to be conscious of none." ~ Thomas Carlyle

I like to give people the benefit of the doubt. I guess that is why it was so easy to allow my addicted loved one to continue to lie to me. Because I was lied to so many times, I felt that I was beginning to lose my ability to trust. My denial of the situation only made things worse and I was turning into a bitter and distrusting person. Because I distrusted the addict, I was always wondering in the back of my mind if people were telling me the truth or if they were taking advantage of me.

Through the Nar-Anon program, my trust of others returned. By detaching from the addict's behavior, I was able to learn to trust again. The support, unconditional love and friendship that I have received from my fellow Nar-Anon members give me the ability to trust again, including the addict. Of course, any change takes time, and I did not develop my sense of trust overnight. However, I was able to look past the lies that the addict was telling and realize that he was allowing himself to remain sick. I had to wonder if my continued resentment and lack of trust meant that I was as sick as the addict was.

It feels good to be able to trust again. I do not have to be thinking in the back of my mind that someone is trying to take advantage of my trusting nature. I do not have to go back to my old sick way of thinking. I can choose to trust and feel good again.

Thought for Today: When I remember the saying "In God We Trust," I think about the meaning of that phrase. I can trust my Higher Power to guide me and keep me at peace.

"I will look to this day with wonder and trust. Everything is okay. I am in the care of a power greater." ~ Each Day a New Beginning – Daily Meditations for Women

At the beginning of every meeting our chairperson reads, "Anything you hear tonight is strictly our own opinions. .....If a member says something you cannot accept, remember they are merely speaking from their own experiences. They are not speaking for Nar-Anon. When you leave our meeting, take home those thoughts that will be most helpful to you, forget those you feel will not be helpful, and keep coming back."

Tradition Six states that we should not endorse any outside enterprise. Tradition Ten builds on and confirms this concept of autonomy. Autonomy is a "personal independence and the capacity to make moral decisions and act on them." In order for this personal independence to thrive, Tradition Ten states that Nar-Anon should not take a position on any public issues. If we were to become involved in an outside issue, we could bring the Nar-Anon program into the public eye, together with any controversy surrounding that issue. This may alienate people who need our help.

Because our fellowship is made up of thousands of people, who represent all races and cultures, taking a position on a public or political manner could certainly divide our fellowship. Nar-Anon's primary purpose of providing aid to the families and friends of addicts could be jeopardized by taking such a stand.

Thought for Today: Tradition Ten allows me to have a relationship with someone who has different beliefs than my own. It even allows me to give and get support from people whose personal politics may appall me. In Nar-Anon, this aspect of their lives is not important. We are all here for recovery from the effects of another's addiction. It is unimportant that one member voted for and another voted against the same drug control proposal. Because of the Tenth Tradition, these issues are not part of our recovery program.

"Patterning your life around other's opinions is nothing more than slavery." ~ Lawana Blackwell

One day during our addicted son's early recovery, I found a sprouting onion in the pantry. I was going to throw it away when he stopped me, saying he wanted to plant it. This surprised me but I gave him the onion. He planted it outside and faithfully watered it. I shared this in a meeting because it was not typical behavior, even before his drug use.

A Nar-Anon friend suggested it might show a feeling of hope for himself and his new growth in recovery. Her words also gave me hope. He moved away before the stalks had grown much but I continued to water it. The stalks grew tall and sturdy and I was amazed when, at their tips, a cluster of buds formed. One day the buds bloomed into tiny, beautiful white flowers.

I took a photo of the white clusters and look at it often. It reminds me of my own wonderful, life-changing growth in Nar-Anon. My recovery was slow in the beginning and, at times, I felt I was not growing at all, but I kept coming back. To my amazement, I kept growing.

Thought for Today: Recovery and growth did not happen overnight. We would like quick fixes when we first come to Nar-Anon. Instead, we learn to release the addict and grasp our own recovery, not the addict's. We can only change ourselves.

"Bigness comes from doing many small things well. Individually, they are not very dramatic transactions. Together, though, they add up." ~ Edward S. Finkelstein

My adult son was college educated, had a good job, a car, and his own apartment. Due to his addiction, he lost everything and was forced to live on the streets where he witnessed some really bad situations. He encountered a young, homeless girl, who was also an addict, suffering a miscarriage in a public washroom. She begged him to help her. He did what he could but both she and the baby died. This lifestyle was very different from how he was raised. He grew up in a sheltered, although average suburban environment, where he was shielded from this type of reality.

Later he was arrested, and spent a month in jail. He was then sentenced to a year in drug rehab. The doctors, who examined my son, before he was admitted to the treatment center, diagnosed him with Post Traumatic Stress Disorder (PTSD), similar to the shell shock of soldiers and others who have gone through horrifying events. He is now seeing a psychologist for the PTSD that he incurred while he lived on the streets.

It hurts me so much to see the addict suffer, but this seemingly cruel and harsh experience may have actually been a lifesaver for the addict and to everyone who loves him. I learned in my Nar-Anon program, that I enable because I do not want to see my addicted love one suffer. I cannot bear to see him in pain so I try to fix everything. In doing so, I am standing in the way of those experiences that may be what the addict needs to find the courage to change.

Thought for Today: My thoughts and prayers are with everyone who is struggling with similar issues and with their own loved ones, whether they are parents, spouses, children, or friends. You are not alone but among true friends who understand as few others can.

"Change is the constant, the signal for rebirth, the egg of the phoenix." ~ *Christina Baldwin*

Violence comes in many forms: physical, verbal and mental abuse and ugly stares full of hate. I have experienced them all. I remember being pushed, hollered at, and pinched by my grandfather who was partially responsible for raising me. He was an alcoholic who was drunk most of the time. His violence extended to sexually abusing us as young children. When my father died, my mother took her grief out on me. She expected me to be her number one assistant because she was left to raise four children. Later, I married a man who was not only violent but also an addict.

I believe those years spent experiencing violence in its various forms gave me an inner strength to carry on in this life. I know I no longer need to allow or tolerate abuse from others. I know because I deserve better treatment. I also gained awareness and sensitivity towards the hurts of others. I am able to listen, learn and guide without judgment. Sharing with someone in Nar-Anon I can trust is a powerful healing tool. With my newfound hope and support, I feel free and able to continue on with my life. I learned in Nar-Anon that I have the power to make my own choices for a healthier and better way of life.

Thought for Today: No one deserves to be abused; we all deserve to be safe. With the help of my Higher Power, I will no longer continue to act like a victim. I will choose to get help and recovery from past abuse and make a better life for myself. I will help others do the same.

"Domestic violence should not happen to anybody. Ever. Period. But it does - and when it does there is help." ~ Domestic Violence Handbook

I have a problem with living in the here and now, just for today. It took me a long time but I finally realized that I could not cure my addicted husband and I separated from him. With four small children, I felt that it was okay for other members of the fellowship to live one day at a time, but I had to think of the future of my kids. What if they blame me for their father's drug use just as he does? What if they become addicts themselves? Could I be Mommy and Daddy for them? I read something recently that finally changed my mind:

> "As we focus on the present moment, we live it deeper, and we derive a satisfaction that we did not know when we were regretting the past and worrying about the future. Whatever happens now is all I can manage and all I need." ~ _Food for Thought_ by Elisabeth L.

Sure, I still worry once in awhile, but that is fine as long as I do not let it consume me. Now I ask myself, "Are my children happy today? Is there anything I can do to make this day a better memory for them?"

I think the reason I can do this is that I am finally at peace with where I am now and who I am. I am grateful for today, for right now.

Thought for Today: I will live in the here and now. I cannot see the future and I may glance back at the past, but I will not stare.

"Finish each day and be done with it. You have done what you could. Some blunders and absurdities no doubt crept in; forget them as soon as you can. Tomorrow is a new day; begin it well and serenely and with too high a spirit to be encumbered with your old nonsense." ~ Ralph Waldo Emerson

Helping is important to me. It was something I was taught to do. I felt I was obligated to help those I love. I became terribly confused about helping before I started attending Nar-Anon. It took time and much introspection to realize that I am supposed to help people in ways that demonstrate my love for them and are not harmful or demanding of something in return. In Nar-Anon, I am learning a new way of helping, a way that I hope will move my loved ones towards courage, independence, a full life, freedom, and joy.

What I used to think of as helping was really interfering or enabling. When I think of helping someone today, first I stop and think:

Why am I helping?
Who am I helping?
Is this really help?
Did they ask for my help?

I also ask myself if the help I am offering is similar to a pair of cement shoes that drags them down and keeps them there, or is my help going to be more like a spring breeze that gently provides a lift to a child's kite.

In Nar-Anon, I am learning I play a role in the family disease of addiction and I do have options. When I am clear about the part I play, I can stop and look at what I am doing before I act and choose my behavior. I now know that when I feel resentment or I am expecting a change as the result of my helping, then it is enabling so I do not have to do it. I only prolong the addict's struggle when I meddle.

Thought for Today: Helping others build personal strength and independence is giving someone a helping hand. Helping them avoid the consequences of their actions or doing for them what they can do for themselves, is giving them a permanent crutch.

"We can stand back, without losing our love and compassion for them and 'Not Do.' It's OK, it doesn't cause a dramatic change, it didn't change when we 'Did' either." ~ The Nar-Anon Twelve Step Program

No matter what kind of group I joined, I always felt like an outsider. I did not feel as though I belonged. That all changed when I found Nar-Anon. I felt it at my first meeting; I had found a second family! I fit in here in these rooms. I could talk about my son's addiction without feeling ashamed. My group understands how I feel, and I do not feel so alone. It is okay for me to be me. It is wonderful to be safe and have Nar-Anon friends I can call because they understand my feelings of going crazy. I am comfortable getting up in front of my Nar-Anon group because I know I am accepted. I am an equal. I do not feel judged or odd. I can sense the unconditional love of the Nar-Anon fellowship. I can experience the healing.

I was having a rough time and had stopped attending meetings for several weeks. When I came back, I was welcomed. No one asked, "Where were you?" I was accepted, hugged and told it was good to see me back. My Nar-Anon group is my family of choice and I am so grateful to belong.

This experience led me to a newfound sense of confidence. This sense of confidence helps me relate to others outside my Nar-Anon program. Nar-Anon has given me back my self-assurance and self-esteem. I know that today, with the help of my Higher Power, I can carry on with my life whether my son is using or not. My life is mine again and it has meaning.

Thought for Today: The unconditional love I receive from Nar-Anon is similar to medicine. It protects and soothes the pain and hurt I have suffered because of addiction, so the healing process of recovery can begin.

"If we make our goal to live a life of compassion and unconditional love, then the world will indeed become a garden where all kinds of flowers can bloom and grow." ~ Elisabeth Kübler-Ross

I am sitting here in a Nar-Anon meeting by myself, not feeling alone. I have checked the literature supply, written a notice for the local newspaper, read the thought for the day, and read part of <u>A Guide for the Family of the Addict and Drug Abuser</u>. I am so grateful to the people that were here when I needed them; so starting a group is one of the ways I can give back.

I remember my old behavior and habits. My busy mind was always going a hundred miles an hour. I wondered where the kids were, if they went to school, if they were fighting, if my husband was using, did he sneak home, were the kids high, would their dad catch them using, what did they do, or say, and what would happen tomorrow? Today in Nar-Anon, my mind moves in one direction at a comfortable pace, one day at a time.

It is such a relief to know that I do not have to make decisions for others. I am not responsible for their actions, or whether they choose to use or stay clean. Sometimes, I think that it is easy for me to say that since my family members are all clean. Then I would start to wonder how I would handle it if that were not the case. A dear friend reminded me "A day at a time – don't worry about what may happen tomorrow, because those worries may never come to be."

Thought for Today: I like myself. Today I can be of service in Nar-Anon and not take charge. Today I can find something to be grateful for in my life. Today I love my husband and my children. Today I believe in a Power greater than myself, and without this program, I would not be where I am. Through total faith, I became ready to let these changes happen within me.

"It is only possible to live happily ever after on a day-to-day basis." ~ Margaret Bonnano

The first time I heard about self-care was in a Nar-Anon meeting. I never knew what it meant to take care of myself. At home, I was taught to put everyone else first, especially my younger siblings. It was my responsibility to care for them. I love what Nar-Anon is teaching me about self-care. Self-care today means to care for myself first. When I do that, I become a better person and I have more energy to be available to others.

I thought my responsibility was to take care of my ex-husband. Through Nar-Anon, I learned that I was not allowing my ex-husband to be responsible for taking care of himself. In the meantime, my five-year-old son was caring for himself. It was not until one of his teachers pulled me to the side to let me know of my neglect that I saw the truth. That is when I sought help.

A professional told me about Nar-Anon. I called him back later and thanked him. I began to take care of my son and myself. Now eleven years later, another son and a fiancé, things are a lot different. I continue to take care of myself, even when it becomes challenging.

Thought for Today: Now when I come home from work, I go to my room and unwind, instead of going straight to the kitchen. When I wake up in the morning, I talk to my Higher Power first before I talk to anyone. I exercise and read my literature daily.

"If I must love my neighbor as myself, it is at least as fair to love myself as my neighbor." ~ Nicholas de Chamfort

I have learned from Nar-Anon that there are several ways to keep myself encouraged while living with an addict. When I go to meetings, read literature, work the steps, get a sponsor, and trust a Higher Power, I am choosing to take care of myself.

But what about the addict? If the addict chooses not to be in a program, I feel there is no one to encourage him except me. I know there is nothing I can do to change the addict, or to make him want to change, but I can constructively encourage him in little ways:

- I can stop trying to control or run his life. Let him choose, fall, fail, and learn on his own. Saving him from the consequences may mean that it takes longer for him to reach his bottom and get help.
- I can trust in him and believe that he can succeed in recovery. This does not mean I have to trust him or believe what he says. My positive attitude and energy will rub off on him.
- I keep expectations low. Instead of a high level of expectation, I note progress from where he was to where he is, not where I think he should be.
- I give verbal reinforcement for accomplishments, progress and growth. I show appreciation for the good things even if it is expected or seems insignificant.
- I trust in a Higher Power to take care of the addict and thereby not interfere with the working out of the addict's process.

Thought for Today: By practicing these few ways to encourage the addict, I stay out of the way of the addict's recovery and I stay in peace and serenity by ridding myself of the responsibility I might have mistakenly taken on to try to get and keep the addict clean.

"Love and let be." ~ *Nar-Anon Blue Booklet*

This is a hypothetical monologue that those of us recovering from the effects of addiction might have:

Who is this "me?" "Me" is who takes care of "them." "Me" is who will be so much better, once "they" are better. Who has time for "me" when there is so much that "they" need to have done? "They" don't appreciate "me"; "they" don't see all the good "I" am doing for "them." "I" know what "they" need, if only "they" would listen. "They" think "they" can take care of themselves, but where would "they" be without "me?" "They" keep making the same mistakes and "I" have to clean up the mess. "I" don't make mistakes; "I" am too busy with "their" mistakes. "They" will listen; "I" will make them. "I" don't give up; "I" will find a way to make "them" better. The pain will go away, then "I" will not be so scared all of the time. "They" will see how much "I" love "them," how much "I" have sacrificed for "them." Then "they" will make "me" happy, and we will all be better.

Thought for Today: We may think it is easier to be a victim of other people's behavior than to take responsibility for our own lives. Nar-Anon puts the focus on us and takes it away from the addict(s) in our lives. It is scary to look inside ourselves and take responsibility for what we think and feel. Nar-Anon gives us a safe environment to take those looks, and a loving program to help us grow.

"Everyone thinks of changing the world, but no one thinks of changing himself." ~ Leo Tolstoy

Time in the Nar-Anon program gave me a false sense of security. Everyone told me what a great program I was working. I had accepted that I could not change my husband, but I still wanted to help. I still thought that I could be an integral part of the addict's recovery. I started out small, a little help here, and a little help there, but I had my program behind me. I felt, "This time I'm okay, I know what I am doing, and I can handle it. This time is different."

One evening I called home and the addict answered the phone. I knew within a few minutes that he had been using. I left work early and went home immediately to confront him. The confrontation soon became mutually physical. The addict attempted to leave by taking my car and I called the police. When the police arrived, we told our stories and we were both taken to jail.

At that time, I had been in the program a year and thought I had my reactions under control. I could have used any one of the many tools I learned in the program to avoid these consequences. I had a lot of time to think that night. I took what I believe was my first honest Step Ten; accepting that I was in that cell, not because of the addict, who was in the cell next to me, but because of my own insane actions and reactions. I was responsible for me.

Thought for Today: Recovery is a process. I may never be all better. I can learn to grow every day if I keep an honest, open and willing mind to new ways of doing things.

"Help them to take failure, not as a measure of their worth, but as a chance for a new start." ~ Book of Common Prayer

Many of the Nar-Anon meetings I attend close with the Serenity Prayer and a few words of encouragement with the collective suggestion: "Keep coming back; it works, if you work it, so work it, you're worth it."

Keep coming back. This was the only thing that I remember hearing at my first meeting. Initially, coming back to Nar-Anon meetings for me was not a choice I wanted to make. I came because I wanted to change my husband who is the addict in my life. One idea that I neither like nor accepted right away was that I had to change myself. I felt I had no character defects and I definitely was not the problem. I listened at meetings and to my surprise, I kept learning. By listening to other members share their experience, strength and hope, I learned two things. I was not alone and I was not without character defects.

I now know that I can go to meetings and share the anger and rage I feel. The people in these rooms understand. They do not judge me. For the first time, I have permission to be angry and I do not need to hide or feel ashamed. Once the anger has passed, I can begin to look at the one thing I can change: me. In Nar-Anon, I can heal and recover if I keep coming back and work it, because I am worth it.

Thought for Today: I know that I am not alone; I have the support of the Nar-Anon fellowship. All I need to do is to keep coming back.

"Since there is no 'arrival', no magical day on which we suddenly achieve serenity and live on forever free of stress or strain, most of us eventually learn to be patient. We find that we can trust the process of recovery to move us ever forward, even if it sometimes feels as if we're moving backwards." ~ How Al-Anon Works

301

At my first Nar-Anon meeting, people referred to "detachment." I remember how foreign that word sounded to me. I remember thinking, "How do I do that?" I left the meeting knowing that I definitely needed to find out more about detachment. I was convinced it could be the answer I had been looking for!

I began to read about detachment. At first, it sounded harsh. I am supposed to let her take care of herself. Just let the addict fall on her face? She needed me so desperately, how could I just stop, and let her take care of her own problems. She will surely crash! How can I do this? All of these panic questions popped into my head.

Now I see that I was just as sick as she was. My sickness was helping her and living for her, while I was neglecting my own life in all her drama. I was not helping her; I was stopping her from seeing there was a problem and trying to fix it on her own. I was playing God trying to bring about the outcome I wanted, not necessarily what she needed.

Since then, I have learned to detach, and I am living a much calmer existence. I tell myself daily to not get plugged into her drama. I have set some boundaries and she is responding to them. She is still in denial that there is a drug problem, but I have hope she will some day see. It is not my responsibility to play God with another's life.

Thought for Today: The addict has to take care of his or her own life struggles, as we have to take care of our own lives. They may not see there is a problem if they never have to experience it. It is my responsibility to take care of me and my life. By detaching, I can allow this to happen with love.

"Do not take life too seriously; you will never get out of it alive." ~ Elbert Hubbard

The Nar-Anon shared experience has assisted me in healing my weak points and recognizing my assets. Working Step Four is difficult, but necessary, in this evolving process.

My character defects have held me in bondage for too long. I accepted bad behavior from people who I love because I was unable to set appropriate boundaries. I chose the victim role of the shame-blame game. It was exhausting and drained my energy. I became ready for a change. This meant I had to start looking at myself for answers. It was time to get off the pity pot and stop asking "why me?"

My past errors in judgment do not define me. They are part of my learning process. My guilt and shame can only hold me back if I allow it. These feelings cannot control or haunt me as long as I use the honesty tool of recovery. I now have the courage to look at my weaknesses, talk about them, and strengthen them. My energy is being restored. My character defects are evolving into personality assets. A healthy outlook is now as much a part of me as the painful past.

I am learning how to balance my life with a new vision. Life is a tapestry of many threads. They complete a life portrait that is all me! I recognize my gifts. I am okay! God did a good job. I am my own masterpiece. I feel whole again – almost. Well, it is a process.

Thought for Today: Recovery is about growing up and now is a good time to get started.

"If you do not ask yourself what it is you know, you will go on listening to others and change will not come because you will not hear your own truth." ~ Saint Bartholomew

Before Nar-Anon, I was always hiding my innermost thoughts. I did not want to bring them to the surface. Revealing my thoughts to others made them seem trivial. However, the pain I was feeling was real, and the emotional wounds that caused that pain were deep. Hiding my thoughts and feelings only increased the pain I felt and did nothing to help me heal and recover.

When I first came to the rooms of Nar-Anon, I did very little sharing. Instead, I just listened. As I heard the other members share their similar problems with their addicted family members, my courage grew, and I felt safe. The first time I did open up, it was clear that verbalizing my fears, anxieties and problems helped me. In that short five-minute share, I felt as though a five-pound weight had been lifted from my shoulders. I felt that others understood my problems. Sometimes I still get scared and my rambling thoughts are not always coherent, but the other members are patient and listen. After so many years of not communicating, I need more practice because it is difficult for me to even speak my thoughts. When I am having a hard time, I write them down first.

My life was unmanageable before I came to Nar-Anon. I have a tendency to forget what is good and positive around me. When this happens, I go to a meeting and find the loving support of the fellowship.

Thought for Today: Words of wisdom are not my forte, but I have found the healing effect of sharing my concerns with others. The times I most want to hide out with my problems are the times I most need to reach out to others.

"You get to the point where your demons, which are terrifying, grow smaller and smaller and you get bigger and bigger." ~ August Wilson

Ever since I heard the words, "I am a drug addict, and I need help," my life has changed dramatically. I never would have thought that the man I married, my best friend and soul mate, would have such a dark secret. When I entered my first Nar-Anon meeting three days later, I was full of bitterness and anger. I felt like such a victim and was desperately searching for answers to questions about my husband's disease. I wanted to learn everything I could about addiction. Little did I know that I would learn about the most important person in my life, me. Nar-Anon taught me to re-evaluate the person I am. I began to feel more comfortable attending meetings, especially as I got to know the people in these rooms. I felt as though I finally had a safe place where I could share my deepest feelings and get the love and support that I needed; where I could explore myself and learn to live a better life.

One day at a meeting, I shared that I was struggling with trust. I had completely lost all trust in my husband. A fellow member stated that sometime ago he had the same problem. He said that he solved it by thinking that his positive thoughts had as much chance of coming true, as did his worst-case scenario. I understood his message and started focusing on the positive side of my husband's personality, benefiting from feeling good because of my positive thinking. Because of this change in my attitude, I began to be grateful for the fact that my husband faced his addiction and asked for help instead of feeling betrayed because he hid his terrible secret for so many years.

Thought for Today: My favorite slogans are "One Day at a Time" and "Let Go and Let God." They have helped me to keep in touch with my positive thoughts. Nar-Anon has helped me to get in touch with my Higher Power, something I had no concept of before I found this program.

"The greatest discovery of my generation is that human beings can alter their lives by altering their attitudes of mind." ~ William James

After several months of meetings and working a program, I still found that I could not let go of things that I knew I had no control over. One in particular that was weighing heavily on me was my qualifier's anger. He was living in transitional housing after a 90-day rehab program – by his own choice – but was extremely angry with me every time we interacted. This anger was driving me crazy. I could not figure out what I had done to cause him to be so angry, and could not convince him that he should not be angry with me.

I finally brought it to a meeting and opened myself up to suggestions from others. Everyone suggested that I let go of his anger, it was his. There was nothing I could do about it. But nobody could tell me how to do this. One gentleman left the meeting and came back with an old peanut butter jar. He had riveted the lid on and painted over the label. He told me that this was his 'God Jar' but that I could use it until he could make me one of my own. He told me to write down anything that I wanted to give over to my Higher Power and slide the paper through the slit he had cut into the lid of the jar. Once it was in the jar I could not take it back. If ever I should find myself worrying about it again, I need only remind myself that it was not mine anymore.

The process of thinking about it, writing it down, and physically giving it over by putting it in the jar, worked wonders for me. The next day, he brought me my own jar, and now the jar is much heavier, but my spirit is much lighter.

Thought for Today: I can't, God can, I think I'll let God.

"Knowledge is learning something everyday, wisdom is letting go of something everyday." ~ Unknown

One day my husband and I went to our property in the mountains. We were starting a much-needed week's vacation. I was feeling worn out from concern about our addicted son who lives in another state. Not knowing how he is and what he is doing is sometimes more than I can bear.

We have an outhouse that I put a plaque on that says "Serenity Place." I took some Twelve Step reading material with me and closed the door. I heard church music from a church camp a couple of miles down the hill. Then there was a slight patter that aroused my curiosity. I opened the door to see what it was. I noticed that it had started to drizzle. As I watched the droplets of rain wet the leaves, I heard a distant crackling of twigs. A mother deer walked into my view. Our eyes locked for what seemed like a minute. She walked forward and past me with her fawn walking close behind. As they slowly strolled out of view, I felt my Higher Power was telling me that we were watched over and that I could let go, let God and enjoy my vacation.

Thought for Today: I will remember that this Power, that is greater than me, has many ways to reach me. I often find conscious contact through the happenings of the world. I will be open minded and willing to receive the messages that come my way.

"Let all things be exactly as they are." ~ The Voice

Sometimes I did things without realizing why I was doing them. For instance, many nights I went out on the streets to look for my son without knowing where to find him, and risking my own safety. I made decisions for him because I thought his decisions were wrong. I would examine his pockets and smell his clothes as soon as he came home. I could feel the tension in my shoulders and back. This behavior caused me to hit bottom and I wanted to come back to a healthy life. Nar-Anon is helping me to do exactly this.

The pain of having an addict in my life will probably always be with me, but the message of Nar-Anon is helping me learn that my happiness does not depend on the happiness of another person. This is the beauty of our program. I have begun the journey of finding serenity once again in my life by following the Twelve Steps of Nar-Anon.

I am able to laugh once again, even though the addict is still using drugs and is on the streets. I now have hope and I am able to wait for the day when he will be ready to start a recovery program. I am able to stop the sadness from overwhelming me. While I miss my son and his lovely smile and laugh, I realize that concentrating on his addiction does me no good. I realize that to take life one day at a time is a path to healing. I must turn my will and my life over to a Higher Power in order for me to survive.

Thought for Today: Recovery is a spiritual journey. I am learning to trust that my Higher Power is capable of taking care of the addict as well as me. This gives me peace.

"Healing cannot come to a desperate person rummaging through other people's lives." ~ T.D. Jakes

During my prayer and meditation time, I try to keep my thoughts focused on my Higher Power and wait quietly for guidance. I ask only for knowledge of my Higher Power's will and the power to carry that out. I trust I will be shown what is best for me.

I have learned in Nar-Anon that my Higher Power can restore me to sanity, so every day I allow myself a half-hour for prayer and meditation. When there is drama and chaos in my life, I allow myself an additional half-hour.

Many addicts come with drama and chaos. Prayer and meditation are tools used to distract us from the source of the problem, the disease of addiction. I do not have to allow the drama and chaos to cloud my vision. Through prayer and meditation I can be still, listen and not be distracted.

Step Eleven is one of the best things I can do to maintain my peace and serenity. It reminds me to turn over my own will and accept direction from my Higher Power.

Thought for Today: Through Step Eleven, I have a conscious contact with my Higher Power. By calming my thoughts, I am able to interpret my path in a peaceful way. Serenity is often my reward.

"There are thousands of paths to a Higher Power and we can choose any one of them. Gratefully we choose at least one and step out on our continued journey to recovery." ~ Paths to Recovery

Prior to attending Nar-Anon meetings, addiction consumed my life. It was like a nightmare that never ended, never went away, and prevented me from getting a restful night's sleep. I lost weight because my stomach was always tied up in knots. I did not take care of myself. My income went down and I became depressed and listless. I must admit that I was allowing addiction to destroy my family and me.

I have now learned through Nar-Anon that I can take back control of my life. I am learning that if I continue to get sick about actions of the addict, I am losing control of myself. I am learning that I am not abandoning the addict by getting on with my life but merely making myself stronger. I am releasing the addict with love.

I realize that I still have a lot to learn and that I have just begun the journey. I can overcome the obstacles that life places in front of me by using this program and its tools and principles. I also realize that the First Step — admitting that I am powerless over this disease and over other people — gives me power over myself.

Thought for Today: There are no victims in this disease, only volunteers.

"Whether you think you can or whether you think you can't, you are right." ~ Henry Ford

310

Part of the Nar-Anon process is to come to grips with myself and how I see life in general. The concept of "I have no control" reminds me that I have to view my situation differently from how I used to deal with the addict.

Before I started attending Nar-Anon meetings, I was under the mistaken impression that I could control my addicted loved one. Now I know that any control that I thought that I might have had over the addict is long gone. I know that any peace that I may achieve will not be from trying to coerce the addict into getting help, but will be due to my understanding that peace will come to me only if I change my reactions to the situation.

Yesterday, the addict came to our house at 7 a.m. When I walked out the door and saw her, I saw something that has eluded me since this disease came into my life. What I saw was not my daughter, but rather a haggard 27 year-old woman. My view of her at that moment was different from what had been in my mind's eye since she went back to the life of a drug addict. Up until that moment, when I thought of my daughter, I saw a lovely young lady who was the light of my life. This new view of her was startling to me.

I think that is part of the initial anguish of addiction; I tend to see my addicted love one as the loving person she once was. I was refusing to let go! I want so desperately to have her back in my life that I cannot see the reality of the situation. I want so desperately to have my life back to normal that I will try anything to achieve that end. More than once I have hoped I will wake up and this nightmare will be over.

Thought for Today: Nar-Anon has helped me to realize that since I have no control over others, I must start viewing my life as changed and adjust to a different kind of reality. Not a reality of my dreams, but one that I must come to grips with; otherwise, I will be doomed to a life of misery as well.

"Life is what happens to you while you're busy making other plans." ~ *John Lennon*

I have only been coming to Nar-Anon meetings for a short time, but I remember being so angry that I felt like getting up, fiercely grabbing the table and turning it over while screaming and yelling. I felt violently out of control. What a terrible darkness I had descended into, and for what? Because a sick person was doing things I did not approve of. That anger and darkness were destroying me.

Attending Nar-Anon meetings has helped me to accept I have no control over my daughter's life. I could talk and threaten her until I was blue in the face and it would have absolutely no effect on her. Nevertheless, it did have an effect on me. When I tried to control her, I became insane.

I did not want my life to be forever in darkness. I want sunshine. I want the gloom to go away forever, yet I realize this can only happen with growth. Nar-Anon meetings and the help of my Higher Power teach me how to bring back the brightness into my life. When I concentrate on improving myself, it is possible to experience the true meaning of serenity.

Thought for Today: Through Nar-Anon meetings and with the help of my Higher Power, I am finding that it is possible to change myself. This is giving me the opportunity to practice gratitude for what I have in my life and to find peace and serenity as I continue to walk my path of recovery.

"If things go wrong, don't go with them." ~ Roger Babson

I came to Nar-Anon almost six months ago at the urging of my older children, as they were concerned about my health and well-being. They recognized the need for me to seek some help for myself. I of course disagreed with them. After all, had I not been handling business as usual and doing damage control for the past sixteen years?

Was I ever wrong! My oldest son said he would attend with me if I would call around and find a support group for drug abuse. That is how I found Nar-Anon. It was the wisest decision of my life. After attending my first meeting and listening to the stories of others, I knew immediately that I was among friends and family. The Nar-Anon family knew and understood exactly what I was going through as no one else could.

The subject that evening was on the importance of detachment, which was what I needed to hear. After listening to my Nar-Anon Family, I understood what my own family was trying to tell me. I needed recovery as badly as my middle-aged son did. I left that first meeting with a great sense of relief and freedom from responsibility. I came away from the meeting with permission to free myself of the burden.

Thought for Today: I cannot do it alone. I need the help of others. Just for today, I will reach out for that help; I will practice my program and drop the burden that is not mine to carry.

"He who would be serene and pure needs but one thing, detachment." ~ *Meister Eckhart*

When I came into the Nar-Anon program, I was one of those people who always had to know the answer. It was my job in life to understand the chaos, to track it, and to be prepared in an instant to do any one of a list of available remedies to keep the explosions from occurring.

After twenty years of living with active addiction, and a few years in the program, I realized I had three options: continue living with active addiction, leave the relationship, or the addict finds recovery.

What I wanted was for the addict to get clean and sober, and for our family to continue intact. However, I slowly accepted that this option was not up to me. I can get clean and sober and detach from my obsessions, but I cannot get the addict clean and sober.

I did not want either of the two remaining options, and I did not know what to do. I continued to stay confused. After a long while, I realized that all I could do was sit with my contradictory feelings and accept the confusion. I decided not to act until I was clear. I learned from the program that being confused is okay. I learned it was okay to just sit, and not make any decisions. I was released from being entangled and enmeshed in the problems of the addict. I regained more and more of myself.

One day, a year and a half later, that moment of clarity came. I have never second-guessed myself since that time, never felt I should have made the other choice. When it finally became clear, I knew it was time for me to go. I waited several more months until I could manage the actual move and then I moved out.

Later, I realized that if I had cut myself off too quickly, I would have left parts of myself behind and taken parts of him with me. We were too enmeshed, like a kitten-tangled in a string of yarn, and it took some time to unravel those twenty years and gather all of me together into my new separate self.

Thought for Today: When I feel confused, I practice awareness and acceptance, waiting for clarity before I move to action.

"It's all right to have butterflies in your stomach. Just get them to fly in formation." ~ Dr. Rob Gilbert

I have a difficult time distinguishing the difference between helping and enabling. The <u>Nar-Anon Blue Booklet</u> has a paragraph on "HELPING" that reads: "Your role as helper is not to DO things for the person you are helping, but to BE things, not to try to train and change his actions, but to train and change your reactions."

I have also heard a program speaker state, "I am not a human doing; I am a human being." Now before I take action, I try to ask myself a few questions:

- Is this a situation where I should be helping?
- Am I cleaning up someone else's mess and allowing that person to avoid the consequences of their actions?
- What is my motive? Am I trying to control this person?
- Am I doing this to teach or perhaps punish this person so that next time they will act differently?
- Is this a situation that the addict could/should handle without help?
- Does my "help" really demonstrate a lack of respect for this person's abilities?
- Do I feel resentful or angry about what I am doing?

If I answer, "yes" to any of these questions, I believe I am enabling and not helping.

Thought for Today: Before I jump in to help the addict or anyone else, I try to take a moment to look at the situation, examine my role, and evaluate my motives and feelings about what I am doing.

"If I am willing to stand aside and let God's will be done, I free myself from personal anxiety and a mistaken sense of responsibility." ~ <u>Nar-Anon Blue Booklet</u>

The addict called me last night (actually, she called four times). Thankfully, I had gone out for dinner and made the decision to leave my cell phone at home. If I had taken the phone and she called, even if I did not answer, I would have allowed a dark cloud to overshadow my thoughts for the evening.

I used to wait anxiously for the calls: where the addict would say she is ready for rehab; where the police would call to tell me that my daughter had been arrested; where I heard that my daughter had been beaten severely and needed to be hospitalized. Do I still worry about the calls? Before Nar-Anon, yes I did. However, since I have been trying to live one day at a time, I have not been worrying as much.

While I realize that my life could change instantly when I receive one of those calls, I am beginning to see that life is not all bad. I have made new friends through this experience – friends who understand and offer me encouragement.

Maybe, as the saying goes, "one should stop to smell the roses." I can realize the positives in my life, even if they seem small. When I think about pleasant and positive things, this can be what life is all about.

Thought for Today: "It all comes down to this: Nar-Anon is for me. I make my life what it is. I can have a good day or a bad day. It depends on my attitude. With these twelve steps, I can only make progress." ~ <u>As We Understood</u>

"You don't have to suffer continual chaos in order to grow." ~ John C. Lilly

Since attending Nar-Anon, I can see that to give opinions, advice, and money to the addict is a message that I do not trust the addict's ability to mature and manage his own life. Just as I want to be in control of my life's decisions, the addict has the right to be in charge of his decisions. Nar-Anon helps me see the boundaries I need to set for myself and to not focus on the addict's decisions.

As I watch different people in my life, I see everyone learns life's lessons differently. Nar-Anon has taught me how to watch and listen to the addict. "To watch is not to love" (Jung). I am practicing patience and letting the addict struggle through his life knowing his Higher Power is with him. I am beginning to realize how important it is for me to accept things in my life that I have no control over. It took me several years to accept the fact that I cannot change the addict.

I am learning that serenity comes to me when I do not judge the addict or give him feedback on what to do. Every day the addict makes his way through life as his Higher Power guides him. I am learning to focus on my life and trust what happens is my Higher Power's plan for me. I am learning to be grateful for my inner peace each day as I let go and let God, one day at a time.

Thought for Today: Calm your spirit, calm your mind. Know and trust that your Higher Power will lead the way.

"Wisdom comes with the ability to be still. Just look and just listen." ~ Eckhart Tolle

My son, in his addiction, was not in the habit asking me for favors. Then he called to inform me that he had been asked to leave a transient hotel in a nearby city and wanted me to pick up his belongings.

At the hotel, the manager informed me that my son had used his room for a bathroom all week and that he had kept other guests up at night. I realized the seriousness of my son's condition. I left with some of his belongings. As I drove north, the sky was ominous. I knew my son's condition was ominous, too. I was afraid that he might not survive the week.

I knew I needed an instant Nar-Anon meeting so I drove twenty-five miles to the nearest meeting. I was the second person to get there and sat in a handy seat. The first person there advised me, "If you sit in that seat, you'll have to chair the meeting."

What a blessing! That is what I needed. I was able to cover all the bases of my anxiety. As I shared, my fears were lifted.

Thought for Today: Whatever I may be trying to achieve, I can look up and breathe a sigh of relief when I remember: help is always right here within me, and things will work out in spite of me. I need to have the Nar-Anon program in my life and, even more, a belief in a Power greater than me. I am grateful to the program and the fellowship.

"You may not think you can reach it. Climb anyway. You may not think you'll be heard. Speak anyway. You may not think you can change things. Try anyway." ~ Maya Angelou

My girlfriend was enabling her addicted son and his addicted girlfriend. Her denial was allowing the addicts to become an issue between us. It was destroying our relationship, as well as my life. My exhaustive effort as the voice of reason only made matters worse. In fact, I was feeling that my girlfriend had turned against me and was siding with the addicts. I expressed my pain and fear in the following poem:

Lost in a wasteland
Barren and dry
As scavengers ruthlessly
Circle the sky

When a lone tree appears!
Abundant with fruit
Beauty and refuge
In sultry green suit

And I just might survive
With her love and affection
But her limbs are all covered
With thorns of rejection

Is tending her futile
As hope turns to doubt
With no food…no water
And time running out?

Lost in a wasteland
While searching for love
As scavengers ruthlessly
Circle above

And should they arrive
To tear at my skin
Will she sustain me
Or will she join in?

Thought for Today: In Nar-Anon, I am learning the fight against addiction is futile. I cannot be the voice of reason to those unwilling to listen. I can forgive others, let go and allow them to choose their own path. Although painful at times, I can make choices that are healthy for me.

"Truth, like surgery, may hurt, but it cures." ~ Han Suyin

After attending Nar-Anon meetings for a while, my greatest secret wish was that my partner would embrace recovery and get clean. I kept my mouth shut – white knuckling it, sometimes – when I thought he needed direction or correction by me. As a result, we were getting along pretty well. I kept speaking of recovery, of how happy my program was making me and dropping big hints; telling him stories of recovery that I was hearing from my new friends in Nar-Anon.

Then the miracle happened. The addict stopped using when he and his Higher Power were ready. Instead of blissful happiness flooding my world, suddenly the addict was telling me that his recovery came first, that my behavior was not helping him stay clean and if I could not get the focus off of him, I would have to leave. What a wake-up call! This was not what I expected. The pain in my heart was enormous and I wondered for the thousandth time why I could not have a normal boyfriend. Then the Nar-Anon program came to my rescue when I remembered to keep the focus on myself.

When I practiced this advice, I realized that deep in my heart, I loved this person, addicted or not, and I was here because of that deep love. To stay and be true to that gift of love, I was going to have to gather the courage to change. To change not the addict but to change myself! This is one of the best gifts I have received from my recovery and I owe it all to Nar-Anon where I learned that it is okay to love an addict.

Thought for Today: I will work my recovery program and let the addict work his own recovery. I will keep the focus on me because that is where I can make a change.

"All changes, even the most longed for, have their melancholy; for what we leave behind is part of ourselves; we must die to one life before we can enter into another." ~ Anatole France

The acronym reminds me that when I am Hungry, Angry, Lonely, or Tired, I am not taking care of my needs. If I am enmeshed with my addicted loved one, I do not take care of myself.

I lived for the addict. When the addict was out using, I could not relax, enjoy a movie, read a book, or even take proper care of myself. I did not eat. I smoked cigarette after cigarette and played game after game of solitaire until I could not think or see the computer screen. I did not call anyone or share my feelings of anger and fear because I did not want to hear what they had to say or hear their advice for the hundredth time. I was hooked. I stayed in this state of tension and misery until the addict came home. I felt better, but then the whole cycle repeated itself with the next binge.

In Nar-Anon, I am learning that feeling good is my responsibility and my feelings should not be connected to the addict's or anyone else's behavior. I am learning how to be a healthier person who takes care of her physical, spiritual, mental, and emotional needs each day. Today, I start my day with prayer and meditation and end it with a prayer of gratitude. This helps me stay connected to my Higher Power. Through this contact, I take care of my own spiritual needs. I eat well, exercise and try to get enough sleep to take care of my physical needs. I read books for pleasure as well as Nar-Anon literature for recovery and I write to keep my mind active and focused on healthy thoughts. I cry when I feel sad, acknowledge my anger and disappointments, and work through my emotions with my sponsor and other friends in the program. In this way, I care for my emotional needs.

Thought for Today: It is my responsibility to take care of me. When I do this, I am not being selfish, but learning self-responsibility.

"Self-care isn't selfish; it's self-esteem." ~ Unknown

As I sat on the patio one day, it appeared that everything was wrapped in fog. It was grayish white, like old cotton batting that I used to get in a jewelry box when one of my great-aunts would give me a present. I was never sure what would be underneath that cotton. It was old, obviously recycled and reused, before it was fashionable. This great-aunt was a bit dotty. Sometimes she would box and gift-wrap odd things such as a broken pencil. Other times, it would be an old piece of costume jewelry, missing most of its faux pearls. Every once in while, she would come through with a stunning piece of crystal or a gold brooch or a pair of earrings.

That day on the patio felt like that. I pondered: What is under this cotton batting fog? Will it be a broken dream such as thinking that my son is in recovery, a faux truth, or the real thing? Are truth, honesty and the priceless gold of recovery awaiting me today? I pray for my son's recovery and I pray harder for my own.

After some time in the Nar-Anon fellowship, I know that I have to live in the here and now and not think about dreams and false realities. I have to work hard to accept the present, believing in a Higher Power who can bring me back to sanity. My son's recovery depends on him. My recovery depends on my own spiritual awakening. If I trust my Higher Power, I will not fear whatever is underneath the cotton batting.

Thought for Today: Living one day at a time and trusting my Higher Power is my new way to live. I shall always remember this lesson.

"What you are is God's gift to you, what you do with yourself is your gift to God." ~ Leo Buscaglia

When I need some peace of mind................... I need a meeting.
When I don't know what to do with my time .... I need a meeting.
When I feel like splitting for a desert island ..... I need a meeting.
When I think I don't need a meeting................ I need a meeting.
When I start thinking I can think for myself...... I need a meeting.
When I am worried about everyone but myself.I need a meeting.

When I think I can cut down because I have attended a meeting every night for a month..................................... I need a meeting.
When I start feeling guilty, sad, or lonely and "need time for myself" ....
.... I need a meeting.
When a family member says, "You can afford to miss just this once in honor of your Aunt's birthday"............. I need a meeting.

When the kids have been sick or my temper's too quick,
When my head is in a fog and I am kicking the dog,
When I can't find my reason, or it's the changing of a season,
When things are good or they are bad, or I am happy or sad,
When I am falling in love, or can't find my glove,
And it's 20 below, or "that guy's driving too slow!"
"This one's driving me nuts," I have squirrels in my guts,
If it's starting to rain, if I am feeling no pain,
Got a zit on my face and a broken shoelace,
And I hear myself saying, "Yeah but..."
....**I need a meeting**

Thought for Today: Meetings are one of the tools the Nar-Anon program gives to me. With these tools, I can find peace and serenity whether the addict is using or not.

"Our Nar-Anon Family Group meetings are a safe place where we can talk to others and express our feelings with members who share our common problems. ...The peace we find in this fellowship has become our lifeline to serenity.." ~ The Nar-Anon Twelve Tools of Recovery

Before I came to Nar-Anon, I was angry. I worried all the time and I was obsessed with the addict. I was always doing something for someone else, putting everyone else first, and neglecting myself. I needed to change because I was self-destructing. Over the years, I had many talks with myself but I could not or would not forgive the addict. This attitude was making me ill. I was so angry and negative. I did not like myself. I was a whirling dervish, never quiet inside. Finally, I realized that I needed help.

I am so grateful that a friend, who also loved an addict, invited me to my first Nar-Anon meeting. When I first came to Nar-Anon, I still heard all the voices of martyrdom, but my Nar-Anon family modeled healthy behavior for me. They gave me the tools, courage and motivation to change my attitude and my life. They helped me find peace and serenity.

In Nar-Anon, I am learning about the power of prayer and meditation. I have learned how to meditate to deal with the insanity I am going through. I can meditate and clear my mind of obsessive thinking. Meditation is helping me to be relatively worry-free and helps me to find peace. My best learning experience happens when I am doing nothing. Through meditation, I am learning a better way to focus. It is helping me to change my behavior for the better. To me, meditation is a mind clearing experience and it helps me find peace

Thought for Today: In Nar-Anon, I have grown and relapsed, but I am getting myself back through the loving presence of my Higher Power, which became real and alive in my life through prayer, meditation, and the voices of my Nar-Anon family.

"Our prayers are answered, our problems find solutions, our worries are eased, if we but attune ourselves to the message." ~ Each Day a New Beginning – Daily Meditations for Women

When I first came to Nar-Anon, I heard a member share that when she forgave others it was a gift to herself. Before that, I always thought I forgave others as a favor to them. In Nar-Anon, I am learning that forgiveness is not a favor; it is something I do for myself. When I hang on to anger and resentment towards others, I am hurting myself. More often than not, the person I am angry with does not give me a second thought. I believe this is especially true if that person is in active addiction.

Today I try to practice forgiveness in those times when I am feeling hurt and abused by the actions of the addict. I remember the addict is sick. My resentment and anger toward the addict keeps me connected to the abuse which is now in the past. My angry thoughts and feelings toward that event keep me experiencing it over and over again. It also prevents me from experiencing serenity and peace.

Anger and resentments are not good for the addict or me. So today I will go to a meeting, I will talk about how I feel, I will ask for my Higher Power's help to let it go and move on. Sometimes this process takes a long time, but if I keep going in the right direction, I will receive the serenity I am seeking.

Thought for Today: No matter how grievous the wrong, I need to forgive because my recovery is my first priority. I have no right to sit in judgment of others and when I forgive others for past harms, it is a double blessing.

"Life is an adventure in forgiveness." ~ Norman Cousins

When I think of unacceptable behavior, the first thing that comes to mind is the actions of the addict. I believed the addict's behavior caused chaos and made my life unmanageable. It was easy for me to blame someone else for my unhappiness. The bills were not paid on time because the money was used for bail and the lawyer. I could not buy clothes for myself because I paid the traffic tickets, the pawnshop, and even the drug dealers.

After attending Nar-Anon meetings, reading the literature, and working the steps with my sponsor, I realized that I also had unacceptable behavior. I am the one who chose to pay the bail, the lawyer and the drug dealer. I chose not to buy myself clothes so money was available to ease the addict's consequences from active using. I made choices that were unacceptable for me. It was easier for me to blame the addict. Blaming the addict was easier than taking responsibility for my own behavior. Blaming the addict was easier than recognizing that my behavior and actions were causing me to be unhappy.

In Nar-Anon, I learned to look at myself and be responsible for my behavior. I have choices and can choose my behavior (just as the addict does) that will make me happy. I can choose chaos or serenity. Unacceptable behavior is in the eyes of the beholder. My behavior and happiness are my responsibility.

Thought for Today: When I am pointing my finger and blaming someone else for my unhappiness, I need to look and see that my fingers are pointing back at me.

"I have a clear choice between life and death, between reality and fantasy, between health and sickness. I have to become responsible – responsible for mistakes as well as accomplishments." ~ Eileen Mayhew

Sharing the Nar-Anon message with those that are in need is important because it is Nar-Anon's main purpose to offer comfort and aid to those that suffer from the effects of another's addiction. However, since anonymity is also the "spiritual foundation of all our Traditions," I should not become too publicly enthusiastic in my promotion of the Nar-Anon program.

On a personal level, I can share how Nar-Anon has helped me and suggest that others may find the same help. However, Tradition Eleven reminds me that this is a personal choice. Some members may not be comfortable publicly declaring their participation in Nar-Anon; nor is any member required to declare their membership.

At a public level (press, radio, films, internet, and other forms of mass media), I should not preach or recruit. Nor should I be over zealous and try to drag my friends and family members to meetings. When I demonstrate a positive change and set a good example by handling my own problems in new ways, with grace, a positive attitude, and a more loving manner, it is this behavior that others will notice. When others see these positive changes happening in my life, they may be attracted to the program.

The second part of Tradition Eleven reminds me that I should always "guard with special care the anonymity of all NA members." As a person who loves an addict, I may be proud of my recovering addict and want to share the addict's success with others, by telling my friends with addicted loved ones "look what NA did for the addict." This is not my place to do so, as the stigma of addiction could ruin the addict's reputation, even after years of recovery. Only the addict has the right to tell others about what the NA program did for him or her, when the addict feels it is the appropriate time.

Thought for Today: I must remember actions speak louder than words. Before I tell people about Nar-Anon, I should be sure they ask.

"Our public relations policy is based on attraction rather than promotion; we need always maintain personal anonymity at the level of press, radio and films. We need guard with special care the anonymity of all N.A. members." ~ Nar-Anon Tradition Eleven

While I was trying to manage and control my loved one's life, I had let my personal appearance go. I looked in the mirror and saw the results of my obsession. I thought that working on me was difficult. I could no longer blame others for how I looked and felt. I admitted that I was powerless over the addict and came to believe that only faith in a Power greater than myself could free me to live in recovery, one day at a time.

As I was powerless over my loved ones, I also seemed to be powerless over doing good things for me. I had trouble getting started; I had so many good excuses. With step work, I began to see that I could be good to myself, regardless of my situation, with my Higher Power's help. I became ready for my Higher Power to remove my excuses and help me start managing my own life.

When I get scared of what might happen next, my program reminds me that projecting the future and bringing up the past keeps me frozen, unable to move ahead in recovery. Faith in a Power greater than me replaces that fear and helps me grow.

Thought for Today: I will be a good friend to myself. I will do a good deed for me. I will pamper myself as I normally do for others. Today, I will focus on my good feelings and fun in my life. I will be thankful. I will laugh today for there is joy in living.

"If you nurture your mind, body, and spirit, your time will expand. You will gain a new perspective that will allow you to accomplish much more."
Brian Koslow

For me, there was so much fear connected with my growth. I had to make decisions that affected my loved ones and me. I was so afraid of what would happen. What would my loved one's reactions be? Alone, I failed to see my choices. When I talked with a Nar-Anon member, I realized I was not trapped and my fear was put into perspective. Now, through working my program, when I experience success, I break the cycle of fear. Another day of growth!

When a new crisis arises, I want to rush in to rescue. I feel it is my fault. If only I had done something different. Why do I always feel I am the reason something bad is happening to my loved one? What is the difference between rescuing someone and working my program? I needed to ask for help to understand. I call my sponsor or a friend in the program. Slowly, by sharing, I begin to see that I have choices. I see that my loved one also has choices. Then I understand that I do not have to react, but that I can make decisions based on my best interests.

As my fear is lifting, I am free to take an honest look at myself. I do not have to give away my identity and my self-esteem. I find in the quiet times, I can fill my mind with constructive thoughts. My Nar-Anon program suggests ways to rediscover myself. It also suggests that there is a better way to live.

Thought for Today: When I make better choices for myself, my life will get better. Nar-Anon suggests that I, too, can direct that change consciously if I so desire. Myself, I can change. Others, I can only love.

"There is nothing like returning to a place that remains unchanged, to find the ways in which you yourself have altered." ~ Nelson Mandela

The slogan, "One Day at a Time," helps me retain my serenity. Before I learned how to put this slogan into practice, I anticipated the worst. I planned in my head what I would do when the addict would have an accident or when any other unlikely event would happen. Without my program, I predicted countless worst-case scenarios. I became all worked up and reacted as though these fantasies were happening. The fantasy pain I felt was so acute, it was as though it were reality.

I realize I was insane at times like those. By the time the addict arrived home, I was ready to jump on him before I knew what had really happened. Other times, I might hide or pretend to be asleep for I felt sure he would jump on me.

As I learn to practice the Nar-Anon program, I find serenity by focusing on what I am doing at the moment, a moment at a time. As clarity of mind grows, I realize that I can decide what to do and how to deal with things that do happen. Most of the time, I find that I do not have to do anything!

Thought for Today: Living one day at a time is the path to serenity. Staying in today, I deal with the reality of what is actually happening. I learn to not trade my serenity for worst-case scenarios.

"I will try to live through this day only, and not tackle my whole life problem at once." ~ Nar-Anon Blue Booklet

One day when I was at church, I looked at my watch. The watch is special. When my husband, retired he gave me this watch with his company's emblem on it.

When I arrived home, I did some chores. I was sweeping up and went to check the time. My watch was gone! I did not even feel or know when it came off. I checked all over and I walked back to church checking the route. I asked if some one had turned it in. No luck.

I felt terrible. My husband reminded me that the watch was a material thing and that I should let it go. Even though I knew he was right, I felt that I had the right to feel what I felt and that I did not want to let it go. In hindsight, I realized I must have seen some value in feeling terrible, although I still do not know what it could have been. Finally, I did manage to let go of my feelings about the watch.

A week later, I was changing the bed. As I grabbed the sheets off, the watch fell to the floor. I was over-whelmed with joy! I cried as my husband stood and watched. I explained that I was crying tears of joy but not for the watch. That moment I thought how hard it is to let the addict in my life go. I realized that until I let them go, they would not come back to me.

It was so evident what my Higher Power was showing me through this incident of the watch. Thank you for being there when I needed you.

Thought for Today: Today I will trust and I will let go and let God.

"It's mind over matter. When you no longer mind, it doesn't matter." ~ *Unknown*

After a terrible fight with a loved one, I was in deep despair. I began to pray, asking for help and guidance. I followed the prayer with a twenty-minute meditation in hope of getting an answer that would ease my suffering. After the meditation, I felt a strong urge to get the phone book. Upon retrieving it, I did not know why I had it. I closed my eyes and thought, what should I look up? The answer came, "drug addiction"! The biggest shock of all was that I was not even aware that the underlying problem with my loved one was addiction!

Using the phone book, I found several listings under "addiction," but I did not know which one to call. Following the guidance from my meditation, I called them all. After many calls, I learned of Nar-Anon, a support program for the friends and family of people suffering from addiction. I attended my first meeting that night and I knew without question that was the answer I had been seeking!

I learned a valuable lesson that day. If I take the time to ask for help through prayer and meditation and listen for the answer, I can find serenity and peace of mind. Through prayer and meditation, the Nar-Anon program was working for me before I even found these rooms.

Thought for Today: Prayer and meditation are invaluable tools at our continuous disposal. Through prayer and meditation, you can find the answer you are seeking, waiting for you to discover it.

"Healing is a matter of time, but it is sometimes also a matter of opportunity." ~ Hippocrates

Acceptance is a powerful tool. When I started to put it to work, I was able to take some giant steps in my recovery. At the beginning, somewhat condescendingly, I looked at acceptance as a cop out. I felt as though I was surrendering or giving in and giving up.

I remember deciding to practice that old saying, "Don't knock it until you've tried it." I had been using all my energies and powers of persuasion on issues that were not of my making. I had no power or control over these issues even though they concerned adults I loved and cared about. When I practiced acceptance in the manner our literature suggests, it fit like a glove and proved to be very beneficial. I guess that is because it makes good sense.

What I decided to do was question myself. "Is this my issue? Do I have any power to change it? Should I interfere with the outcome or allow the person who made this choice handle it?" Once I had answered these questions, I sometimes decided that silence on my part would be a good tool. Now that I have tried it, I am okay with acceptance because I know it works for me.

Thought for Today: Today I know for sure that things work out the best for me when I make the best of how things work out.

"Acceptance is not submission; it is acknowledgment of the facts of a situation, then deciding what you're going to do about it." ~ Kathleen Casey Theisen

All my life, I have been surrounded by dysfunction, alcoholism, depression, and drug addiction. At an early age, I began covering up my feelings. I was sure if I was happy and helpful to those around me, everything would be okay. I took care of everything and everyone, but I forgot to take care of myself. I thought I was in control. After many years in an abusive marriage, I realized I had no control over anyone, not even myself. When I found Nar-Anon and its Twelve Steps and the spiritual principles, I was able to see that I am worthy of a better life. I am finally learning how to take control of my life and take care of me.

That abusive relationship is many years in the past. I did not change the addicts in my life; I changed the way I responded to them. By working the Twelve Steps, I found recovery over my old dysfunctional behaviors. Attending Nar-Anon meetings has given me a sense of well-being and support. The shared experiences of those in the program give me strength and hope. I will be forever grateful to Nar-Anon for showing me a better way to live.

Thought for Today: "When we fully understand and accept that addiction is a disease, that it is both mental and physical, and that we are powerless over it, we become ready to learn a better way to live." – *Nar-Anon Blue Booklet*

"I can be changed by what happens to me. But I refuse to be reduced by it." ~ Maya Angelou

I once heard a Nar-Anon convention speaker say, "Anger is my drug of choice." Why am I so angry all the time? It seems that every time I feel I am done with anger, it comes back with a vengeance and I am even angrier. I go to meetings, I do my daily readings, I focus on changing my reactions to the addict, yet it continues. I still continue to beat my head against the wall.

I am angry that the addict cannot see what her addiction has done to her family, her friends and her life. Why can't she get out of her denial, accept that she is an addict, and finally get treatment? I did everything humanly possible to help her see her illness. Now, I am done! I am no longer going to assign a role or function for someone else to fulfill. Anger occurs as a result of the failure of a person or situation to fulfill the function I have assigned to them.

Nar-Anon has helped me to see that anger is an emotion that I must deal with in my own recovery. Anger does come and go along with many other emotions, and I am no different from anyone else suffering through the insanity of dealing with addiction. Knowing that I am not alone and that others are going through the same emotions as they work in the recovery process brings me comfort.

Thought for Today: Anger is an emotion that comes from unfulfilled expectations. As I work my program, I learn not to create expectations for others. We are in control of our thoughts. We can choose to see anger as part of the process we go through in recovery or we can let it eat away at us and make us cold, bitter and resentful. Why not make the choice to use anger as a stepping stone and climb the ladder to recovery?

"How much more grievous are the consequences of anger than the causes of it." ~ Marcus Aurelius

One of the principles of the Nar-Anon program is gratitude. Through gratitude, I can appreciate the good things in life. Some years ago, I was watching a TV show about gratitude. It suggested that our lives could be more successful if we focus on the positive things in life instead of the negative. We can change our thoughts, and this, in turn, changes our whole focus of life.

That day, I started a gratitude journal and wrote down five things that make me feel grateful. As I began focusing daily on gratitude, I noticed a difference in my attitude and in my life.

I learned that even in my darkest moments, there is something to be grateful for if I but take the time to acknowledge it. My worst days can then become better days. I can create a better life for myself by thinking positively because the negative thoughts do not overwhelm me as they had in the past. This daily exercise also brought with it the realization that the blessings in my life are limitless in every area: physically, emotionally, and spiritually. With that knowledge, I gain more confidence in myself and I make better choices.

Thought for Today: The Nar-Anon program teaches me that I can choose to see the positives or the negatives in life. Every day I can feel sorry for myself or I can choose to find something positive to be grateful for, even in my darkest moments!

"What a wonderful life I've had! I only wish I'd realized it sooner." ~ Colette

One night in a dream, I learned something about myself that I did not realize nor did I like much. I dreamt that in my backyard there was a cage full of people. When I saw them, I knew I was the one putting them in there and I thought what an awful person I must be to keep all these people chained and in a cage. I was not aware that I was that controlling.

Each time I went back to check, there were fewer and fewer people in the cage. In my dream, there was a special, healthy and wonderful little child who was also in that cage. I realized that child was secretly helping these people to escape. I was so grateful to him and proud of him. I told him I was glad he was letting the people go. He was surprised and said, "Really?" "Yes," I said, "Really." I now realize that the healthy little child was the new me. Before Nar-Anon, I was sick and controlling and now I was letting these people control their own lives. I was still little and new but I am getting better. Even in my fantasies, I have made a box where my world exists and I am in control. It is not the real world, but it is and has been my real world.

With the help of the Twelve Steps, my Higher Power and the fellowship of Nar-Anon, I can let myself out of the cage I have created and let everyone else I meet out as well. Gradually, maybe I can start to live in the reality where my Higher Power is in control, not in the facsimiles of illusionary control I have attempted to create.

Thought for Today: I have no right to control others. It is as cruel as putting them in a cage. I will try to release myself from this insane behavior.

There can be no happiness if the things we believe in are different from the things we do." ~ Freya Stark

I experienced a painful feeling of despair when I realized I could not control the addict, cover up the problems created by his addiction, or change the events caused by the addict's behavior. I found that my life had become unmanageable, because I was allowing the addict to have full control of my life.

I thought that the addict had the problem and was the problem. If the addict would just stop using, everything would be normal. Since my life revolved around the addict and the addict's behavior, my involvement in the addict's life kept me in a downward spiral of despair. I thought the only way out was to remove myself from the situation.

When I came to Nar-Anon, I heard other members talking about similar situations. However, they had a hopeful attitude about their lives. They lived with an addict, yes, but were not focused on the addict's life. Over time, the personal despair I felt seemed to lift and I saw a way to change my life for the better. By using the Twelve Steps of the Nar-Anon program, I am finding a way to remove myself from the feelings of despair. I can now replace these feelings with serenity and peace.

Thought for Today: Despair and pain can be motivators and I can release myself from them by working the Nar-Anon program to change myself.

"Pain nourishes courage. You can't be brave if you've only had wonderful things happen to you." ~ Mary Tyler Moore

Through the years of coming to Nar-Anon, I have come to recognize that the program is working in me. Often this work is not one of my intentions, but rather one of following my instincts and listening in the moment.

Recently, I had an experience that was an example of "being in the moment." I lost many friends when I divorced my husband of twenty years. These friends were cordial but the sharing of family dinners, picnics and weekly phone calls stopped.

When my son married, one of these friends made contact and I spent a rare afternoon at her home talking with her. It was delightful! While chatting, I learned that a girl, who had been my student for many years, was addicted and struggling with recovery. I felt as if my own child had been afflicted and it hurt to know this sweet and caring person had turned to drugs!

That evening I felt compelled to attend my home meeting, which I had missed for almost a year because of an out-of-town job, so off I went. When I arrived, unexpectedly, there was my other friend, the mother of the girl discussed earlier that day. This mother was lost, frantically trying to find the Nar-Anon meeting room. I led the way, all the while listening to her story. We shared a meeting.

Thought for Today: If I follow my instincts I am able to help others find what we all find in Nar-Anon: we are not alone and there is hope.

"For it is in giving that we receive." ~ Saint Francis of Assisi

Letting go was one of the most difficult lessons I had to learn. I felt strongly that if I could control the behavior of the people in my life then my life and my world would be better. I truly thought I would be the happiest person in the world if my husband would live his life the way I wanted him to live it. I believed with all my heart and soul that if he would stop using drugs everything would be all right. I assumed his abuse of drugs was the reason I was unhappy and miserable.

It was hard for me, but in Nar-Anon I learned to let go and turn my controlling impulses over to a Power greater than myself. I stopped expecting others to make me happy. Today I know I have to let go of yesterday, stop living for tomorrow and live for today.

Thought for Today: Letting go of trying to control others lets me take responsibility for my own life. These old habits are not easy to change, but when I do give them up and I do let them go, I begin to find the happiness I wanted others to give me.

"What life means to us is determined not as much by what life brings to us as by the attitude we bring to life: not so much by what happens to us as by our reaction to what happens." ~ Lewis Dunning

Virtue, like muscles, must be exercised to be strengthened. The only way to exercise virtue is to have opportunities to use them. This has taught me to be careful of what I pray for – I just may get it.

I prayed for the addict to get clean. When he did, I needed more patience. I continued to try to control him. I wanted to know if he was going to enough of his meetings. Then I wanted to know why he was going to so many meetings! Someone once told me that if I prayed for patience, I would be given something to be patient about. I have found this to be so.

One day I wanted to use a copy machine that was warming up. This turned into another opportunity for me to practice patience. I kept pushing the button thinking that would hurry it along. My co-worker asked if I noticed that it said, "WAIT." I realized that is how I pray. I want the answer yesterday! I am learning that as the copier will copy when it is ready, I must learn to trust the process. It unfolds when it is ready!

Thought for Today: The gift of patience can be as simple as staying in the moment. I want to enjoy whatever is happening while I am waiting for the answer. Whether a smile from a passerby, holding a door for a stranger, a sunset, or the laughter of a child, I want to enjoy it all. Sometimes the answer is that simple.

"Yesterday is history. Tomorrow is a mystery. And today? Today is a gift. That's why we call it the present." ~ Babatunde Olatunji

Yes, it hurts; I have tried to deal with my addict boyfriend and the insanity that comes along with addiction. Yet, ever since I went to my first Nar-Anon meeting, I have found hope. Maybe not the hope I expected, but hope nonetheless.

From the program and my fellow members, I am learning a different way to cope with my situation. I see how it has helped the people around me at meetings and I know it is going to be worth it. I think the most profound understanding that I have reached so far is that letting go does not mean leaving him. It does not mean that I cannot think about the person, love him, and pray for him. It means that I must let him do what he has to do right now, and not worry about him because God will help him take care of himself.

It makes me undeniably jubilant to know that I will not be making impulsive road trips at all hours of the night in the vain hope of running across him, just because I cannot think of anything else to do.

I still get crazy and I still cry. I still have a long way to go, but I am more at peace with myself and able to be more supportive of him in my own way. It is a great feeling.

Thought for Today: Just for today, I will smile and be unafraid!

"Practice easing your way along. Don't get het up or in a dither. Do your best; take it as it comes. You can handle anything if you think you can. Just keep your cool and your sense of humor." ~ Smiley Blanton MD

I find that I have an amazingly self-centered disease. Being at the center of the world carries a lot of responsibility! I have to tell everyone what I want and what I expect of them. After all, how would they know what to do without me directing them? Knots in my stomach and tension headaches are par for the course when I am in charge and the center of the world. It is only natural that I become angry when so many people let me down after all I have done for them!

The Nar-Anon program has taught me that I can experience relief when I let go of all my imaginary control and my real anger. Now I have so much more time to work on my own changes that will lead to my own recovery.

My expectations and wants for other people's lives are a source of anger that I do not want to pick up again. I know that when I write down all the things others do that make me angry, I find that many of them are things I do also! I want to get to work on my own recovery!

Thought for Today: I can practice the adage, "Don't let the sun go down on your anger."

"Anger is but the failure of a person or a situation to fulfill the function I have assigned to it. I can be free of the anger by releasing the assignment." ~ Robert Perry

I know from working the Nar-Anon program that the only person I can control is me. Yet occasionally, I still continue to try to control people and situations. When will I learn? After celebrating his second year of recovery, my husband relapsed, plunging my life and my own recovery into a deep hole. I stopped attending my meetings and I stopped using the phone list. My urge to control the situation returned instantly. My whole focus was on getting my spouse back into his program. I even left our small children at home alone to search abandoned buildings where I thought he might be. I tried many things to get the addict to see what he was doing to our family. When that did not work, I blamed myself for not seeing the signs sooner. I never once realized how out of control and damaging my own behavior was. Finally, my sponsor reminded me of the importance of minding my own business, and remembering what is my business and what is not. My loved one's sobriety definitely was not my business.

Thought for Today: When I take another person's inventory, my urge to control returns instantly. I must learn to focus on myself and stay out of other people's business. Today I can practice the basics. Step One begins with admitting we are powerless. If I practice this step each time a situation arises that causes me to want to control a person or situation, I will be able to mind my own business. I will gain time and energy to work on myself.

"There is only one corner of the universe you can be certain of improving, and that's your own self." ~ Aldous Huxley

Many mornings I wake up full of fear. My fears are not based on my present circumstances, as I am safe and warm in my bed. My thoughts are either in the past, replaying some situation, or in the future, worrying about what might happen. I am usually focused on someone else. An example of this is when the addict has been out all night or using for days, and although I have not heard from him, I am already afraid. I am worried about what this latest binge may bring. All I want to do is roll-up in a ball and hide under the covers. Today, I know I can choose to use my Nar-Anon program and find an answer that helps me throw back the covers, get out of bed and get on with my life.

The Nar-Anon program suggests there is a better way to live. At Nar-Anon meetings, I learn fear is a lack of faith. I now know that yesterday is history, tomorrow is a mystery, and today is the present. Living this day fully is the one sure way for me to have a life. Most importantly, I know I am not alone. I have a Higher Power who is my "partner in this business of living." I can finish my prayers and start my day with confidence and determination. I find relief when I trust in my program and a Power greater than myself. I can replace fear with faith.

Thought for Today: When I am full of fear, I read my Nar-Anon literature and take a few minutes to quietly ask for guidance. I need only be willing to try a new way of living and to trust.

"Just for today I will try to live through this day only, and not tackle my whole life problem at once. I can do something for twelve hours that would appall me if I felt that I had to keep it up for a lifetime." ~ Nar-Anon Blue Booklet

It was a leap of faith for me to start a Nar-Anon Family Group. The request to start a meeting had come from an unlikely source - my son, who is a recovering addict. He had been successfully following a twelve step program for a year. When the Twelve Steps were put under my nose, I was drawn by a strong desire to take a closer look. I decided I would appreciate a spiritual way to handle my life. Apart from attending a relatively new meeting on the other side of town, I knew absolutely nothing about Nar-Anon. I had felt completely out of place, as my son was now clean. I wondered why I would need to be there. Then, I remembered, I attend Nar-Anon meetings for my recovery.

I finally sought out a place to start a meeting. I was nervous, as I had never openly used the word "addict" or "addiction." These words were conveniently tucked away, out of sight. How wonderful it was when I approached the person in charge of the facility, to be welcomed with open arms. She had experienced a similar trauma and said, without a doubt, that she would support a Nar-Anon meeting.

Many times, I receive calls from people who are considering Nar-Anon. I am asked, "What happens when I go to the Nar-Anon meeting? Do I have to give my full name?" No. "Do I have to give my address and where I work?" **NO.** I tell callers that Nar-Anon meetings are a safe place; whatever is said is not repeated outside our meeting rooms. Sometimes that same person will phone back, even after a year and say, "I remember your voice and can you help me?" I have always been able to reply that our meetings are still open, anonymous, and welcoming. The Nar-Anon Family Groups survive because of our Traditions. The Twelfth Tradition is especially important as it protects our members and ensures our meetings are a safe place.

Thought for Today: The Nar-Anon program offers me a safe place because of the groups' commitment to anonymity. I am grateful to do my part to protect the anonymity of all Nar-Anon members.

"Anonymity is the spiritual foundation of all our traditions, ever reminding us to place principles above personalities." ~ Nar-Anon Twelfth Tradition

As a child growing up with seven boys, grandparents, my mother, and aunt, there was little, if any, praise. Everything I did or accomplished was dutifully expected of me. I learned to think of praise as false flattery. I learned that pleasing others should always be my goal. Doing otherwise was neglecting my obligations to my family and selfish. Pleasing others led me into relationships with addicts.

When I came to Nar-Anon, my understanding changed. I learned that subtle and real praise gently spoken could transcend and inspire people. By accepting and giving praise to others and myself, I could see a change. I felt positive feelings beaming from me as I spoke words of approval to others. I saw the same transformation as I allowed myself to experience and believe the praise I received from others.

In Nar-Anon, praise is the unconditional love I give and receive from others. Praise is now a part of my everyday life. I learned to give praise to those I love. I have also learned to accept it with a simple thank you. I believe praise is as essential to the spirit as breathing is to the body. I believe that everyone can benefit from praise. We can be lifted and inspired to conquer the challenges of life and to change negatives into positives.

Thought for Today: Praise is an expression of love and love is the divine force that connects us all. I will accept and give praise to those I love.

"Love is a sacred reserve of energy; it is like the blood of spiritual evolution." ~ Pierre Teilhard De Chardin

I have been in Nar-Anon for a few years and continue to be excited about what I hear and see at meetings. I love to watch the new members grow. The program depends on the growth of the newcomers as well as on the continued growth of long time members. I am sorry to see new members stop attending meetings as soon as they feel better.

My own spiritual awakening has helped me so much that I feel I owe it to the fellowship to keep coming back so I can share my experience, strength and hope with the new members. Nar-Anon depends on the attendance of all members to keep the fellowship healthy and growing.

By being a sponsor, I have gained guidance and tremendous wisdom from my sponsees. Being a sponsor is a good way to carry the message.

Other ways to practice the principles include being on a committee, to serve as program coordinator or meeting chairperson and to participate by making a telephone list for the newcomers. I believe that Step Twelve is about service. Carrying the message through service and practicing the principles of the program gives me the opportunity to help others. This in turn helps me and helps Nar-Anon grow.

Thought for Today: I am grateful that the long time members were there when I walked into my first meeting. So today, I will practice Step Twelve and be there for the newcomers. This is the way the Nar-Anon program survives, and I believe I owe my survival to the Nar-Anon Family Groups.

"However many holy words you read,
However many you speak,
What good will they do you
If you do not act upon them?" ~ Buddha

I have been blessed to find Nar-Anon through my family and friends whose addictions affected my well-being. I say blessed because it brought me to recovery and serenity, once I had suffered enough to let myself come through the door.

Imagine me as a shy 17-year-old girl from a small farming community at my first week at college. Throughout the freshman orientation week, I became familiar with fraternity jackets and was in awe of the college men. The various student organizations made their pitches for the freshmen to join some kind of group. I was feeling insecure, and overwhelmed and lonely. Throughout the week, it rained. I was faced with crossing the campus without an umbrella. Just at the worst downpour, a tall blonde fraternity hunk stepped out of his dorm and offered to share his umbrella. As we walked and talked, I learned that he too was shy and unsure of himself. We were two people, one with a little more experience, taking shelter from the storm. This is my image of sponsorship.

The fabric shield (umbrella) represents our Twelve-Step program bringing me shelter from the pain of addiction and dysfunction. I must carry it and use it first for my own protection, and then I must share it. This shield cannot be effective unless I consider the whole picture. While I may work on one step at a time, the benefit of the program is from the whole program philosophy working together through regular attendance at meetings, the daily reading of literature and service work. The lifeline of the program is the calls I make to another as a sponsor and friend. All these threads of understanding and caring in the program weave a most useful and comforting respite from the storm of addiction and co-dependency. Sponsorship is the lifeline of the program, the handle of the umbrella of our Twelve Step recovery.

Thought for Today: Sponsorship is Twelfth Step work. It is one way we carry the message to others and ensure the survival of the program. I can only keep true recovery if I am willing to give it away.

"A sponsor is someone we can relate to who has achieved the level of recovery that we are also seeking." ~ The Nar-Anon Twelve Tools of Recovery

Today, I am learning the importance of setting healthy boundaries for myself. I learned from past experiences that all my efforts to control and change my addicted loved one by pleading, crying, praying, and shaming would not make him stop using. My behavior made me emotionally sick. My anger turned inward and resulted in depression. My depression took such a strong hold of me that I feared being emotionally damaged for life.

At Nar-Anon meetings, I am learning that I can set boundaries and reclaim my life. Boundaries are limits I set for myself, what I will or will not allow in my life. Boundaries are not limits I set for others. For example, I can choose to leave a party if someone's behavior affects me in a negative way. I can change an old pattern of enabling and say no. I used to engage in circular arguments with the addict. One of my new boundaries is to stop this behavior because it never improved anything. It only made me upset. Now when I see I am arguing in circles, I stop. I look at the addict and say, "You may have a point. I would like to talk about something else." It does not mean I have to cave in to the addict's demand to be rescued from consequences. It simply means I stop arguing.

Setting boundaries is a change in my behavior and it does not always come easy. Many times, others criticize me when I change. However, I can set another boundary and choose not to let others' reactions change my decision to take care of myself. In Nar-Anon, I am learning a better way to live. I feel as if a ton of bricks has been lifted from my shoulders.

Thought for Today: I do not have to let someone's reaction to my changed behavior discourage me from doing something good for me. I will choose to set healthy boundaries.

"If others put me into emotional bondage, my boundaries are not yet defined." ~ Unknown

When I first learned of my son's addiction, I rode an emotional roller coaster. Nearly a year passed before I heeded the advice of my son's Narcotics Anonymous sponsor, who suggested I attend a Nar-Anon meeting. My first response was that I was not the one with the problem.

Little did I understand that an emotional roller coaster is a problem. The first meeting I went to was small; only two other women were there. I wondered what good this meeting would be to me. The first lady shared how her son had overdosed and died. My son had also over-dosed, but he had lived. Not only did that give me something to be thankful for, but I had also finally met someone who understood what I was going through. I felt some healing take place immediately at that first meeting. I was so glad I had gone to this meeting. I continue to attend Nar-Anon meetings for the strength it offers me. Hearing others' experiences lets me know that I am not alone.

Attending Nar-Anon meetings is one of the most important ways I can carry the message. Even when things are going well in my life, I attend meetings. I pray that when I share my experience, strength and hope, I may help someone else feel the healing I experienced at my first meeting. Each time I attend a meeting I pray that it will help me or give me the opportunity to help others.

Thought for Today: I can carry the message by sharing my experience, strength and hope with others. Only in this way can I continue to heal and recover.

"When we share openly at meetings, this is also part of Step Twelve. Our experience, strength and hope will benefit someone. Even our early shares about our pent up frustration, grief and pain living with an addict, before we are able to focus on ourselves, helps newcomers realize they are not alone. Newcomers' stories remind old timers how grateful we are and how far the Twelve Steps to recovery has taken us." ~ The Nar-Anon Twelve Step Program

You were there to greet me as I came through the door,
You listened to my story, though you'd heard it before,
And as I recall at my meeting number two,
The people I recognized were all too few,
On a different day, in a different place,
I felt secure seeing a familiar face,
You didn't say much, but you nodded a lot,
I thought to myself, "She has what I've got!"

There was strength behind your words,
That through my fears somehow I heard,
I could tell when you talked you didn't pretend,
And it didn't take long 'til you felt like a friend.
At my first convention, I was feeling alone -
Until I ran into you and soon felt quite at home,
I see how you work hard to do all you can,
You're a credit to service, always lending a hand.

I treasure the way you share as you grow,
You've helped me in ways you'll never know,
"It works if you work it," I know that part is true,
But it only works for me because of people like you.
So let me take a minute, my hand in your hand,
To thank you from my heart, I know you understand.

Thought for Today: The Nar-Anon program and fellowship is here for me because of the service given by other members. They carry the message and support the program. Today I will give to the program as I can only keep what I have by giving it away in the form of service to others.

"Carrying the message is essential to our personal recovery. It is a way of offering hope to the families of addicts who still suffer and it is part of our Twelfth Step work." ~ The Nar-Anon Twelve Tools of Recovery

Change! Well, I am learning that I definitely cannot change the addicts. I cannot make my addicted loved ones do anything they do not want to do. I cannot make them stop their obsessions with drugs, food, smoking, gambling, sex, golf, or computers. Their obsessive/compulsive behavior continues and will until they desire to change and seek the help they need.

Every now and then, I still take their inventory and talk to them about their behavior. That does nothing to improve our relationships; instead, it causes more resentment and creates more distance between us. I need to remember they will work their own programs with their own sponsors when they are ready. The only thing I can do today is look at my behavior. Am I obsessed with cleaning my house, working long hours, and taking on more than I should to fill my time so I do not have to feel or see the addicts' behavior? Am I avoiding my own shortcomings?

I know that I have a choice today to change what I can. I also know I can only change me. I can do this by working the Twelve Steps with my sponsor, going to meetings, being of service in Nar-Anon and taking care of me. I have to stay on my side of the street to be healthy.

Thought for Today: Today I will only work on changing my attitudes and myself. I cannot change the addict, only my reactions to the things the addict and others do. Today I choose to have peace and serenity in my life.

"The sages do not consider that making no mistakes is a blessing. They believe, rather, that the great virtue of man lies in his ability to correct his mistakes and continually to make a new man of himself." ~ Wang Yang-Ming

When I was young, I felt a strong connection with my Higher Power, who I believed linked all human beings to each other. I experienced an electric current of connection as we held hands during the closing prayer of a spiritual ceremony. But as I grew up in the traditional, patriarchal organized religion I was familiar with, I found little or nothing to offer a young adult. After living with my partner's active addiction for twenty years, I lost any connection to a Higher Power that I once had.

Upon coming into the Nar-Anon program, I reconnected through that familiar activity – holding hands for the closing prayer. Although I liked that, it was different from my childhood prayers. I began to feel connected to the people in the group – my first step in a new relationship with my Higher Power.

During the many years of my son's battle with active addiction, I had to accept that this disease might kill him. I had to release the addict with love into the care of his Higher Power, not mine. I slowly accepted that my Higher Power is in charge of my life. My addicted son survived, made a new life, matured, married, found a new career, and bought a home.

With six years of clean time, this adult now has aggressive cancer. More than ever, I must turn my will over to my Higher Power. I am grateful that I have reconnected with God while dealing with addiction. Yet again, with this deadly disease, I am powerless and my role as "helper" is exactly as described in "Helping" in the Nar-Anon Blue Booklet.

Thought for Today: My Higher Power connects me to others. He is the loving link between each of us. We are strong because we are all of the same cloth.

"It is better to practice a little than talk a lot." ~ *Muso Kokushi*

When I lived with active addiction, everything I did seemed necessary from crisis to crisis. I was in survival mode. My life was similar to an emergency room triage. What is the most urgent of the three or four crises currently facing my family today? I found myself always choosing the response that would cushion the addict from the consequences of addiction. Needless to say, things became worse.

I have learned in the Nar-Anon program to shift the focus onto myself and away from the addict. The meaning of what is necessary has changed and it now includes me. It is now necessary for my survival that my recovery program is my first priority. The addict has his own path to recovery and his own program. If he is going to win against this deadly disease, he has to fight his own battles. I cannot fight, let alone win for him.

Now after several years of clean time, the addict has another deadly disease. I can give him support but I cannot fight this new battle for him. But I worry: If the addict has to take prescription drugs with his new health problem, will a relapse follow? Then I remember I do not know the future. How the addict copes with severe pain is between him and his doctor. It is not necessary for me to be paranoid about whether the addict relapses into severe addiction. If that happens, he will have to find his way out. When I am paralyzed with terror that the addict will die, I remember that a negative attitude will only send a negative message. What I can do is have hope that the addict will survive and heal one more time. I need to keep a positive attitude and remember with the help of his Higher Power he found the way from impending death back to life from this deadly disease of addiction.

Thought for Today: All I can do is love and pray for the addict and that is enough.

"Never be afraid to trust an unknown future to a known God." ~ *Corrie Ten Boom*

I once read a book entitled: "<u>Do Not Be Afraid</u>." This book is full of words of wisdom, and talks about life and the pitfalls that it presents to us. The words, "Do not be afraid" help me put my life in perspective.

"Do not be afraid." I am coming to understand that Nar-Anon for me means just that. While I may want the best for my addicted loved ones, I am concentrating on what I am learning in my program. I am focusing on that phrase "Do not be afraid" and finding that I do not need to be afraid for the future of the addict. She is in the care of her Higher Power, just as I am in the care of mine.

"Do not be afraid" means to me that I can turn my life over to the will of my Higher Power as it says in the Third Step, and have faith that all will be as it should. I believe that I will have the strength to deal with whatever lies ahead.

Thought for Today: These few words, "Do not be afraid" are powerful in my recovery. When I practice the Twelve Steps of Nar-Anon, I learn to replace my fear with faith.

"Never fear shadows .... that always means there is a light shining somewhere." ~ Jonathan Santos

I have been thinking about the Nar-Anon slogan, "One Day at a Time." Thinking that the addict might straighten out if she gets arrested is worrying about the future and projecting. This is something that contradicts the notion of this slogan. I project as I think of her possible arrest, being sentenced to prison time, and possibly seeing the error of her ways. In my mind, this event will, of course, lead to her recovery.

While no parent wants their child to be arrested, this scenario made sense to me. Rather than wishing she would get her life together, my thoughts seem to be about her suffering the consequences of her addiction. Why did I have to think this way? Why did I have to worry about the future?

In Nar-Anon, I am learning that I do not need to worry about the possibility of my addicted loved one "seeing the light." Nor do I have to be disappointed if she is arrested, spends time in prison, and then goes back to her old ways. I can cease projecting my sense of morality onto her.

As many people who are going through this know, I so desperately want my once beautiful daughter to stop her life of self-destruction and to rejoin our family. However, I have learned that I will be on the path of self-destruction as well, if I continue to try to manipulate her or this disease as I have no control over either situation. I try not to project my will on the addict's life.

Thought for Today: The Nar-Anon slogan of "One Day at a Time" helps me realize that I have no control over the future. I must face the problems of today and today only. Trying to predict events and worry if they will come true is merely wasting energy that is better spent in focusing on me.

"Advice is what we ask for when we already know the answer but wish we didn't." ~ Erica Jong

I am beginning to sense the changes arising from my attendance at Nar-Anon meetings. My wife does not attend these meetings and she seems to be in a constant state of anxiety and nervousness that I have not felt for some time. I am drawing my strength from the others who attend. I would share this experience more with my wife, but she has asked me not to and that is her choice.

I think that my wife would get so much out of the meetings were she to attend. I witness the bonding when one of the group members shares and I see the recognition in the eyes of another member going through a similar experience. That demonstration of help is rewarding to me. If nothing else, perhaps my wife could connect with another who is going through the same situation that we find ourselves experiencing. I repeat to myself, "God grant me the serenity to accept the things I cannot change, courage to change the things I can" because this applies to everything in my life, if I but see it. This does not exclude my wife and I must accept this.

Thought for Today: I am learning that the message of Nar-Anon is not only carrying the message to others but also practicing the principles in all my affairs. I hope that a change in me will be noticed and others will want what I have gained through my program. I can remember that Tradition Eleven reminds me that ours is a program of attraction rather than promotion. Step One suggests that I am powerless over others and that trying to exert power over them most likely will bring some insanity into my life. Live and let live is probably my safest course of action.

"The world is new to us every morning; this is God's gift, and every man should believe he is reborn each day." ~ The Baal Shem Tov

"Having had a spiritual awakening" – I remember hearing that statement when I first came through the doors of Nar-Anon. I wondered what that meant. I decided that it meant that I was going to be a perfect, spiritual person, that I would have no more problems or concerns and that I would be able to completely trust in my Higher Power for all things. I was ready for that experience. I also decided that in order to accomplish my spiritual awakening, I needed to get the addict in my life clean and into recovery.

In the beginning, I was only able to take what I could and leave the rest. That is what makes this program work. I was not forced to learn it all at once. How glad I am that I stuck around and allowed the tools of this program to work in my life. I am learning along the way that my spiritual awakening came "as a result of working the Twelve Steps." It was not something I could claim and use without the work that preceded it. I also need to use what I learn to "carry this message to others and to practice these principles in all my affairs."

Thought for Today: My spiritual awakening will come as a result of working these steps. We try to carry this message to others who suffer as we have, hopeful that it will be received, remembering always that Nar-Anon is not for those who need it but for those who want it.

"It had long since come to my attention that people of accomplishment rarely sat back and let things happen to them. They went out and happened to things." ~ Leonardo da Vinci

When I first came to Nar-Anon, I was not able to give of myself. Most of the time, I was confused and did not even know who I was. I was so addicted to the addict that it was difficult to shift the focus back to myself. I was his caretaker and fixer. This made me angry and resentful. The thought that my son's problems were because of addiction never entered my mind. I thought only other people suffered with this problem. I then found myself fighting the disease of addiction as if it was a battle to be won.

How wonderful that Nar-Anon gave me the opportunity to face reality and admit that my life was not working with me in charge. Now I have the choice to give up the control I thought I had and let my Higher Power take over; otherwise, I would continue to go on suffering. Now I know that I do not need to have all the answers. I can feel my feelings. I can have my own life and be happy in spite of what is happening in the addict's life. My happiness does not depend on the happiness of anyone else.

By working the steps and using the tools of the program – the slogans, meetings, sponsorship, literature, and doing service, I realize that what I am learning not only helps me but also could help others. By practicing Step Twelve and Tradition Five, I can give back to the other members of Nar-Anon what was so freely given to me.

Thought for Today: I have the responsibility to give to others the gift that was given to me by the Nar-Anon Family Groups.

"Generosity is giving more than you can, and pride is taking less than you need." ~ Kahlil Gibran

The fourteen years that my son was doing drugs put me on an emotional roller coaster. For a long time I surmised, guessed, assumed, but never had actual proof that he was using drugs. When the proof finally came, his life and mine were completely out of control. My days were consumed with looking for him at 3:30 in the morning, bailing him out of jail, making good on credit card bills that he had no intention of paying, and patching holes in the walls of his room, while the holes in my heart grew deeper by the day.

I could not bear to look at pictures of him, as they were only a sad reminder of what he had been and what was taken from him. I missed his sweetness, his innocence, his loving nature, and his honesty. That was my son, not the shadow of the person he was now. I was losing him and myself while my family was being torn apart. The only thing I was sure of was the fact that I was powerless.

Walking into a Nar-Anon meeting was my only hope of bringing sanity back into my life. It allowed me for the first time to cry, to vent, and to be unmasked without pretense and not to worry what other people thought. There was no judgment, only understanding. There was no inquisition, only compassion. I was aware that I was among people who have traveled this same road.

My son has now been in recovery for nineteen months, and has graduated into independent living while still in rehab. I am proud and hopeful. I pray and I am thankful. I have my son back again. My husband, daughter, son, and I are a family again. I can now allow myself the right to dream again.

Thought for Today: Nar-Anon gives me the tools to deal with what lies ahead. It is a crazy ride but there is laughter, joy and hope. I am not afraid of facing tomorrow whether the addict in my life is in recovery or not.

"As we change in such ways as these, we change the world around us and all the people in it for the better." ~ *Nar-Anon Blue Booklet*

Years ago my wife contracted breast cancer. I was scared and angry. After several months, I asked her doctor if he could think of anything or anyone else who could help her. With a caring, compassionate voice he said, "Your problem is you haven't accepted the fact that your wife is dying, and until you do, you will not be any good to yourself or to those who rely on you." His words finally helped me to see things as they really were. I went home and cried, but from that moment on, I was calm and focused on keeping my wife as comfortable as I could. She died within six months.

Twenty years later, my son told me he had been using heroin for over a year and could not stop. I was struck dumb and stunned beyond belief. We both cried hugging each other. Finally, I understood some of his unexplainable behavior. I made up my mind that I was going to help my son become clean and sober.

I smile now at my innocence. I have gone through all his lies and deceptions, collect calls from jail, residential treatment facilities, and his heartfelt promises that were all broken. My son could not stop using and I could not understand why.

A friend recommended I join a Nar-Anon family group. I balked at the idea because I am shy, but I went because my desperation overpowered my shyness. I went only to learn how to help my son. I listened as people spoke openly and lovingly about themselves and their addicted loved ones. I did not know any of the people in the group but I felt a sense of kinship with them. I came back to the next meeting, and I kept coming back. During one meeting, I felt a God moment. No one had asked or spoken about my son, but I felt as if the members were kindly and tacitly saying to me, "Your problem is you haven't accepted the fact that your son is a heroin addict." From that moment on, I became calm and focused on my own recovery.

Thought for Today: Acceptance means that I can admit that I cannot end my son's chemical dependency nor can I make a healthy person sick. If I can accept this, it means that I can go on with my life.

"We must accept finite disappointment, but never lose infinite hope." ~ Martin Luther King Jr.

The Nar-Anon fellowship has given me the tools to deal with the hardships that have come into my life. I am grateful for the program and the friends I have made who have been sharing and teaching me many good things. I have learned the following:

- do not be afraid every time I see a patrol car in my neighborhood;
- do not be afraid of reading the crime log in newspapers for fear of seeing the addict's name in the write-up;
- do not jump when an unfamiliar voice on the phone asks for the addict;
- do not trust as easily as I used to, but do not be cynical either;
- do not feel guilty about an event that is out of my control;
- do not be ashamed of something someone else does; and
- do not dismiss the past as wasted time and do not let go of the happy memories either.

I have also learned these things:

- do examine all sides of a situation;
- do know that some things are beyond my control no matter how hard I try to manage them;
- do believe it is true that good people sometimes have bad things happen to them;
- do believe that dreams can be destroyed but life goes on, just in a different direction;
- do give up thinking my suggestions are helpful when in reality they are enabling tools;
- do detach from the disease, not from the addict;
- do embrace each day in spite of the sadness I might feel; and
- do believe I could not have reached this point in my life without help.

Thought for Today: Today I have a new perspective on life and the person I want to become. I want my actions to always be spiritual. I have a much improved relationship with the addict I love and I thank recovery and Nar-Anon for helping me to change my life for the better.

"By learning you will teach, by teaching you will learn." ~ Latin Proverb

Many years ago, when my daughter was about four years old, friends took us to a surfing beach. Although the tide was out, I found the scene rather daunting. My daughter, however, ran after some adults heading towards the surf. We were playing in fairly shallow water about fifteen meters from the shore when suddenly someone shouted, "Run for it, here she comes!" I grabbed my daughter's hand and we ran towards shore. I realized we would not make it to safety before the wave hit us. Many thoughts were racing through my mind in that moment of panic. I thought that if I held onto her hand I might pull her shoulder out of its socket because we would tumble at different speeds. I thought that I might drown and take her with me, or let her go knowing that her body was light and would float to shore. I had to make a split-second decision, so I let go of that precious little hand. I was hit by the water, thrown and pounded. My little girl had floated to safety and shook herself with hair flying, water spraying and shrieking with laughter. This all seemed a marvelous adventure to her. I was bruised black, blue and purple from my left shoulder to my ankle for several months, by trying to maintain control.

Many years later, during my first month in Nar-Anon, once again I knew I had to let go of my daughter's hand. She was already in recovery and no longer wanted to be dependent on me. This time it was so much harder for me to let go. It was like letting go of the habit of a lifetime. All my thoughts started with "yes, but" and "what if?" I realized that without faith in a Power greater than myself, I could not do it.

Thought for Today: Today I know that letting go of her hand was an act of faith, although then I would have denied that strongly. I realize that the effort it takes to control still causes bruising and damage, not only to my daughter's life and other people, but to my own life, too.

"The successful people of this world take life as it comes. They just go out and deal with the world as it is." ~ Ben Stein

Today, I look forward to another Nar-Anon meeting. I am uplifted and energetic. My Nar-Anon meetings are a special place where I can share my situation with others experiencing similar pain and powerlessness. Often our friends and family do not understand these feelings. Most of all, I come to hear the experience, strength and hope of my Nar-Anon Family. It is a safe place where I will not be judged for my actions or reactions. It is a place where I can grow at my own pace, set my own boundaries and work my own program as the Higher Power of my understanding guides me.

Without Nar-Anon's Twelve Step program, I would not be able to understand the addict in my life. I am learning to detach with love and compassion. When I admit I am powerless and quit trying to change my addicted loved one, I can face adversity that comes my way by using the Twelve Steps and principles of the program. I am grateful for my newfound courage and strength. Nar-Anon has taught me a new way to live and think.

Thought for Today: Wherever I am in practicing my Nar-Anon program, there is a place for me to learn and to grow. At the end of each meeting, I feel a little better than when I arrived.

"God expects but one thing of you, and that is you should come out of yourself insofar as you are created being made, and let God be God in you." ~ Meister Eckhart

Every day can be a new beginning; but New Year's Eve is special and different. There is no other time of the year when people of the world simultaneously focus on the same phenomenon. Each country and its people acknowledge the passing of time and change as we recognize the end of the old year and the beginning of the new.

Nar-Anon is a worldwide fellowship and I take great comfort in the thought that millions of recovering people take this time to reflect on the events of the last year and commit themselves to continued recovery in the new year.

I look at my own personal growth in this process of recovery. Last year I finally asked someone to be my sponsor and this year I have been asked to be a sponsor. This could not happen without the support of my fellowship and my willingness to keep an open mind to the Nar-Anon program and its principles.

I reflect on the long-time members who shared their experience, strength and hope with me to show me that I can change. I see my pain, anger and confusion lessen as I choose to be happy whether others choose recovery or not. I reflect on the newcomers because they give me an opportunity to share my recovery. I see my progress and I can have that same hope for them.

Thought for Today: Today is the end of the old and beginning of the new. I look forward to the New Year with hope for continued recovery and growth. I thank my Higher Power for showing me the way. Today I am exactly where I am supposed to be.

"New Year's Eve is like every other night; there is no pause in the march of the universe, no breathless moment of silence among created things that the passage of another twelve months may be noted; and yet no man has quite the same thoughts this evening that come with the coming of darkness on other nights." ~ Hamilton Wright Mabie

THE TWELVE STEPS OF
NAR-ANON FAMILY GROUPS

1. We admitted we were powerless over the addict – that our lives had become unmanageable.

2. Came to believe that a Power greater than ourselves could restore us to sanity.

3. Made a decision to turn our will and our lives over to the care of God as we *understood* Him.

4. Made a searching and fearless moral inventory of ourselves.

5. Admitted to God, to ourselves, and to another human being the exact nature of our wrongs.

6. Were entirely ready to have God remove all these defects of character.

7. Humbly asked Him to remove our shortcomings.

8. Made a list of all persons we had harmed, and became willing to make amends to them all.

9. Made direct amends to such people wherever possible except when to do so would injure them or others.

10. Continued to take personal inventory and when we were wrong promptly admitted it.

11. Sought through prayer and meditation to improve our conscious contact with God as we understood Him, praying only for knowledge of His will for us and the power to carry that out.

12. Having had a spiritual awakening as a result of these steps, we tried to carry this message to others, and to practice these principles in all our affairs.

THE TWELVE TRADITIONS OF NAR-ANON FAMILY GROUPS

Our group experience suggests that the unity of the Nar-Anon Family Groups depends upon our adherence to these traditions.

1. Our common welfare should come first; personal progress for the greatest number depends on unity.

2. For our group purposes there is but one authority – a loving God as He may express Himself in our group conscience. Our leaders are but trusted servants – they do not govern.

3. The relatives of addicts, when gathered for mutual aid, may call themselves a Nar-Anon Family Group, provided that as a group, they have no other affiliation. The only requirement for membership is that there be a problem of addiction in a relative or friend.

4. Each group should be autonomous except in matters affecting other Nar-Anon Family Groups, or N.A. as a whole.

5. Each Nar-Anon Family Group has but one purpose; to help families of addicts. We do this by practicing the Twelve Steps of Nar-Anon, by encouraging and understanding our addicted relatives, and by welcoming and giving comfort to families of addicts.

6. Our Family Groups ought never to endorse, finance or lend our name to any outside enterprise, lest problems of money, property and prestige divert us from our primary spiritual aim; but although a separate entity, we should always cooperate with Narcotics Anonymous.

7. Every group ought to be fully self-supporting, declining outside contributions.

8. Nar-Anon Twelfth Step work should remain forever non-professional, but our service centers may employ special workers.

9. Our groups, as such ought never to be organized, but we may create service boards or committees directly responsible to those they serve.

10. The Nar-Anon Family Groups have no opinion on outside issues; hence our name ought never be drawn into public controversy.

11. Our public relations policy is based on attraction rather than promotion; we need always maintain personal anonymity at the level of press, radio, films, internet, and other forms of mass media.. We need guard with special care the anonymity of all N.A. members.

12. Anonymity is the spiritual foundation of all our traditions, ever reminding us to place principles above personalities.

THE TWELVE CONCEPTS OF
NAR-ANON SERVICE

Just as freedom for the individual comes from the Twelve Steps and freedom for the group springs from the Twelve Traditions, so freedom for the service structure flourishes from the Twelve Concepts.

1. To fulfill our fellowship's primary purpose, the Nar-Anon Family Groups have joined together to create a structure that develops, coordinates, and maintains services on behalf of Nar-Anon as a whole.

2. The final responsibility and authority for Nar-Anon services rests with the Nar-Anon Family Groups.

3. The Nar-Anon Family Groups delegate to the service structure the authority necessary to fulfill the responsibilities assigned to it.

4. Effective leadership is highly valued in Nar-Anon. Leadership qualities should be carefully considered when selecting trusted servants.

5. For each responsibility assigned to the service structure, a single point of decision and accountability should be clearly defined.

6. Group conscience is the spiritual means by which we invite a loving Higher Power to influence our decisions.

7. All members of a service body bear substantial responsibility for that body's decisions and should be allowed to fully participate in its decision-making processes.

8. Regular, two-way communications are essential to the fulfillment of all these concepts and the integrity and effectiveness of our services themselves.

9. All elements of our service structure have the responsibility to carefully consider all viewpoints in their decision-making processes.

10. Any member of a service body can petition that body for the redress of a personal grievance, without fear of reprisal.

11. Nar-Anon funds are used to further our primary purpose to carry the message, and must be managed responsibly.

12. In keeping with the spiritual nature of Nar-Anon, our structure should always be one of service, never of governance.